PRAISE FOR *SHOW.*

"With apologies to President Ken. represent the highest concentration of intellectual rigor in one place, since any single essay of William F. Buckley.

--*Robert C, McFarlane, National Security Advisor to President Reagan, Chairman and CEO of McFarlane Associates, Inc.*

"If you're tired of political correctness and of euphemisms about our enemy -- the nefarious alliance of radical Islam and the hard left -- search no further. Jamie Glazov and his 29 brilliant and articulate interviewees deal such fuzzy thinking and fuzzy talk a blow reminiscent of those delivered superbly in an earlier era by George Orwell."

--*R. James Woolsey, Director of Central Intelligence 1993-95.*

"Jamie Glazov knows how to gather the sharper minds, and he knows how to probe them. He has one of them himself: a sharp mind. This collection of interviews and commentary is a guide to our perilous times."

--*Jay Nordlinger, senior editor, National Review.*

"In my other life, at the top of the Soviet bloc, I witnessed how its redistribution of wealth ruined every country it touched, and how its appeasement of terrorism brought the world to the brink of nuclear war. Alas, now the fatal virus of Marxism, with its nauseating cult of personality, its governmental nationalizations and its coddling of nuclear terrorism, has begun infecting our shores as well. The author has dedicated his life to preventing these catastrophes from happening. Dr. Glazov's *Showdown With Evil* is his crowning effort."

--*Lt. Gen. Ion Mihai Pacepa, the highest ranking Soviet bloc official granted political asylum in the U.S.*

"Be careful! As always with Jamie Glazov's work, the contents of this package are highly explosive - and are guaranteed to singe any leftists in the vicinity."

--*David Frum, editor of FrumForum.com.*

"Jamie Glazov has produced the most important book in America. This compilation of interviews describes the dangers of the Obama administration and the President himself with facts that will enlighten the American people for the coming elections. Do we have a Manchurian candidate in the White House now trained by Frank Davis and Saul Alinsky? Read it and find out!"

--Lieutenant General Thomas McInerney, USAF (Ret.).

Showdown With Evil:

Our Struggle Against Tyranny and Terror.

By Jamie Glazov

With a Foreword by Richard Perle

Published by
Mantua Books
Brantford, Ontario N3T 6J9
Vancouver B.C. V6K 4C4
Email: Mantua2003@Hotmail.com

Library and Archives Canada Cataloguing in Publication

Glazov, Jamie, 1966-
    Showdown with evil : our struggle against tyranny and terror / by Jamie Glazov ; foreword by Richard Perle.

Includes index.

ISBN 978-0-9734065-5-9

    1. Interviews--United States. 2. Islamic fundamentalism. 3. Terrorism. 4. Right and left (Political science)--United States. I. Title.

BP190.5.T47G63 2010   **201'.763325**   **C2010-907041-0**

First Printing October, 2010

Cover Design by Linda Daly; Author photo by Ron Jocsak, JOSCAK Photography

To Mamochka

Table of Contents:

Acknowledgements i
Foreword by Richard Perle iii
Preface viii

Part I: Obama's Destructive Path

Introduction: 2
1. Brown's National Security Victory – Andy McCarthy 3
2. The Obama Tragedy in the Terror War – Ralph Peters 9
3. Obama's Tortured Rendezvous With Reality – Victor
   Davis Hanson 13
4. Obama, Fort Hood and CAIR – Rep. Sue Myrick 18
5. Why He Shouted "Allahu Akbar" – Robert Spencer. 23
6. Obama's Human Rights Disaster - Elliott Abrams 26
7. Catastrophe - Dick Morris 32

Part II: Unholy Alliance

Introduction: 36
8. Unholy Alliance - David Horowitz 37
9. Jewish Collaborators - Kenneth Levin. 48
10. The Islamist Lobby in the House - Steve Emerson 57
11. Jimmy Carter and the Middle East - Rep. Howard
    Berman. 65
12. The Death of Feminism - Phyllis Chesler 68

Part III: Islam: The Religion of Peace?

Introduction: 78
13. Defeating Radical Islam - Brigitte Gabriel 79
14. Sex in the Islamic City - Mohammad Asghar 87
15. Allah's White Faces – Abul Kasem 105

Part IV: The Terror War

Introduction: 116

16. World War IV - Norman Podhoretz 117
17. The Case for Democracy - Natan Sharansky 120
18. Banquo's Ghosts - Rich Lowry 133

Part V: The Evil Empire

Introduction: 140

19. Spies – Harvey Klehr and John Haynes 141
20. Putin's Spies in America - Konstantin Preobrazhenskiy 146
21. Ted Kennedy and the KGB - Paul Kengor 154

Part VI: Leaving the Faith

Introduction: 164

22. My Way Into and Out of the Left - Andrew Klavan . . . 165
23. Gay and Leaving the Left - Charles Winecoff 172
24. A Terrorist Who Turned to Love - Walid Shoebat 189

Part VII: The Titans

Introduction: 198

25. Miles Gone By - William F. Buckley Jr. 199
26. god Is Not Great – Christopher Hitchens 207
27. Treason – Ann Coulter 218
28. Vixi: Memoirs of a Non-Belonger – Richard Pipes 227
29. Romancing Opiates -Theodore Dalrymple 234

Part VIII: Looking to the Future of Freedom

Introduction: 240

30: Showdown with Evil – Jamie Glazov 241

Acknowledgements

I am most grateful to all the superstars in this book who gave me their time and energy in our interviews. I am indebted to Richard Perle for his superb foreword to the book and to David Swindle for his commentary throughout the sections.

I owe deep thanks to David Horowitz. Thank you David.

John Corrigan, I cherish your friendship and all your help throughout the years.

I am indebted to Professor Jack L. Granatstein, my academic mentor, who helped me build the foundation on which my career, and books like these, became possible.

I am grateful to Stephen Brown, Anton Wright, Ivan Wright, Rudy Chavarria, Shane MacDonald, Natty Jackson, Anna Atell, Christine Williams, Jamie Griffin and Jerry Griffin. Thank you for your support and your friendship that sustained my perseverance.

I thank Lynne Rabinoff, my agent, for all her superb help in making the publication of this work possible.

To Camille Flynn, thank you for your love throughout all of these years -- and for all the precious things you brought into my life.

Thank you Peter Collier, Mike Finch, Stephanie Knudson, Elizabeth Ruiz, Jeffrey Wienir and Sharon Schuster – my valiant colleagues at the Freedom Center who have stood by me over the years and helped me a great deal.

I am also grateful to my colleague at Frontpage, Jacob Laksin, whose friendship, loyalty and moral support has sustained me throughout the years.

To my brother Grisha and his family. To my sister Elena, her husband Kevin and their whole family. I am grateful for all your prayers, love and support. Thank you Yuri and Arielle.

To Nonie Darwish, I cherish your helping, loving and magnanimous hand in a tough hour of need.

To my Papochka, looking at me from above: thank you for being a noble knight and a courageous hero -- and for your effort to instill your priceless values in me. I treasure all that you are and that you gave me. I love you dearly and we will see each other again.

And to who is most divine to me on earth: my Mamochka. I am forever grateful to you for everything. I thank you that, from the moment of my birth, every time I awake from sleep anywhere in your vicinity that, upon seeing me, you begin to cheerfully celebrate -- as if the most joyous occasion on earth has transpired. This precious dynamic has implanted an indelible mark in my soul. You taught me the true nature of love and bestowed tremendous wisdom upon me.

Whatever you touch becomes gold for me.

I love you.

This book is for you.

Foreword

In this extraordinary collection of interviews, Jamie Glazov demonstrates that consistent, searching questions can both enrich and impart coherence to disparate answers: for what emerges from 29 interviews conducted over eight years is an illuminating and important commentary on the largest issues facing America and the West.

It is a commentary whose preoccupation reflects history— Jamie's Glazov's history, rich in the issues of identity, freedom, truth telling and courage. Jamie, it may be said, has had rather more history than he needed—as a man whose parents were dissidents in the Soviet Union and who was taught the values of freedom and the courage to fight for it from the beginning. It is no wonder that he is so wholly absorbed in understanding and opposing, radical, political Islam and its apologists. Today's "useful idiots," like those who preceded them, are drawn almost entirely from the Left. Indeed, many of the individuals are the same, as is the intellectual foundation of their obsessive disdain for the liberal values of an open society. In one way or another nearly all the interviews in this book touch on the readiness of the Left, in an often ludicrous pursuit of political correctness, to accept, and even to advance, the Islamist agenda that has replaced communism as the principal threat to western values and civilization.

Part I, "Osama's Destructive Path," certainly deals with the destructive qualities of a number of policies—but, sadly, support for these policies goes well beyond Obama and his administration. The refusal to recognize that we are gravely threatened by Islamist terror— by deeply ideological extremists who are prepared, even eager, to die in the act of killing infidels (that is, all of us including "moderate Muslims")—is neither original with President Obama nor limited to his administration. Ranging along a spectrum from myopic to willfully blind, the community of academics, journalists, politicians, clerics, establishment lawyers, non-governmental organizations and others who believe we are confronted only by a small number of miscreants who can be effectively dealt with by our criminal justice system (after being Mirandized, of course) is alarmingly large. The idea that those who hate and wish to kill us have been given reason and cause by failures of our own making—aggression against Saddam's murderous regime or the Taliban or support for democratic Israel or the failure to censor blasphemous words or drawings or the use of harsh methods of interrogation, and the like—goes well beyond the current administration (and is likely to outlast it).

Like Bush before him, Obama has done nothing to recognize publicly the Islamist nature of the terrorist threat. But, unlike Bush, his apologetic tone when addressing the Muslim world implies that we are somehow responsible for Islamist extremism. Victor Davis Hanson knows what the President should, but will never say: "Dear radical Muslims, you, not us, created your present misery through religious intolerance, gender apartheid, statism, corruption, tribalism, anti-scientific fundamentalism, and autocracy, and we have neither regrets about our own success nor responsibilities for your own self-induced miseries, unfortunate as they are."

No one, least of all Jamie Glazov, would be surprised at the Media and liberal Left's misplaced sympathy for Islamist militancy, sympathy that obscures the underlying Islamist motives in even such obvious cases as the Fort Hood massacre. As Robert Spencer sagely observes: "They reflexively deny and ignore these conclusions because they are completely sold out to the idea that Muslims, as non-white, non-Christian, non-Westerners, cannot possibly be anything but victims."

Steven Emerson has been relentless in exposing seemingly moderate Muslim organizations that are, in reality, working to "… infiltrate the corridors of power (Congress and the government), the media, Hollywood, the intelligentsia and even law enforcement, an agenda Emerson sums up as secretly aspiring to a "civilizational-jihadist process". More than anyone, Emerson has exposed one such organization, the Council on American Islamic Relations (CAIR), for what it truly is: a Muslim Brotherhood associated political/propaganda organization with a concealed history of support for Hamas, posing as a civil rights group interested only in protecting Muslims from alleged discrimination. Emerson exposes CAIR's collaboration with other radical groups including J Street, an organization that feigns sympathy for Israel while working with CAIR against it. Congresswoman Sue Myrick's interview is a reminder that there are intelligent, diligent members of congress—though not as many as a majority driven institution requires. Her patient, sustained criticism of CAIR stands in sharp contrast to the uncritical acceptance it has gained in some parts of the Congress and the media. Taken together, Emerson and Myrick demonstrate that serious analysis and reporting can have a real impact when members of Congress are armed with facts.

Fascinating, informative interviews with Brigitte Gabriel, Mohammad Ashgar and Abul Kasem shed light on Muslim ideology as reflected in the Koran and propagated by extremist clerics, charitable organizations, educational institutions and states purporting to be friends and allies of the United States. As one learns of the venomous intolerance of Muslim extremism—towards women, homosexuals, Jews and other infidels—the Left's romance with Islam and its opposition to combating the menace it has become is almost inexplicable. But Jamie Glazov and his mentor David Horowitz understand the Left and are keenly aware of the parallels between the Left's indifference to Soviet totalitarianism then and Islamic fundamentalism now. They understand that the "peace" movement of the Cold War threatened our security in much the way that civil libertarian opposition to dealing effectively with Islamist terror threatens us today.

Norman Podhoretz understands that we are at war with, as he rightly calls it, Islamofascism, "…as precise a characterization as I could find of the religio-political totalitarian force that we are up against." His defense of the Bush doctrine as our strategy in this war is clearer and more compelling than the case made by Bush himself.

Natan Sharansky is Jamie Glazov's hero. Jamie is not alone in this. Anyone who followed Sharansky's struggle for human rights before, during and after his 11 years in the Gulag was certain to become an admirer of his personal courage, his dedication to individual liberty and, in recent years, his deep insight into the nature of democracy and the human dimension of life under totalitarian rule. As I look back at 11 years on the staff of Senator Henry "Scoop" Jackson, the task I found most gratifying was drafting speeches for Scoop supporting

Sharansky's struggle and demanding his release from prison. Sharansky captured George W. Bush's imagination with his book, *The Case for Democracy*, but the hapless Bush was never able to mobilize his own administration to develop policies reflecting Sharansky's astute analysis, the essence of which is contained in his interview in this book. Ironically, Bush's decision to support elections among the Palestinians, which led to the rise of Hamas, flew in the face of Sharansky's argument that elections in the absence of a civil society cannot be expected to promote democracy. It didn't.

The three essays in Part V, "The Evil Empire," shed fascinating light on the operations of the KGB during the Cold War and since. It is not surprising that the operational code of the KGB under the Soviet Union continues in Vladimir Putin's Russia. How could it be otherwise? Putin is a man of, by and for the KGB even if it is now called the FSB. That the continuing oppressive role of the KGB/FSB is so little appreciated in the United States—and most especially among policy makers and bureaucrats eager to "reset" American-Russian relations—is at least partly the result of the failure of mainstream media in the U.S. to pay attention. Klehr, Haynes, Preobrazhenskiy and Kengor, who all have interesting things to say in their books and in their interviews in this volume, have received almost no coverage. This reflects a troubling trend evident in the way the New York *Times*, the Washington *Post*, and the major networks increasingly ignore—blackout might be the better term—books and viewpoints that differ from their own. There's a world out there that we would learn little of were it not for FOX and volumes like this one.

Andrew Klavan, like David Horowitz, has changed sides. So have Charles Winecoff and Walid Shoebat: four personal histories that bring an immensely valuable depth to their understanding of the mindsets and ideologies they have abandoned. Klavan, once on their side, now says this of the Left: "So desperate are they to display their tolerance, to claim virtue and open-mindedness for themselves, so secretly ashamed and guilt-ridden and self-hating are they, I guess, that they will give aid and comfort to a philosophy that turns everything they're supposed to stand for on its head. Anti-female, anti-gay, anti-religious liberty, anti-humanity, radical Islam is a cancer on the face of the earth. Ignoring it, pretending it isn't there, moral equivalence, relativism – all the various forms of false piety in which the Left specializes – are as helpful with radical Islam as they are with other cancers."

Buckley, Hitchens, Coulter, Pipes and Dalrymple are always a pleasure to read. There is no point commenting on their commentary: read and enjoy.

Richard Perle
Assistant Secretary of Defense for the Reagan administration,
now a fellow at the American Enterprise Institute.

Preface

From the year 2002 to the present, David Horowitz gave me the privilege and honor of being the editor of Frontpagemag.com. During that time he encouraged me to do interviews with the big newsmakers and thinkers of our time. This collection of some of the best interviews is the result.

I've asked my colleague and NewsRealBlog.com editor David Swindle to introduce each section of interviews. For the final discussion of this collection David will be interviewing me on what can be done to triumph in our showdown with tyranny and terror.

Part I: Obama's Destructive Path

Introduction:

When Barack Obama emerged as a credible presidential contender in the spring of 2008 he was an ideological enigma. Obama spent his entire life amongst the hard Left – mentored by communists like Frank Marshall Davis, ministered by anti-Americans like Reverend Jeremiah Wright, and trained in the community organizing methods of the notorious Saul Alinsky.

Yet during the campaign Obama actually positioned himself to Republican John McCain's right on foreign policy. He cited Indiana Senator Dick Lugar as a key influence, and vowed to hunt down al-Qaeda in an aggressive fashion. It fit with the entire tone of his campaign – one of centrism and bringing together a country that had grown weary of the partisan street fights of the previous 16 years.

So when Obama triumphed in the election it was certainly anyone's guess which direction he would actually lead the country. In the Fall of 2008, *Frontpagemag.com* featured several articles by Jacob Laksin in which Obama's betrayals to his anti-war base were celebrated. *Frontpage* Editor-in-Chief David Horowitz noted approvingly of Obama's choice of Hillary Clinton as Secretary of State and further endorsed the president's war cabinet as "center-right." For a moment it appeared as though a disastrous foreign policy course might be averted.

Since then, however, any optimism that Obama might actually execute a sensible foreign policy has evaporated. And the interviews collected in this first chapter explain why. Dr. Glazov discusses Obama's first year in office with numerous foreign policy experts and startling conclusions emerge about where this country is headed as it continues to face a tenacious enemy. -- David Swindle.

1.   Brown's National Security Victory – Andy McCarthy

Frontpage Interview's guest today is Andrew C. McCarthy, a senior fellow at the National Review Institute and a columnist for *National Review*. His book *Willful Blindness: A Memoir of the Jihad* (Encounter Books, 2008), has just been released in paperback with a new preface. Check out a description from Encounter Books.

FP: Andy McCarthy, welcome to Frontpage Interview.

I would like to talk to you today about Scott Brown's victory in Massachusetts and how it was the issue of national-security that put Brown over Coakley.

Can you talk a bit about that? The people seemed to have cared about terrorism and the treatment of enemy combatants, yes?

McCarthy: Jamie, great to be here as always. And you're right. The Brown campaign's internal polling told them something very interesting. While it's true that healthcare is what nationalized the election and riveted everyone's attention to it, it was the national security issues that put real distance between the two candidates in the mind of the electorate—in blue Massachusetts of all places. Sen.-elect Brown was able to speak forcefully and convincingly on issues like treating our jihadist enemies as combatants rather than mere defendants, about killing terrorists and preventing terrorism rather than contenting ourselves with prosecutions after Americans have been killed, about tough interrogation when necessary to save innocent lives. Martha Coakley, by contrast, had to try to defend the indefensible, which is Obama-style counterterrorism. It evidently made a huge difference to voters.

FP: What do you think of how Bush was treated on this whole issue?

McCarthy: As many of us predicted during the Bush years when the president was being hammered by the Left and the press, history is treating him much more kindly on the national security front. His movement of the country to a war-footing rather than treating international terrorism as a criminal justice matter was common sense, but common sense cuts against the Washington grain so it took a strong president to do it. Now, on issue after issue, he is being vindicated—he and Vice President Cheney, who has become the country's leading voice on national security, after spending years being vilified.

FP: What role did McCain play?

McCarthy: Sen. McCain is, as ever, a mixed bag. He's recently been very good on the need to treat the enemy as an enemy, not as a defendant. So that was helpful to Brown. But it can't be forgotten that McCain was the force behind the libel of Bush as a torture monger and the consequent ruination of our interrogation policy. And it was the "McCain Amendment" that gave us, as a matter of law, the extension of Fifth Amendment rights to our enemies overseas, which has had awful ramifications even outside the issue of interrogation practices. McCain is responsible for a lot of the fodder that made Obama possible.

FP: What lessons should Republicans take from Brown's success?

McCarthy: These national security positions resonate with voters. Healthcare, TARP, and the economic issues in general are very important, but they're complex and make people's eyes glaze over sometimes. The national defense issues, besides being the most important ones confronted by a political community, are comparatively easy to wrap your brain around. And strong, unapologetic national defense in a time of terrorist threat is appealing to voters. So we should be arguing these issues forcefully, and not worry about the fact that the left-wing legacy media will say nasty things about us. Their instinctive America-bashing is why they are speaking to—or, better, speaking *at*—a steadily decreasing audience.

FP: The Left pretends that its positions in how to confront terror (or not to) are somehow founded on the Constitution. What's the mindset here?

McCarthy: Yes, because they reject the foundational fact that the Constitution is a compact between the *American people* and the government they created. They think every person on planet earth is an American waiting to happen, born with the full panoply of American constitutional rights that can be asserted against the American people. And they think the courts, rather than being a peer branch of our government, stand over and above our government: a forum where the rest of the world, including enemies of the United States, is invited to make its case against the United States. That's a warped understanding of the Constitution.

FP: What hope does Brown's victory give? What do you think Obama, Holder and Napolitano are thinking – or not thinking?

McCarthy: Well, I think it's Brown combined with what's happened in New Jersey and Virginia, with Obama's plunging numbers, the unpopularity of the Democrats' healthcare, employment and national-security policies, and the disgusting wheeling-and-dealing the supposedly "transparent" Left is doing behind close doors (i.e., not on C-SPAN). All these things give hope that freedom is on the march, that people are broadly rejecting statism. But I don't think Obama is a normal politician and that his administration is a conventional "let's modulate to remain viable" administration.

Enacting their agenda is more important to them than being re-elected, and they are not to be underestimated.

FP: Why do you think that when I see or think about Janet Napolitano I am engulfed with a profound sense of doom and despair?

McCarthy: Well, if I have this right, she is an official who is in charge of securing the homeland but — after ballyhooed, years-long investigations, including by the 9/11 Commissions — she didn't know how the 9/11 hijackers got here, thought they snuck in from Canada, and believes that what they did when they got here was a "man-caused disaster" that had nothing to do with jihadist ideology (indeed, she thinks that saying "jihadist" is problematic). She does see ideology as a problem, of course, but only if it is … *conservative* ideology. That is, she thinks the *real* terror threat comes from people with radical ideas like limited government, the sanctity of life, and the Second Amendment — especially if they're military vets who've served in George Bush's wars of aggression. And she is in charge of enforcing the immigration laws but wasn't aware that entering the country illegally is a criminal offense.

I can't imagine why you'd have a problem with any of that, Jamie.

FP: Who needs horror movies or a tragic film to make you cry when you have things like this to think about?

Well, let's move on:

What was this whole thing about Brown's pick-up truck and Obama making fun of it? I thought Obama represented the common man?

McCarthy: This president has lived a very different kind of life from most Americans. He lived his early, formative years in Indonesia, a majority-Muslim police state. After he returned to America at age ten or so, he dove into the fever-swamps of the Left and was steeped in the cynicism and nihilism of Saul Alinsky. For years, he's surrounded himself with fawning sycophants who've told him he's "The One." And he's extremely insulated from the real world of everyday Americans. I don't think the sudden burst of Obama-style populism is going to fly — and going after Brown's pick-up is a good indication of why. He thinks people who like their pick-up trucks are bitter-clingers. Actually, they're Americans.

FP: Brown vs. Obama, 2012?

McCarthy: I don't think we should get ahead of ourselves. Brown's an impressive, talented guy, but he's also someone no one outside of Massachusetts had heard of until a few short weeks ago. But this does underscore something I've been saying for a long time. As late as 1991, few people really knew who Bill and Hillary Clinton were, and yet they've towered over our politics from 1992 forward. The world changed on a dime on 9/11.

A year ago today, with President Obama just inaugurated and with the Democrats having wide margins in Congress, the Republican party seemed dead and even conservative intellectuals were telling us we had to abandon Reagan conservatism—the conservatism that's leading us out of the woods. This is all a long-winded way of saying: We may not yet know, even today, who the leaders will be when 2012 rolls around. We've got a ton on our plate right now, and the unknown tomorrow. You know the old saw, "You want to make God laugh—tell Him about your plans." Right now, I'm worried about today, and content to figure 2012 will take care of itself.

FP: Well before we say goodbye for now, what is on your mind the most right now? What can you tell our readers that will give us all some hope that America, despite its current leadership, can prevail against the threats it faces?

McCarthy: After slumbering for too long, the public — the great swath of Americans that is basically conservative, patriotic, and thinks the country is the best the world has ever known, not in dire need of transformative "change" — has asserted itself. But even if he's held to one term, Obama will leave us in a deep hole. The reckless borrowing and spending would take decades to dig out of even if we stopped it tomorrow. There is a lot of mischief a sprawling executive bureaucracy can do in four years, and Obama is likely to stock the federal courts with very left-wing judges who will try to impose transnational progressivism by fiat if the Republicans don't have the gumption to stop the president from appointing them. And that last point is what I think about most.

The challenge for Republicans is not to win the next elections. The smart Democrats have already factored elections in. Obama Leftists are not conventional politicians. They are true-believers. Of course they hope their friends at ACORN and similar outfits will soften the blow come November. But if not, they are willing to endure electoral losses for what they see as the greater good of using this one-time opportunity they have to transform this country radically.

Republicans don't so much need a plan to win elections — the Democrats' statist policies and their irresponsible positions on national security will take care of that. Stopping bad government is not enough. Republicans need a plan, after they win elections, to roll back what the Left has done and is doing. That will require courage and skill. I hope we have it, but I confess to worrying about whether we do.

FP: Andy McCarthy, thank you, and a pleasure and honor as always to speak with you.

[Jamie Glazov, "Brown's National Security Victory,"
Frontpagemag.com, January 25, 2010.]

2.   The Obama Tragedy in the Terror War – Ralph Peters

Frontpage Interview's guest today is Ralph Peters, a retired U.S. Army officer, a controversial strategist and world traveler, and the author of 25 books, including the recent bestselling thriller, *The War After Armageddon*, and the forthcoming *Endless War* (March, 2010), which examines the history–and future–of conflict between Islam and the West. An opinion columnist for the *New York Post* and popular media commentator, he became Fox News Network's first Strategic Analyst in 2009.

FP: Ralph Peters, welcome to Frontpage Interview.

Peters: Great to reconnect with you, Jamie.

FP: What are your thoughts regarding the recent botched terrorist attack on Christmas Day on Flight 253?

Peters: Well, I have to separate my thoughts and my feelings. First, the feelings: Outrage. Not so much at the bomber, who was just fulfilling his duty to commit jihad against Christians on their most important holiday (with any dead Jews as a bonus), but at the stunning lack of interest or concern on the part of our partying president and his paladins. Hey, why interrupt your holiday just because an Islamist terrorist (well, they don't exist, right?) tried to kill 300 innocents and almost pulled it off? And, of course, we were all instantly reassured when Secretary of Homeland Security Janet Napolitano (whose real interest seems to be harassing law-abiding citizens at airports, while preparing to push through citizenship for millions of illegal immigrants) told us that the system worked. I mean, God help us, you and I don't live in the same universe as our "leaders."

On the thoughts side: President Obama, sooner or later, has to take responsibility for something. His call for yet another review in the wake of the failed attack had the primary purpose of deflecting blame from the administration. Well, the military maxim applies: A leader is responsible for everything his subordinates do, or fail to do. All his adult life, Obama wanted to be president. Now it's time for him to actually be a president. That means taking responsibility.

FP: How much confidence, exactly, do you have in this administration providing safety to Americans against our enemies?

Peters: Unfortunately, I have no faith–none–in the administration's seriousness, when it comes to protecting Americans. A president who insists, in the face of overwhelming evidence, that every next terrorist is just an "isolated extremist" with no connection to Islam isn't interested in solving the problem.

FP: How about our intelligence system in this case?

Peters: It failed. But, to be fair, many things that seem obvious in retrospect weren't necessarily obvious in advance. Our intelligence system has two pertinent problems (among many others): It's dealing with a literally unmanageable volume of data, and (according to my friends still inside the system), the post 9-11 "reforms," such as creating a Director of National Intelligence and the National Counter Terrorism Center, simply created additional layers of bureaucracy. We're fighting a lean, mean, fast, ruthless enemy. Our response? Bring more of yesterday's senior officials out of retirement and hire more lawyers. Maybe we should just sue al Qaeda and see how splendidly our civilian-justice approach to terror works.

FP: Your view of Janet Napolitano? Why is she still heading Homeland Security?

Peters: I'd rather not view Janet Napolitano at all. This woman is so far out of her depth that it can't be measured with Newtonian metrics. She was a politically correct appointment, period. On the positive side, word is that she'll be gone in the next few months–Obama's too vain to fire her right now, while the administration's under fire over the Christmas terror attempt, but he realizes what a political liability she's become.

There's another, unfortunate, side to this. When representing our country, especially on security matters, appearance and physical presence matter. It would be great if that were not so, but facts are facts. Even if Napolitano were a security genius, she doesn't project a forceful, capable image to our deadly enemies (or to our allies). Again, every one of Obama's cabinet-level appointments has been about domestic politics, not about their effectiveness on the world stage.

Well, at least he can't blame Bush for Napolitano.

FP: Your perspective on how the wars in Iraq and Afghanistan are going? What strategies that are in effect are wrong? What strategies would be more effective?

Peters: Strategy? We still don't have a strategy for Afghanistan-Pakistan. We just have a collection of disjointed techniques we're desperately trying to apply, hoping something, anything, will work. A troop surge is a tool, not a strategy. And you can't nation-build where there's no nation to build. I'm disheartened. American soldiers and Marines are dying and being maimed for fairy-tale counterinsurgency strategies that insist that digging wells for illiterate Afghans will deter al Qaeda's Arab fanatics from killing Americans. The only wise and effective thing we're doing is applying UAVs (drones) and our special operations forces to the indispensable task of killing terrorists.

I've never been threatened by a dead terrorist. And when a terrorist believes he's on a mission from his god to kill you, killing him is the only plausible response.

As I've written recently, what little analysis of the Afghan problem we do obsesses on our continuing failures. But the real question, which we refuse to ask, is "Why are the Taliban successful?" And, of course, we go on pretending that Islam has nothing to do with anything. Political correctness is killing our troops, defeating us, and facilitating terror around the world.

FP: Potential threats in 2010? Where have we taken our eye off the ball?

Peters: Good Lord, where do you start? The usual suspects will still be with us: Iran, al Qaeda, Chinese subversion of our economy (brought to you by WalMart, among others, thanks), piracy, Hugo Chavez's apparent determination to precipitate a border war with Colombia, the Kirchner regime's attempt to hobble democracy in Argentina, Islamist aggression in Nigeria (which is intensifying again), and, above all, Mexico–where the narco-insurgency constitutes the real number-one threat to the welfare of our citizens. It bewilders me that we're obsessed with "saving" Afghanistan, a worthless piece of dirt in the middle of nowhere, when the crucial struggle is right on (and crossing) our southern border. Mexico is the most important country in the world to us–for better and worse–and we treat it as problem number 47.

Where have we taken our eye off the ball? Please, tell me where the Obama administration has an eye on any foreign-policy or security balls. This ultra-left administration isn't concerned with security (except to the extent that it impacts on politics), but with a hard-left, destructive and divisive vision of "social justice." Which means, of course, punish productive citizens to reward the Lumpenproletariat. We're a greater threat to ourselves, in the long run, than al-Qaeda is to us.

FP: Ralph Peters thank you for joining us. It was an honor to speak with you.

[Jamie Glazov, "The Obama Tragedy in the Terror War,"
Frontpagemag.com, January 8, 2010.]

3. Obama's Tortured Rendezvous With Reality – Victor Hanson

Frontpage Interview's guest today is Victor Davis Hanson, a classicist and historian at Stanford University's Hoover Institution. He is a columnist for National Review and a recipient of the 2007 National Humanities Medal.

FP: Victor Davis Hanson, welcome to Frontpage Interview.

First things first, let me ask you this.

If our government was serious about fighting Islamic terrorism and saving lives, wouldn't Abdulmutallab be getting water-boarded just about now?

We know that the use of "enhanced techniques" of interrogation on al-Qaeda leader Khalid Sheik Mohammed – which included waterboarding – forced KSM to give up crucial information that ended up preventing countless terrorist attacks and saving an infinite amount of innocent lives. It allowed, for instance, the U.S. to capture key al-Qaeda terrorists and to thwart a planned 9/11-style attack on Los Angeles.

But now, thanks to the Obama administration and its approach to the terror war, Abdulmutallab will probably be getting a lawyer and not have to say anything. This, naturally, drastically increases, rather than minimizes, the possibilities of a future terror attack on our soil and against our citizens.

Your thoughts?

Hanson: I don't think right now the question is over interrogation techniques, but rather not giving this foreign national would-be mass murderer full rights, as if he were a common criminal rather than a non-uniformed soldier at war.

Abdulmutallab apparently, has been happy to tell all he knows without even being interrogated formally, which makes the entire foiled attack even more absurd: a Nigerian radical Muslim buys with cash a one-way ticket, carries no check-in luggage, was previously reported by his own father as a threat to America, and boards a plane to America after previous stays in Yemen?

Before we even get to questions of interrogation, how about first some sanity? And in reaction to all this, Secretary Napolitano nonchalantly talks about the system working like "clockwork"? I think very soon we will hear of no more "overseas contingency operations" and "man-made disasters"—and no more Janet Napolitano as head of our homeland security.

And when the next official struts and says "Bush did it", the public will sigh "Thank God, he did", since in comparison with the seriousness with which the prior administration dealt with terrorism, the Obama team seems to consider radical Islam an interesting catalyst for a civil liberties debate. "Reset" button probably won't be used any more either—the phrase is too ironic now, and would mean going back to our anti-terrorism policies from 2001-9, which are preferable to the present mess. In political terms, one cannot ask millions of Americans to take off their belts and shoes, and then not put someone like Abdulmutallab on a no-fly list.

FP: The fate of Gitmo?

Hanson: With over 100 Yemenis in Guantanamo, I doubt the facility will be closed; perhaps it will be virtually closed like the Iranian deadlines to stop building a bomb, or the health-care deadlines. I doubt too that Khalid Sheik Mohammed is ever tried in New York; that partisan gambit will be quietly Guatanamoized.

The present Obama diffidence—trash the Bush anti-terrorism protocols, bow, and apologize abroad, contextualize the US in the Al Arabiya interview and Cairo speech, promise to try KSM in New York, shut down Guantanamo—does not quite work in the context of a new series of human IEDs being unleashed against the US. Surely there are one or two astute advisors who will take the President aside and quietly say, "Your present rhetoric and policy are nuts! And you will destroy the Democratic Party for 30 years if you continue!"

FP: Abdulmutallab doesn't seem to come from the ranks of the poor, the oppressed and the downtrodden. What does this do to the Left's belief that the devil made them do it when it comes to our enemies?

Hanson: Well that debate was over long ago, when we learned of the past profiles of the 9/11 killers, the West Bank suicide monsters, and many of the human bombs who went off in Iraq.

The angriest at the West are those with enough money, and education to have developed a full sense of inferiority, self-disappointment, envy, and jealousy. A Major Hasan or Abdulmutallab or Atta inside the West sees the prosperity, liberality, informality, and success around him, begins to figure that no such thing exists in the world of the Middle East and Islamic world, and, presto, believes America and the Jews ensured that there is no resurgent majestic caliphate. We excite the appetites in these characters faster than radical Islam can repress them. That we too often apologize and convey a sense of shame about our own culture only emboldens these killers in their fantasies.

Every bit as important as our military response and vigilance, is our moral tone, which should be along the following lines: "Dear radical Muslims, you, not us, created your present misery through religious intolerance, gender apartheid, statism, corruption, tribalism, anti-scientific fundamentalism, and autocracy, and we have neither regrets about our own success nor responsibilities for your own self-induced miseries, unfortunate as they are." Until they get that message, we will have the sort of image conveyed by Obama in Cairo and his Al Arabiya interviews: pleasing to the world, but a signal to those who despise the US that we really do not believe in our own exceptional history and institutions.

FP: You mentioned Napolitano, her moronic statements, and how she might not be around much longer. What's the psychology here of this administration and its overall dance with denial?

Hanson: They seem very naive and inexperienced, almost as if to say: "This is not supposed to be happening to me; I was elected to undo George Bush's anti-constitutional, so-called war against terror, not actually fight real life terrorists." In this administration everything is "isolated" and "allegedly", unless you're the Cambridge police, and then we really can snap to instantaneous judgement.

Again, I think the Obama administration felt that it would prance in, and end the bad war in Iraq, finish off the good war in Afghanistan, and dismantle the unnecessary Bush crusade against mythical dragons. Instead, they learned that Iraq was essentially won by Bush, Afghanistan is heating up, and there are thousands of al Qaeda terrorists who hate us for who we are, and don't give a damn that our President's middle name is Hussein. We are no longer dealing here with college deans and TV pundits who are wowed by split-the-difference, hope-and-change soaring rhetoric.

FP: Two of the four leaders behind the Northwest Airlines passenger jet appear now to have been released by the U.S. from the Guantanamo prison in November, 2007. Significance?

Hanson: It reminds us of what happens when the Bush administration caved to the popular slur that Guantanamo was a veritable Gulag, and also reminds us that those in Guantanamo were there for a reason.

We have this la-la land fantasy that there are perfectly good and bad choices. But there are no such things. We are targeted by premodern killers, out of uniform, who are keen students of Western doubt and guilt. And in dealing with them, there are no easy solutions, as is always true when the postmodern meets the premodern.

Guantanamo was a bad solution amid far worse alternatives. Candidate Obama demogogued the issue, as he did tribunals, renditions, and the Patriot Act, and now, invested with responsibility rather than mere rhetoric, can't close it when he promised. 'Guantanamoize' is a good verb for incessant rhetorical deadlines that are never met. Ask Ahmadinejad.

FP: Concluding thoughts? What most worries you about the threat we face and the people who are supposedly overseeing our protection?

Hanson: Our well intentioned leaders see radical Islam more as an alternative world view that has grievances, rather than a sick, perverted Nazi-like creed that wants to take the world back to a 7th century theocracy, where freedom is denied, heretics and gays stoned, and women relegated to servile status–all overseen by rather creepy autocrats that destroy almost any modern institution they encounter.

Too often Obama, Biden, Holder, Napolitano, etc. see terrorists in terms of domestic criminals, not as enemy combatants. But once one wades into that legalistic mess of war being a judicial circus, nothing good comes from it: is it a supposed sin to water-board the confessed architect of 9/11 to find out about future mass murdering, but OK in legal terms to be district attorney, judge, jury, and executioner in a nanno-second when sending Predator drone hellfire missiles into the mud-brick compounds of suspect terrorists and their families in Waziristan?

We are in a race between sober people around Obama trying to apprise him of the danger, and his natural Carter-like take on America's partial culpability for world tensions. Let us hope that the serious people win.

FP: Victor Davis Hanson, thank you for joining Frontpage Interview.

[Jamie Glazov, "Obama's Tortured Rendezvous With Reality," Frontpagemag.com, December 31, 2009.]

4. Obama, Fort Hood and CAIR – Rep. Sue Myrick

Frontpage Interview's guest today is Representative Sue Myrick (R, NC-9), who is leading the charge nationally on issues related to terrorism. The founder of the Congressional Anti-Terrorism Caucus, she has recently called for an investigation of the Council on American Islamic Relations (CAIR).

FP: Rep. Sue Myrick, welcome to Frontpage Interview.

Myrick: Thank you Jamie.

FP: It is an honor to speak with you.

I'd like to talk to you today about a few things connected to our terror war, especially the tragedy that just occurred at Fort Hood and also your call for CAIR to be investigated.

Let's start with the jihad at Fort Hood. What are your thoughts?

Myrick: My first thoughts were of the families of the victims. These are our soldiers, the people who sign up to defend our country, and you just can't imagine what their loved ones are going through. But this isn't something that we can ignore. The shooter was radicalized and was a jihadist. The several terror plots uncovered across the country over the past few months all have one common thing: they are all connected by a radical global ideology that is self-identified by its believers as jihadist, or "jihadiyya." These men were from different backgrounds and races, yet they were all guided by this radical ideology. The American people need to wake up and realize this is not going to stop. We need to seriously address the issue of this radical ideology. That is why I have been working with many mainstream moderate Muslims, and trying to help empower them to speak out and confront this radical ideology within their community.

FP: And this radical ideology has been very much been protected and bolstered by groups like CAIR.

Tell us why you have called for an investigation of that supposed Muslim "civil rights" organization.

Myrick: The FBI has publicly stated CAIR has ties to HAMAS, a designated terrorist organization. This was clearly stated in a letter the FBI sent to Sen. Jon Kyl on April 28, 2009:

"As you know, CAIR was named as an unindicted co-conspirator of the Holy Land Foundation for Relief and Development in the United States v. Holy Land Foundation et al. (Cr. No. 3:04-240-P (N.D.TX.). During that trial, evidence was introduced that demonstrated a relationship among CAIR, individual CAIR founders (including its current President Emeritus and its Executive Director) and the Palestinian Committee. Evidence was also introduced that demonstrated a relationship between the Palestinian Committee and HAMAS, which was designated a terrorist organization in 1995. In light of that evidence, the FBI suspended all formal contacts between CAIR and the FBI."

If CAIR has been successful at placing interns on the offices of Members who serve on the Homeland Security, Intelligence, and Judiciary Committees for the purpose of influencing policy, the Members have a right to know. The American people have a right to know.

Why would anyone allow a group, who the FBI says is tied to terrorism, to influence national security policy, or any policy for that matter? If the FBI has cut ties with CAIR, Congress should wake up and do the same.

FP: Why do you think Congress has been so slow moving in on CAIR?

Myrick: We are not the first Members of Congress who have raised questions about CAIR. In February of this year, Senators John Kyl, Charles Schumer and Tom Coburn sent a letter to the FBI expressing support for the Bureau cutting ties with CAIR, and called for a government-wide policy of not working with CAIR. However, the first thing that CAIR does when anyone – government or otherwise –

speaks out against them is to label them as hate mongers, bigots and racists. It's this type of negative image that has probably kept more Members of Congress from speaking out against CAIR, which has ties to the terrorist organization HAMAS.

FP: David Gaubatz and Paul Sperry just came out with their new book, *Muslim Mafia*. You wrote the foreword to this revealing book, which exposes how a Muslim mafia has infiltrated many layers of our government and society. What do you make of the book and its message?

Myrick: It's a very eye-opening book that I think the American people should read so that they have a better understanding of just how pervasive the influence of this radical organization is within our government. I find it *very telling* that CAIR has only attacked the authors of the book and has not disputed any of the claims made in the book or the validity of any of the documents.

FP: CAIR has filed suit against the David Gaubatz, one of the *Muslim Mafia* authors. Your thoughts?

Myrick: I'm not surprised that CAIR has filed a lawsuit against Gaubatz, but I'm glad that this matter is getting attention. I say that we investigate everything. Let's investigate the claims made by the authors and how they got the material. And let's investigate and shine some light on CAIR's books, operations, and to whom they are connected. No matter what happens, we need to make sure that the facts prevail.

FP: Brigitte Gabriel's organization *ACT! for America* has launched a national petition calling for a government investigation of CAIR. People can join in signing this petition at ActforAmerica.org.

Your take on an effort like this?

Myrick: I'm thankful for any group that's willing to take a stand on this issue. The American people aren't going to get the facts about CAIR from the mainstream media, so it's important that groups like *ACT! For America* get the information out to their membership.

FP: Your views on the Obama administration's handling of national security so far as it pertains to the threat of radical Islam on our territory?

Myrick: The President's actions with regard to national security haven't helped us at all, especially when talking about radical Islamists and self-proclaimed jihadists. Earlier this year, the administration decided that "jihadists" would be called "violent extremists" and the "global war on terror" is now a "transnational conflict." What the President seems to be missing is that the terrorists call themselves "jihadists." If you look at recent FBI reports regarding the terrorist plots uncovered in the US over the past few months – all of them state the suspects wanted to commit "jihad." Again, this is how the terrorists label themselves. If we would label them as such, we could know our enemy, and their goals, objectives and beliefs, to ensure we can defeat their efforts to harm us.

The administration has also released our interrogation techniques to the world. No matter where you stand on interrogation in general, we can agree that letting the bad guys know what's going to happen to them when they're caught doesn't make us safer.

CIA agents are also being investigated, for a second time on the same evidence, based on what we asked them to do to keep us safe. What incentive do current agents have to do their jobs if they know they're going to be punished for it?

FP: What do we need to do to more effectively confront Islamic jihad?

Myrick: We must identify our enemy. We are fighting against radical Islamists who are using political Islam to advance their agenda to create a Caliphate, an Islamic state, and jihadists who use violent means to do the same. We need to educate the American public about our enemy, so they know their goals, objectives, and strategies, so that we can stand together and confront them. We must also make sure that we maintain, and strengthen our national security policy as well as ensure our intelligence officials, and military, have the resources and the freedom that they need to do their jobs and keep us safe.

I also encourage people to visit my website and learn more about the work we are doing on these issues. We have recently released the "Wake Up America 2.0 Agenda", which tries to set a national security agenda on these issues.

FP: Rep. Sue Myrick, thank you for joining Frontpage Interview. It was a pleasure and an honor to speak with you today.

Myrick: It's been my pleasure. Thank you.

[Jamie Glazov, "Rep. Sue Myrick Takes a Stand on Obama, Fort Hood and CAIR," Frontpagemag.com, November 11, 2009.]

5. Why He Shouted "Allahu Akbar" – Robert Spencer

Frontpage Interview's guest today is Robert Spencer, the director of Jihad Watch, a program of the David Horowitz Freedom Center. He is the author of nine books on Islam and Jihad, a weekly columnist for Human Events and Frontpagemag.com, and has led numerous seminars for the U.S. military and intelligence communities. He is the author of the new book, *The Complete Infidel's Guide to the Koran*.

FP: Robert Spencer, welcome to Frontpage Interview.

What do we now know about the Fort Hood shooting and what conclusions can we make?

Spencer: Jamie, we now know from the testimony of various eyewitnesses that this act was carefully planned. Nidal Malik Hasan some time ago told his landlord he would not be renewing the lease on his apartment. He gave away his furniture along with copies of the Qur'an on the morning of the day he committed mass murder. This indicates that he thought he was going to die – in other words, that he was planning a suicide attack. As he began firing, he shouted "Allahu Akbar."

We also know that he was disciplined for proselytizing for Islam during his stint at the Uniformed Service University of the Health Sciences. Law enforcement officials flagged Internet postings written by a man named "Nidal Hasan" and he was praising suicide attacks, but they couldn't be sure that he was the man who had written them. Still, it was in character: one of his colleagues recalled that he had said that Muslims must rise up against the U.S. military, and had spoken approvingly of Sgt. Hasan Akbar, a Muslim soldier in the U.S. military who lobbed a grenade at American troops, killing two, several years ago.

And we know that during a lecture he was supposed to be giving on a medical topic, he instead preached Islam, warning the assembled unbelievers of hellfire in such lurid Koranic terms that some left the hall wondering if he might end up shooting someone someday.

FP: Why does the media and liberal-Left so reflexively deny and ignore these conclusions?

Spencer: They reflexively deny and ignore these conclusions because they are completely sold out to the idea that Muslims, as non-white, non-Christian, non-Westerners, cannot possibly be anything but victims. (The facts that there are white Muslims, and that the jihad doctrine and Islamic supremacism are not racial issues, but constitute an ideological and societal challenge, are completely lost on them. Likewise the non-white victims of the jihad matter nothing to them.) We can see from the avalanche of "backlash" stories in the main-stream media – even in the absence of any actual backlash – that it is simply impossible for these people to conceive of a paradigm in which Muslims can perpetrate any kind of evil at all. In the lenses through which they view the world, only white Judeo-Christian Westerners can do anything wrong.

FP: What does this massacre, and the media response, indicate about what is coming down the line for our country?

Spencer: The more we remain in denial about how these things happen, and from what wellsprings they come, the more we will see of attacks like this. Why? Because nothing is being done to pre-vent them. Instead of the endless stories about backlash that we are seeing, we should be seeing stories about authorities calling the American Muslim community to account. We should be seeing stories about authorities demanding transparent, inspectable programs in American mosques and Islamic schools, teaching against the Islamic doctrines that inspired Nidal Hasan. This is not a religious freedom issue – these are political doctrines with a lethal edge, as Nidal Hasan illustrated. It is an entirely Constitutional matter of self-protection to move to restrict it.

But that won't happen. Political correctness has the media and government in a stranglehold. That will only ensure that nothing will be done to address this problem at its root, and we will see many more Nidal Hasans.

FP: Robert Spencer, thank you for joining us.

[Jamie Glazov, "Why He Shouted 'Allahu Akbar,'"
Frontpagemag.com, November 9, 2009.]

6. Obama's Human Rights Disaster – Elliott Abrams

Frontpage Interview's guest today is Elliott Abrams, senior fellow for Middle Eastern Studies at the Council on Foreign Relations. He was a deputy national security adviser in the Bush administration.

FP: Elliott Abrams, welcome to Frontpage Interview.

I would like to talk to you today about America's human rights policy under Obama.

What is Obama's human rights policy exactly? The recent visit to the U.S. of Egyptian president Hosni Mubarak was kind of illuminating in this context, yes?

Abrams: It seems clear to me that the Obama Administration has no human rights policy. That is, while in some inchoate sense they would like respect for human rights to grow around the world, as all Americans would, they have no actual policy to achieve that goal-- and they subordinate it to all their other policy goals.

In the Middle East, for example, they have decided to go for an Israeli-Palestinian deal at all costs. That means our relations with Egypt (and Saudi Arabia, Syria, etc.) are all about Israeli-Palestinian matters, not about Egypt itself as a country. Human rights and democracy in Egypt become a small issue, a side issue.

The Mubarak visit was illuminating, as was the President's choice of Cairo to give his speech a few months ago, for Obama pretty much forgot about freedom. He did not utter the word (or words like democracy, human rights, free elections) sitting there next to Mubarak at the White House. Democracy activists in Egypt have been abandoned.

Clinton's remarks about China are another example. Mitchell's visits to Syria are yet another: dead silence about human rights, smiles at dictators. That's the norm.

FP: What are the consequences of this lack of a human rights policy?

Abrams: There are four major ones.

First, we have a foreign policy that does not reflect the greatest ideals and principles of America. America was not founded to improve health care or housing; it was founded for freedom. The "shining city on a hill" was not supposed to be a model for urban planning or social policy, it was supposed to be a model of liberty and self-government.

Second, we let down the people fighting for human rights and for democracy and who look to America for help. The help can be moral or verbal rather than material support, but when we refuse to give them even that we abandon them to dictators who seek to suppress them. What message could Egyptians have taken, for example, from the Mubarak visit to Washington when the President didn't even say the word freedom or democracy or human rights?

Third, we weaken the cause of human rights globally. That cause always has enemies who seek to rule in place of the people, and they are sometimes restrained or defeated by people fighting for freedom-- sometimes with American support. When that support dries up, the oppressors are more likely to win.

And fourth, our own freedom is safer in a world of democracies, so by abandoning the cause we actually help create a world where America is less safe.

FP: What is the Obama administration afraid of when it comes to speaking about freedom and democracy? Is there the leftist seed here that America should apologize to the world rather than teach it anything?

Abrams: I think there are two explanations for Obama policy. The first is that they associate the freedom agenda and the promotion of democracy with President Bush, so they reject it. The desire to dissociate from a previous Administration is understandable, but not when it comes to human rights. Promotion of human rights was also Carter policy and Clinton policy, in some ways, so what they are actually abandoning is decades of foreign policy consensus.

The second explanation is the one you suggest, left-wing politics. These apology tours suggest a view that America has been a source for trouble, violence, oppression and not an inspiration for freedom. It's a version of the old McGovernite view that we are a bad country and the more we do in the world the worse off everyone will be. Reagan won in 1980 in part because he did not believe that, and the American people don't believe it; they believe we are the greatest influence for good on the face of the earth. And they are right.

FP: What is it that Obama just doesn't understand? And why doesn't he understand it? Is it an ignorance and inexperience? Or is it also just a destructive ideology? Or both?

Abrams: I think it's mostly ideology, the long-time view of the left wing of the Democratic Party, which he represents. It is impossible for him and his advisers, it appears, to imagine that the more powerful and active in the world America is, the better off we and the world will be. American power remains today what it was in the Second World War and the Cold War: the greatest force for freedom in the world. They seem to have a hard time with that notion.

Hillary Clinton recently espoused a view of human rights that we really haven't heard since it was a Soviet argument during the Cold War: that we need a "broad" definition of human rights that doesn't just focus on freedom of speech, or freedom of the press, or free elections, or religious freedom, but includes better housing or the right to a job. That is pure ideology, and it means the AID approach to human rights takes over: we press dictatorships to build more schools, but we don't press them to allow freedom of thought in those schools. We build roads and forget about free elections.

But there is also an element of incompetence here. I'm not sure Obama or Jim Jones or Hillary Clinton fully realizes they have more or less destroyed the effectiveness of the democracy directorate at the NSC and the democracy bureau at State. I imagine none of them issued an order saying "destroy that place." It has happened because they have paid no attention and have allowed real ideologues to seize pieces of the turf and undermine the work that used to be done in those offices-- going back to Carter days in the 1970s. Human rights activists around the world don't really know where to turn in the US Government these days to get a friendly ear and some help.

FP: A recent piece in the Washington Post noted that the only country in the world with which the U.S. has worse relations since Obama took office is Israel. Why do you think this is? Would it be fair to say that there is a strain of anti-Semitism in the Obama administration? A black pastor recently reflected on this issue. Your thoughts?

Abrams: I don't think anti-Semitism has anything to do with it at all, and some of the key people promoting Obama's policy are Jews. No, that isn't the explanation. I think it is partly ideology, once again: the old Leftist view that Israel is the source of the world's troubles and is an aggressive, militarized state. Support for Israel in the Democratic Party and among liberals and leftists is far lower than it is among Republicans and conservatives.

The Right is simply more pro-Israel than the Left. Obama also seems to believe that the Arab position regarding Israel is the result of bad conduct on Israel's part, and will change if that conduct (such as settlement activity) stops. But in truth the real problem isn't any particular conduct by Israel, it is the fact that most Arabs have yet to make peace with the idea that Israel exists, and has a right to exist forever, as a Jewish state in the middle of the Middle East.

The President also seems to think that distancing the US from Israel will gain us points with Muslims around the world. That's an ignoble position-- abandoning an ally in the hope that some other people will smile at us more. It will also not work.

A final part of it I attribute to the accident of who are some of the personalities involved. Rahm Emanuel seems to think he knows

Israel very well, and that the way to treat that country and its democratically-elected government is the way he treats all opponents in politics: by attacking and attacking. I have little doubt he urged the President to pick a fight with Prime Minister Netanyahu early and publicly, which the President then did. And George Mitchell seems to be clinging to the view he expressed in the Mitchell report of 2001, that "settlement expansion" is an absolutely critical issue in moving toward peace in the Middle East.

FP: Overall, what would you say is the best human rights policy for the U.S. to pursue? Why? What President, in your estimation, pursued an admirable and effective human rights policy and should be held up as an example?

Abrams: Look, the United States Government is not an NGO and we must always balance the many interests we have: economic and financial, commercial, military and security, human rights and the expansion of freedom. There will be many cases where we cannot do what we'd like and where realpolitik must govern our behavior; for example, I don't know anyone who's in favor of invading China to free Tibet. But that's a good example: what President Bush did do was to meet repeatedly with the Dalai Lama, including at the White House, to show exactly what his real views were, and make sure we had programs in place to help Tibetans.

Two presidents pursued human rights policies that were serious and effective, Reagan and George W. Bush. They understood that American support for human rights activists is a moral imperative for us and also makes the world safer for us. Under Reagan the huge rollback of military governments and dictatorships began, from Chile, Argentina, Uruguay and Brazil to Central America, from Taiwan to the Philippines to South Korea. President Bush met repeatedly with human rights activists and freedom fighters from all over the world, to give them encouragement and protection and to advance their cause. Under both these presidents, we had active NSC and State Department offices pushing the regional, geographic offices to do more for human rights.

What you need is a clear instruction from the very top that the President cares about this and demands action and results. It has to be clear that the President sees the support for human rights as critical to his Administration and indeed his view of American and the world. And you need political appointees in the key jobs who also believe it and will act on it all the time, seeing it as central to their jobs and not some annoying addition to their "real" responsibilities. In all this, the Obama Administration is failing- and failing very badly.

FP: Elliott Abrams, thank you for joining Frontpage Interview.

[Jamie Glazov, "Obama's Human Rights Disaster," Frontpagemag.com, August 25, 2009.]

7. Catastrophe – Dick Morris

Frontpage Interview's guest today is Dick Morris, who heads *DickMorris.com* and is the co-author (with Eileen McGann) of the new book *Catastrophe*.

FP: Dick Morris, welcome to Frontpage Interview.

What inspired you to write this book?

Morris: Worry, concern, fear, anger, frustration and a few similar emotions.

I think that President Obama is taking America down a very dangerous road which will fundamentally change us in negative ways. My gripes with his policies kept piling up -- the deficit, the increased spending, the borrowing, the takeovers of car companies, the bank nationalization -- in effect, his health proposals, immigration changes, muzzling talk radio. Finally, they boiled over into a book.

FP: How radical is Obama's political agenda and what are the consequences if he fully implements it?

Morris: He will divide America into two classes: the tax eaters and the taxpayers. The former group will be about 60% of the nation that realizes a net profit on their dealings with the IRS. April 15th is a great day on their calendars. The latter group will be about 20% that pays all the taxes. With this arithmetic, he can raise taxes with political impunity.

But the most dramatic consequences are economic. The budget deficit is so big and the borrowing so immense that it will send interest rates way up, deepening the recession and prolonging it. Then, when times improve, we will face mega-inflation as all the money the fed has been printing comes out of hiding and floods the marketplace all at once and as doubts about the currency multiply, impelled by the expansion of the money supply.

And then there is health care. He will ask 800,000 doctors in the U.S. to treat 300 million people as opposed to 250 million who are now insured. But there won't be any more doctors. In fact, with fee restrictions, there will be fewer. That means that less care will have to suffice for more people. The result will be rationing as in Canada. There, the cancer death rate is 16% higher than in the U.S. because of this rationing of medical care. It takes an eight week wait to get radiation therapy for cancer.

FP: You predicted a lot of the ingredients of the present catastrophe and the looming catastrophes didn't you?

Morris: Yes, in *Fleeced*, written in Feb of 2008, we predicted the stock market crash of the fall of that year and in *Outrage*, our previous book, written in Feb of 2007, we predicted the implosion of *Fannie Mae*.

FP: What can ordinary people do to stop the implementation of this agenda?

Morris: In each chapter of the book, we have an action agenda listing specific steps people can take to fight back. We give the names of the key congressmen to pressure, the places to send money, the arguments to use in convincing your neighbors. Particularly on health care, we need to stop the Obama agenda now.

FP: Can you talk a bit about Obama's foreign policy so far? Your thoughts on how he is handling the war on terror, Israel, Iran and North Korea?

Morris: The fruits of appeasement are that rogue nations think they can get away with thumbing their noses at the US and they are correct. Here's what Obama should do in Iran: 40% of Iran's gasoline has to be imported because it lacks refinery capacity. The US Export Import Bank, funded by the taxpayers, gave a $500 million loan guarantee to Reliance Industries, an Indian firm, to expand the refinery that sells Iran 3/4 of its imported gasoline. We need to cut off that funding. Congressman Sherman (D-CA) and Kirk (R-Ill) are proposing an amendment to do so that just passed the House Appropriations Sub-committee. Obama should support it immediately.

FP: Who are some people surrounding Obama who frighten you and who no President should be listening to?

Morris: Eric Holder, the Attorney General, who pushed the FALN pardon of the Puerto Rican terrorists who committed hundreds of bombings and who pushed a pardon for Marc Rich. He is opposed to any aggressive strategy against terrorists and is a real danger to the nation.

FP: Is Obama just naïve? Or does he have some malicious intent with these plans of his? Does he really not perceive the destructive consequences of what he is doing?

Morris: He never believed that the stimulus spending was the way to solve the recession. He used the recession to pass the spending he wanted to do anyway in the stimulus package.

FP: Dick Morris, thank you for joining Frontpage Interview.

[Jamie Glazov, "Catastrophe," Frontpagemag.com, June 30, 2009.]

Part II: Unholy Alliance

Introduction:

In our terror war today, we witness a disturbing but predictable phenomenon: the progressive Left is collaborating with violent Muslim extremists. Leftist feminists and gay rights activists are in cahoots with those who keep women in burqas and hang homosexuals with nooses.

What explains the Left's yearning to reach out to the enemies of freedom – just the way it did throughout the entire Cold War? To those who actually understand radicalism, the answer is simple: because the enemy of my enemy is my friend and the ends justify the means.

The political Left and Islamofascism both possess the same opponent whose very existence sabotages the implementations of their very different utopias: the United States and the principles of her constitution.

Once one accepts this reality and begins looking at the evidence – a sampling of which is presented in these five interviews – a continual pattern begins to emerge of leftist apologists' romance with Islamic jihadists. -- David Swindle

8. Unholy Alliance – David Horowitz

Frontpage Interview is joined today by Frontpage's founder and editor-in-chief David Horowitz to discuss his new book *Unholy Alliance: Radical Islam and the American Left.* One of the founders of the New Left movement in the 1960s, he is a best-selling author, a lifelong civil rights activist, and today the president of the David Horowitz Freedom Center.

FP: Welcome Mr. Horowitz. First let me congratulate you that *Unholy Alliance* has, at this moment, reached to 20 on the Amazon list -- out of several million books. What do you think accounts for this remarkable success?

Horowitz: Well, let's not get carried away here. The key here will be sustaining the success before concluding that it is remarkable. Nonetheless this book has started out with greater velocity than my previous books, which I suspect has to do with its subject matter. Everyone knows there is something strange going on when large numbers of individuals are protesting a war that liberated 25 million people from a sadistic monster, and when the Democratic Party has opted out of a war that we are winning and that we have to win.

FP: Ok, let's begin. What inspired you to write this book?

Horowitz: In some ways, this is a book I was born to write. It distills more than fifty years of experience in the left or studying the left. I was struck by the audacity of radicals I had known in volunteering to be frontier guards first for the Taliban and then for Saddam Hussein. It was one thing to work as overt or surrogate allies of the Communist enemy. After all the Communists claimed to stand for social justice and other radical fantasies. But here were regimes and enemies who were Islamic and fascist fanatics and would as soon saw the heads of Medea Benjamin and Leslie Cagan -- two of the leftist organizers of the protect Saddam movement -- as give them the time of day.

Why would people who thought of themselves as "progressives" and champions of human rights -- and these include many of my former friends -- volunteer so readily to put their bodies on the line to defend the forces of such primitive evil? That was one of the questions I set out to answer with this book. Another was how the hard left had managed to take so much of the "soft" left with it.

FP: *Unholy Alliance* touches on a truly bizarre contemporary phenomenon: the Left's partnership with militant Islam. Islamism is a totalitarian ideology that extinguishes women's rights, gay rights, democratic rights, and numerous other rights that are supposedly at the core of leftist ideology. Yet the Left has enthusiastically embraced this fascist despotism. Illuminate for us the ingredients of this leftwing mindset.

Horowitz: In a long section called "The Mind of the Left" I attempt to describe its evolution from the Communist heyday to the present. I deliberately did not pick an easy (because mindless) target like Michael Moore, but selected figures like Eric Hobsbawm, Gerda Lerner, Noam Chomsky, Eric Foner and even Todd Gitlin, a leftist despised by the radicals themselves for his decent instincts, to show how a broad and in many ways intelligent cross-section of the left could be of a common mind-set. This common mind-set is a view of their own (democratic) homeland in terms that allow them to lend their support to Saddam Hussein by obstructing America's war to overthrow him. Allow me to say here, before I go any further, that I do not put all critics of the war in this category. It is possible to criticize the war as tactically unwise, as risky over-reach and so forth. What the above named individuals have in common is a view of America that is so negative that it approximates the image of the Great Satan that motivates the terrorist savages who want to kill us.

In describing the evolution of the left from Communist progressivism to contemporary anti-war progressivism I come to two conclusions. First that there hasn't been much of an evolution. The analysis of America that drives the left today -- even leftists as otherwise sensible and "democratic" as Todd Gitlin -- is remarkably similar to the views of America held by Stalinists fifty years ago (and of

Hamas and al-Qaeda as expressed in their manifestos) . Of course they don't use quite the same language as the Stalinists or the Islamo-fascists. But the bottom line differences are really quite small. In all of their analyses of American history, there is the "genocide" of the Indians, the rape of the Africans, the oppression of the workers, and the imperialist crusade waged by evil corporations in quest of world domination -- in short the same mythology that one finds in Lenin and Stalin and Mao and Fidel and Osama bin Laden in their indictments of America and the West. And if this doesn't lead them to fly hostage filled planes into tall building, it does prompt them to find excuses for those who do, and for attempting to disarm the victims instead of defending them.

The second conclusion I come to is that the driving force of this leftism is a nihilistic assault on America rather than a positive agenda of socialist construction as was evident in the past. There is no unifying agenda or theme that solidifies the current leftist movement, a fact that often causes people on the left to claim that there is no left, absurd as that may sound. What actually unifies them is their hatred for the United States as it exists in the present. It is much like the election: they don't much like Kerry, but they passionately want to get rid of Bush. In the same way, they may not like the Islamic fascists (although many of them actually do), but they passionately want to get rid of the corporations whom they see as predators but who in fact organize what is the most prosperous, the most democratic, the most egalitarian societies that have ever existed.

FP: In your book, you demonstrate how the Left turned the Democratic Party presidential campaign around and reshaped its views on the War on Terror. Why do you think the Left has such a stranglehold on the Democratic Party? What do you think is the future of this party?

Horowitz: I describe in the book how this happened and I won't spoil the story by telling it here. However, I will say that the left has been taking control of the Democratic Party apparatus for more than thirty years ever since the McGovern campaign. The catastrophe of the Communist dream acted as a check on their arrogance for awhile. (And don't kid yourself, every progressive in one way or another thought of the Soviet Union as a progressive state that would evolve into a worthy future no matter how flawed they might have thought it. They did not disown "actually existing socialism" until it disowned itself.

Up to the fall of the Berlin Wall they were prepared to defend it against the real villain, the United States. They were anti-anti-Communists; in other words, they knew who the enemy was, and it was us.) But a decade of low profile organizing in the Clinton era, and then the assault of 9/11 which they saw as the revenge of the Third World and the Iraq War (and which they as an Imperialist strike) and the fact that they then got away with attacking their own country under attack has emboldened and inspired them. Maybe it was the fantasy of the return of Vietnam that did it. In any case, they have openly revealed their power -- in the streets, in the media, and in the Democratic Party electoral apparatus -- and I hope my book has documented it enough for all to see. As to their future, I am sure a reckoning is coming at the polls. It may not be this election and it may be this election. But it will come. The Democratic Party are too far removed from reality for this reckoning to be delayed much longer.

FP: Like it does now, the Left sided with a totalitarian entity throughout the 20th century: Soviet communism. All historical evidence and empirical reality has completely delegitimized the Left's position in the Cold War – which entailed siding with genocidal, despotic, sadistic and vicious enemies. And yet, as you point out, the Left remains completely unchastened and simply continues its same behavior. All that has changed is that Islamism has filled the void of communism. Why do you think the Left is so incapable of reflecting on its own record and mistakes?

Horowitz: As I have pointed out in all of my works, the left is really a crypto-religion; it is a collective delusion. It is based on the inability of its adherents to come to terms with the real world, the actually existing world, with their own mortality, with human limits. Leftists -- as I show in this book through analyses of the self-revealing memoirs of Eric Hobsbawm and Gerda Lerner -- leftists who are honest with themselves-- admit that they cannot live without the illusion of a social redemption, even if it is not anchored in any reality. They need to believe in a future redemption that will bring socialist world (or a world of social justice) to pass. This fantasy is as necessary to them as the air they breathe. But it is this fantasy of a redeemed world that also creates their hatred for the one they live in.

FP: You have stated that we "have to win" in Iraq. Hypothetically, let's say that the Vietnam process is replayed all over again and we cave in to the anti-war movement, lose our backbone, withdraw and lose. The consequences?

Horowitz: The consequences will parallel those in Indo-china but for us will be much worse. In Indo-china when Kennedy, Kerry, Dean and the other antiwar activists (myself included) were able to prevail in the political argument, and America cut and ran, the result was a bloodbath in Southeast Asia in which the Communists slaughtered two and a half million people. If we were to lose in Iraq and be forced to withdraw, there would be a bloodbath of all those who fought with us, and who resisted the terrorists, and then all those in the terrorists' path. It would not probably reach the proportions of the Vietnam and Cambodian catastrophes immediately, but it would spread to other Muslim states whose governments the radicals are seeking to overthrow and eventually come home to the United States, something that did not happen in the Cold War with Communism.

It may or may not happen immediately. But if the tide of radical Islam is not stopped in Iraq it will spread to other states, which are much larger and even nuclear -- Pakistan comes immediately to mind -- and then we will reap the whirlwind. Iraq as someone has said is not Vietnam, it is Guadalcanal. We are in a war with radical Islam which is seeking first of all to control the lives and resources of one and a half billion Muslims, and then to take on the "Crusader" west. The threat to us can decrease only if we stay on the offensive and keep winning and thus keep them losing and off balance and on the defensive. This is why the efforts of Kennedy and Al Gore and Jimmy Carter to repeat the disaster of Vietnam are infinitely more dangerous than what John Kerry and Ted Kennedy did in Vietnam. Communism, as we didn't fully realize at the time of Vietnam, was already a dying system and an unraveling creed. Radical Islam is not. Radical Islam is a far more fanatical religion than Communism (I never thought I would be saying this!) and – in the short run -- does not depend on the success of an actually existing utopian Mecca to sustain it as Communism did.

FP: You ask why people who think of themselves as "progressives" and champions of human rights would risk their lives to defend despotism – the "human shields" for Saddam, the Taliban etc. Mr. Horowitz, haven't we seen this all before – i.e. the Western progressives who went to help build socialism in Russia after the Bolshevik revolution, only to be slaughtered by the Stalinist terror, etc?

Not to get too heavy or deep here, but isn't this all the same death wish, the yearning to sacrifice one's life for a utopian idea? What else can explain leftist feminists going to anti-war rallies in the nude wearing Saudi headgear, when they know they would be extinguished within 30 seconds if they even showed an ankle under the regimes with whom they now side? Could you comment on this yearning for self-extinction on the part of the Left, or do you disagree with this interpretation?

Horowitz: Well I have drawn the parallels in *Unholy Alliance* and applied the same term that Trotsky used to describe the international progressive movement when he said they were "frontier guards" for the Soviet state. Since 9/11 the progressive left and its "international solidarity" units have acted as frontier guards for the terrorists and the terrorist states. They are once again a radical "fifth column" as they were for our Communist enemies in the Cold War, this time for Islam. As for the radical death cult, this parallel was noted before me, and quite eloquently by Paul Berman, a leftist himself, in his book *Liberalism and Terror*.

Progressives are best viewed as social redeemers, people deluded into thinking they can change the world and usher in a future in which there are no fanatics, Islamic or otherwise. On day one of the revolution in their unhappy minds, the Islamic lion will lie down with the Jewish, Christian and feminist lambs. People who believe that Palestinian suicide bombers are reasonable individuals acting out of political desperation and not sick enthusiasts of a religious death cult, are themselves partial believers in that cult. Their dementia is to believe that if only enough Israelis/Christians/neo-conservatives are eliminated, the world will become a livable and just place. This is the group psychosis that afflicts our time, just as the group psychoses of Communism and Nazism afflicted previous generations.

FP: As a former believer in the progressive faith, what advantages do you think you have to dissect the leftist mindset? Also, if you had remained a leftist you might have today been marching in an anti-Bush rally, cheering for the victory of our Islamist enemies. But that is not the case. What do you think it was in your character and outlook that made it impossible for you to continue along a journey in which you would have ended up doing what I just hypothetically described?

Horowitz: In *Unholy Alliance* I have shown the parallels between the thinking of secular radicals and Islamic radicals. Sayyid Qutb, the theoretical inspiration for Islamic Jihad has even written a book called *Social Justice in Islam*. The idea of "Social Justice," which is really a code for communism and a religious concept is the political left's sha'ria -- the divine law instituted on earth. The Islamic radicals want to impose sha'ria or God's law on the world as a way to redeem it from the corruption into which it has fallen and make it holy. Since God obviously is not going to have a say in this and what they are imposing is their own rule, and a rule that will be comprehensive and all pervasive, they are totalitarians in exactly the sense that Communists and Nazis were in the past.

The revolutionary agenda of progressive leftists is to impose or bring about the similarly universal and all inclusive rule of "social justice," whose only practical meaning is to impose their will through the power of the state on the rest of us. This is the same totalitarian agenda (although some of the words they use to describe it have changed) that they supported in the century just past, and that cost 100 million innocent lives. Like the Bourbons, they never learn and they never forget.

Why am I no longer part of the totalitarian cult (even though I never for a second would have conceded that I was a part of it at the time)? Ultimately, I don't really know. What broke my faith, however, is that I could not close my eyes to the practical results of our efforts. We -- the anti-Vietnam left -- helped to kill two and a half million people in Indo-China. We supported (however "critically") a bankrupt socialist system or an impossible socialist future without regard for the consequences of the destructive acts we committed to make it possible. I don't know why it disturbed me that our efforts led to a slaughter in Southeast Asia and did not disturb others -- John Kerry for example. Tom Hayden seems to have been disturbed for a nanosecond while writing his memoir, before quickly shifting the "real" blame for the genocide in Cambodia to Nixon and Kissinger who tried to prevent it, while exonerating himself and Jane Fonda and John Kerry and Vietnam Veterans against the War who were so instrumental in bringing it about. I do not know why all those progressives (who are in fact reactionaries and who number in the millions) continue to go about their work of attacking and undermining the corporate order and the capitalist system when they haven't a clue as to the future that might replace it, but they do. The archetype of this casual insanity is probably Ralph Nader who has spent a lifetime railing against corporations without having the foggiest idea of how they work or what they do or how any other entities could do better.

FP: One of the greatest gifts you have given this country in its battle, internally and externally, against despotism is your knowledge of how to fight political war – as well as your own personal willingness and determination to do it. As you have shown in your work, Conservatives are extremely weak in fighting political war. Now we have someone from the other side who effectively uses leftist weapons right back against the leftists themselves.

So my question: if we are going to win this war against the *Unholy Alliance*, what tactics must we employ?

Horowitz: The most important element in defeating the left is understanding it -- who it is and what its agendas are. The assault on the war effort would never have gotten as far as it has if our political leaders had gone on the offensive early and not given the saboteurs of the war effort such a wide latitude. Ted Kennedy thinks nothing of implying that if and when there is a dirty bomb set off by the terrorists in this country, George Bush will be responsible. Ted Kennedy is already responsible for the deaths of Americans and freedom loving Iraqis in Iraq. The path on which Al Gore and Jimmy Carter have led the Democratic Party is a treacherous one and they should have been made to pay a political price early on in their sabotage effort.

A year and a half ago the Democratic Leadership began undermining the credibility of the commander-in-chief by calling him a liar over 16 perfectly true and relatively unimportant (if untrue) words in the State of the Union address. This assault was unconscionable and unjustified and has cost many American lives. It was a political war declared that the Democratic Party leaders on the President in the midst of a war, and it should have been fought as such. Instead, the White House apologized for the innocent words thinking that this would discourage the saboteurs. Since their agenda was to derail the war effort and unseat the President it did not discourage them. In fact it inflamed them. And we are paying the price with an election that should not have been this close and with a commander-in-chief gravely weakened in handling the threats not only in Iraq but from Iran and Syria as well.

Democrats pretend to be appalled that patriotism would be an issue. But of course patriotism -- understood as rallying to the defense of America's security -- is an issue. Al Gore understands that -- which is why he attacked the President as unpatriotic -- as betraying Americans. So does John Kerry and the Democratic political apparatus which is accusing Bush of encouraging the terrorists and making the world a more dangerous place. There is no way to avoid this issue. The task is to put the shoe on the foot that it fits.

We have not begun to fight the war at home properly. The coalition of so called civil liberties groups that is conducting a full-out assault on the Patriot Act is a coalition that includes terrorists like Lynne Stewart and Sami al-Arian and their political sympathizers. It is spearheaded by the same organizations and individuals who defended our Communist enemies for the same reasons during the Cold War and whose motivation is not the defense of the Constitution -- a worthy cause -- but the exploitation of the Constitution for their radical agendas (not a worthy cause).

Defending a democracy is always problematic. We must protect our Constitutional rights and democratic processes as vigilantly as possible. We must distinguish between earnest and loyal critics of our war policies and defense measures, and treacherous critics; and we must distinguish between treacherous critics and treacherous criticisms which are not always the same thing. I don't pretend to know what Ted Kennedy's motivation is when he makes remarks that are obscene and disloyal. I don't know whether he's merely getting senile and allowing the bitterness of his personal failures and political defeats to run away with his judgment. But I do know how to assess their political impact. Analyzing the sources of Al Gore's bizarre outbursts would be a challenge for a professional. On the other hand, Michael Moore is a transparent and self-proclaimed member of the enemy camp.

Those who embrace and praise Michael Moore's anti-American, jihadist propaganda undoubtedly do so from a multitude of inspirations, among them the ordinary mean-spiritedness of partisan politics and the normal stupidities of the species (particularly its Hollywood genus). But the effects of these efforts to divide us internally in the face of our enemies and sabotage our efforts to defend ourselves are not so easily dismissed and should not be so readily forgiven. First we need to win the war; then we can forgive. The left likes to confuse the political argument with a legal proceeding. No one in the United States has been charged with treason (let alone convicted) since the Second World War. So take a deep breath and calm down. I am not suggesting anyone should be charged with treason now (though John Walker Lindh and Lynne Stewart would surely qualify). But this does not mean that we should not spell out the implications of political arguments and positions or assess the recommendations of those who oppose our war efforts. The Constitution is a sacred covenant, not a suicide pact.

FP: Thank you Mr. Horowitz, we are out of time. It was a pleasure to speak with you.

Horowitz: My pleasure as well. Thank you.

[Jamie Glazov, "Unholy Alliance," Frontpagemag.com, Parts I and II, September 30 and October 1, 2004.]

9. Jewish Collaborators – Kenneth Levin

Frontpage Interview's guest today is Kenneth Levin, a clinical instructor of psychiatry at Harvard Medical School, a Princeton-trained historian, and a commentator on Israeli politics. He is the author of *The Oslo Syndrome: Delusions of a People Under Siege.*

FP: Kenneth Levin, welcome to Frontpage Interview.

There have been some stories circulating of Ahmadinejad's supposed Jewish roots, but it appears that there is no substance to these stories. Even if it were true, however, no one should really be very surprised because it has been a recurrent phenomenon that some Jews would choose to join the Jews' tormenters and even seek a leading role among them.

Frontpage's new *Collaborators* series deals with this phenomenon. David Gutmann has also written a very profound analysis on this issue for us at Frontpagemag.com.

As a psychiatrist and the author of the *Oslo Syndrome*, what would you bring to the table on this phenomenon?

Levin: Well, it's certainly true, Jamie, that time and again we've seen Jews joining forces with those who would do other Jews ill. But, as I wrote in *The Oslo Syndrome*, this is common within many communities under siege, whether minority communities under assault by the surrounding majority or small states under attack by their neighbors. Inevitably, some elements of the besieged group will embrace the indictments of the besiegers, however bigoted or absurd. They will do so in the hope of thereby extricating themselves from the wider group's dire predicament.

Some will simply abandon the community and seek to immerse themselves in an alternative identity. Within Jewish communities under siege, such people would convert to the dominant religion, whether Christianity or Islam, to escape the Jews' plight. Some among them, however, to more emphatically establish their distance from other

Jews, and to allay any potentially dangerous suspicions among the majority that their conversion was insincere, would become spewers of anti-Jewish venom and high-profile endorsers of attacks on the Jews.

FP: And there's a long history of this.

Levin: Absolutely. This was, for example, a recurrent phenomenon in both the Christian and Muslim worlds throughout the Middle Ages and into modern times. One notable such individual was Solomon ha-Levi, who was chief rabbi of Burgos in Spain when, in 1391, a wave of murderous anti-Jewish riots and forced conversions decimated Spanish Jewry. Solomon was well enough connected that he could have escaped the choice of conversion or death, but – rather than remain a Jew under straitened circumstances and see his place in the world much diminished – he converted, underwent clerical training in Salamanca and Paris, and, as Paul de Santa Maria, ultimately became bishop of Burgos. When a second vast wave of forced conversions began in 1411, Paul took a leading role in the assault on Spain's remaining Jews and was responsible for drawing up edicts that isolated the Jews, stripped them of many communal rights, and, most importantly, deprived them of almost all means of earning a living, leaving them with the choice of death by privation for themselves and their families or conversion.

FP: What was this story about Ahmadinejad being a Jew?

Levin: The story was that Ahmadinejad's family converted from Judaism to Shi'a Islam when he was a child. It is apparently false. But, reflecting a recurrent pattern in Persian lands, there were many episodes of forced conversion and massacre of Jews in Iran in the nineteenth century and in the early part of the twentieth century, episodes typically instigated by Shi'a clergy; and it is a virtual certainty that some among the converts became themselves enthusiastic persecutors of those who remained Jews, if for no other reason than to demonstrate the sincerity of their conversion to their fellow Muslims.

A variation on the same theme can be seen in nineteenth century Europe. Jews were no longer subjected to waves of forced conversion, at least in western Europe, but they lived with severe limits on the educational and vocational opportunities available to them and with other significant social disabilities. Many chose to convert to improve their prospects, and some again joined forces with the Jews' persecutors. Friedrick Julius Stahl, whose conversion enabled him to win a position on the law faculty of the University of Berlin, became head of the anti-Jewish Christian Conservative Party early in the nineteenth century and fought against the extension of political rights to Jews.

But those who abandoned their Jewish identity and became themselves defamers and attackers of the Jews did so much more typically from the political Left than from the Right, with Karl Marx being the leading example. Marx's father had converted, apparently for the sake of professional advancement, and had had his son baptized at age six, in 1824. From his earliest entry into the public arena, Marx was clearly interested in distancing himself from "the Jews," and he did so largely by rabidly attacking them. For example, his essay "On the Jewish Question" is both a regurgitation and an amplification of popular anti-Jewish calumnies. Marx – who knew virtually nothing about Judaism – declares that the religion of the Jews is "huckstering," that the capitalist system reflects the Judaizing of the Western world, and that the radical agenda is therefore the quest to liberate the world from the ethos of the Jews.

In eastern Europe, which then meant mainly Czarist Russia, Jews retained a greater sense of national identity than in the West, and those who embraced socialism did so largely because they had lost faith in left-of-center liberalism bringing an end to czarist anti-Jewish depredations – including forced impoverishment, forced conversion and state-instigated physical assaults – and hoped socialist reforms would improve the lot of the Jews. Very few embraced what ultimately became Bolshevism, with its own anti-Jewish tenets. In contrast, in western Europe most Jews who joined socialist or communist movements did so as an alternative to a Jewish identity – it meant for them conversion to a new religion – and it was common for such individuals to endorse and even embellish the anti-Jewish cant that was typically a fixture of European socialism and communism, and indeed continues to be so today, if transmogrified somewhat into "anti-Zionism."

Today, the Jews' high-profile enemies, such as Ahmadinejad, other leaders of the Iranian theocracy, and key figures in Iranian satellites such as Hezbollah and Hamas, may not themselves have Jewish roots, but there are certainly Jews among their boosters and fellow travelers.

Hezbollah head Hassan Nasrallah has declared that "If [the Jews] all gather in Israel, it will save us the trouble of going after them worldwide," and Hezbollah has in fact gone after them worldwide, as in its 1994 bombing of the Jewish Community Center in Buenos Aires that claimed 87 lives. But none of this has constrained Noam Chomsky from visiting with Nasrallah and other Hezbollah leaders, praising the organization and Nasrallah, and advocating the arming of Hezbollah. Norman Finkelstein has likewise met with Hezbollah leaders and praised the organization. It is not surprising that Nasrallah has at least temporarily exempted Chomsky and Finkelstein, and other like-minded Jews, from Hezbollah's general death sentence on Jews.

Hamas's charter quotes a Hadith according to which Allah declared that the Day of Judgement will not come until the Jews are all killed and even the stones and trees will help in killing them. The charter adds that Hamas "aspires to the realization of Allah's promise, no matter how long that should take." Hamas has perpetrated innumerable attacks targeting Israeli civilians, including suicide bombings and rocket and mortar barrages, and Hamas children's television instructs its young audience to kill Jews. Yet Jewish member of Britain's Parliament Gerald Kaufman has affectionately compared Hamas to Jewish fighters in the Warsaw Ghetto.

FP: And there were Jews who opposed Israel taking defensive measures in Gaza.

Levin: To be sure. For years Hamas attacked Israel from Gaza, only accelerating its rocket and mortar assaults in the wake of Israel's total withdrawal from Gaza in 2005. It built and cached its rockets and other arms in, and unleashed its attacks from, heavily populated civilian areas. When Israel finally responded forcefully to Hamas's terror campaign, in December, 2008, myriad Jews – who almost invariably had been silent about the Hamas attacks – condemned Israel's actions and largely maintained their silence on Hamas's terror, instead often parroting Hamas's skewed version of events during the war.

Jewish groups across the world – such as Independent Australia Jewish Voices – rushed for media podiums from which to publicize their censure of the Jewish state. Jewish South African Richard Goldstone's recent report for the so-called United Nations Human Rights Council offered his conclusions from an "investigation" whose mandate preemptively condemned Israel and whitewashed Hamas. His report largely follows Hamas's narrative of events, minimizes Hamas crimes, ignores Israel's documented rebuttals of Hamas claims, and would deprive Israel of the right to defend itself against Hamas's genocidal campaign against the Jewish state. Goldstone is simply among the most notable examples of Jewish participation in such travesties.

Other Jews and Jewish groups, in their stances on Middle East issues, largely choose to ignore the genocidal Jew-hatred that pervades the media, mosques and schools of Israel's enemies. They likewise ignore or play down or relativize the explicitly trumpeted genocidal goals of Iran, Hamas and Hezbollah.

FP: Your thoughts on the Jewish group J Street?

Levin: It has honed the relativist tack in its characterizations of last December's Gaza fighting, declaring that "neither Israelis nor Palestinians have a monopoly on right or wrong" and there are "elements of truth on both sides of this gaping divide".

J Street has curried support from Jews and non-Jews who have been rabid critics of Israel and supporters of, or at least apologists for, those in the Middle East who seek the Jewish state's destruction. They include Israel critics with close ties to Saudi Arabia, such as Ray Close, and Stephen Walt, co-author of the factual-error-filled anti-Israel screed *The Israel Lobby and U.S. Foreign Policy.*

Former Senator Chuck Hagel was among the senators least supportive of Israel during his tenure and often exhibited greater sympathy for the Jewish state's enemies. When 88 senators wrote to the EU urging it to add Hezbollah to its list of terrorist organizations, Hagel was one of the handful who demurred. Yet J Street has seen fit to enlist Hagel as keynote speaker at its First National Conference this month.

In addition, while J Street incessantly declares itself to be "pro-Israel" its advisory board includes Jews and others who have long been not merely critics but defamers of the Jewish state and have even questioned the wisdom of its continued existence. For example, advisory board member Ayelet Waldman has been quoted as declaring, "I can't help fearing that the Zionist enterprise will one day be seen to have done the Jewish people more harm than good. Our tenacious hold on this strip of homeland has become the scapegoat for the world's terrorism and this wouldn't be the case if we remained a people of the diaspora."

The quote from Waldman, like perhaps most of the attacks on Israel by Jews, reflects a variation on the phenomenon of some within communities under siege seeking to separate themselves entirely from the community. In many instances, elements of communities or nations under attack will see the assault as directed at a particular segment of the community, and will seek to emphasize their own belonging to a different segment – a segment sympathetic to the besiegers' indictments – and so deserving of exemption from the attack. Here, Waldman directs no criticism against those who regard Jews as uniquely unfit for national self-determination and want Israel destroyed. Rather, she takes that bigotry as a given and reserves her criticism for Jews not readily bowing to it. Instead of criticizing the scapegoating of Israel, she embraces the delusion that if Israel would just disappear and Jews became again only a Diaspora community – the community of which she is a part – her life and that of Jews like her would be better.

FP: How about Tony Judt?

Levin: Judt is perhaps the poster boy for this kind of thinking. He has called for Israel's dissolution and sought to justify his stance by arguing that Israel's creation came too late, that a state based on religious or ethnic identity is passé, and so it should be discarded into the dustbin of history.

While singling out Israel for dissolution, Judt ignores the fact that most of the world's states, including the other states of the Middle East, are based on a dominant ethnic or religious identity, and, Rip Van Winkle-like, he seems unaware that in the last two decades at least twenty new nations have been created based primarily on a dominant ethnic or religious identity.

But, in fact, this rationale is not the true spur to Judt's attack on Israel. Rather, as he makes clear elsewhere, he is upset that the circles in which he travels – primarily, academic circles – include many people who are not only censorious of Israel but regard all Jews suspiciously as likely sympathetic to the Jewish state. He feels this unfair, wishes therefore to trumpet his lack of any such sympathy, and desires the demise of the Jewish state, removal of the root cause, to more definitively spare himself – as well as others who may be similarly misunderstood – from coming under such unfair suspicion and suffering such discomfort.

The Jews thus far cited as ignoring or rationalizing the genocidal agenda of Israel's enemies and even in many instances siding with those enemies have all been Diaspora Jews. But even among Israeli Jews there are many who do the same, despite the fact that they and their families are directly threatened by Iran, Hezbollah, Hamas and those many others in the surrounding states who seek Israel's destruction.

The editors of Haaretz, for example, persist in downplaying the genocidal agenda of Hamas, urging Israel to be more forthcoming to the Islamist group, and castigating the government for not doing so. Haaretz writers such as Gideon Levi, Amira Haas and Akiva Eldar rarely have a critical word for Hamas or others of those dedicated to Israel's destruction, and when they do have something critical to say they almost invariably find a way nevertheless to lay the ultimate blame on Israel. The same pattern can be seen in the work of many Israeli academics, and even in the views of various Israeli politicians. This is true even though – in the wake of the terror war launched by Arafat and the PLO against Israel in 2000, the Second Lebanon War, and all that has transpired around Gaza in the period since Israel's total withdrawal from the area – many fewer Israelis entertain such thinking than did so formerly.

Of those Israelis who do embrace such thinking, some, like Diaspora Jews who choose such a course, may seem to do so out of far Left ideological commitment, according to which Israel must be condemned as representing Western imperialism and its enemies embraced as embodiments of transcendent Third World virtue. But even those devoted to such an ideology have the option to change when confronted with the reality of murderous assault and genocidal intent. Many apologists for Stalin and the Soviet Union changed their politics after the Hitler-Stalin pact while others did not. Similarly, many American devotees of far Left orthodoxies had a change of heart after 9/11, while of course many clung to their former views and blamed American policy for the attacks or even embraced the madness that the U.S. was itself the agent of the attacks.

So ideological commitment is not in itself an explanation for why some Israelis cling to blaming Israel for its enemies' hostility and ignoring or rationalizing those enemies' genocidal intent.

FP: So what are other explanations?

Levin: Some – like many of those who abandoned the Jewish community in past centuries – no doubt do so for personal gain. For example, Israeli academics who cultivate a reputation as critics of Israel are much more likely to win visiting professorships and other desirable academic perks in Europe and the U.S. Indeed, the more extreme their attacks on Israel the better their chances.

But most Israelis who adopt and cling to blaming Israel first, and who avert their eyes from the dimensions of the genocidal threat, do so out of wishful thinking – which is yet another response by some within communities under chronic attack. Some will rationalize the threat, close their eyes, ears and their minds to what the community's enemies are actually declaring to be their objective, and will embrace selected elements of the attackers' indictments in the hope that if the community will only reform itself in ways that address those elements – if Israel would only give up enough land, for example – the attackers will be appeased and peace will be won.

Yet whatever the psychological dynamics driving any particular individual, one thing is certain: As the genocidal threat facing Israel from Iran and its allies and satellites, and indeed from others among Israel's neighbors, persists and perhaps grows even more ominous, some Jews, in the Diaspora and in Israel, will respond by recognizing the threat and urging efforts to confront and defeat it, but others will respond by distancing themselves from the Jewish state and even embracing its genocidal enemies, or by seeking to rationalize the threat and advocating self-reform and appeasement, or by taking some other, related course that will likewise add to the threat rather than help diminish it.

FP: Thank you for joining us Kenneth Levin.

[Jamie Glazov, "The Psychology of Collaborators in the War against Israel and the Jews," Frontpagemag.com, October. 19, 2009.]

10. The Islamist Lobby in the House – Steve Emerson

Frontpage Interview's guest today is Steve Emerson, terrorism expert and founder of *The Investigative Project on Terrorism.*

FP: Steve Emerson, welcome to Frontpage Interview.

There are some Congressional Democratic stooges operating on behalf of Islamist groups. Can you tell us what is going on?

Emerson: We obtained a letter sent on July 24 by seven House Democrats to Attorney General Holder on behalf of 9 radical Islamic front groups relaying the complaints of the groups about law enforcement techniques in terrorist cases, including the use of informants.

The Congressmen acted as virtual lobbyists for these militant groups, asking that the AG stop employing tried and proven counter-terrorist techniques and also echoed information that was blatantly false claiming the FBI was engaged in racial profiling. The Congressmen asked that the AG meet with these groups, which are almost all derivatives of the Muslim Brotherhood.

FP: CAIR (Council on American Islamic Relations) is one of the groups, yes? Tell us about CAIR.

Emerson: Yes, they included CAIR, an un-indicted co-conspirator in the Hamas (Holy Land Foundation for Relief and Development) funding trial last year in which an FBI agent labelled CAIR a front group for Hamas and ISNA, another un-indicted co-conspirator in the same case. CAIR has defended suicide bombings and ISNA has featured anti-Semitic speakers and terrorist supporters at its most recent conference a month ago in DC.

Another group represented by the Congressmen included the Muslim American Society (MAS) which is the defacto arm of the Muslim Brotherhood in the US (by its own admission) and whose leaders have openly called for jihad and support for Hamas and Hezbollah.

FP: And we have members of Congress actually working on behalf of these terrorist-related groups? Who are these Congressmen?

Emerson: The letter was signed by California representatives Loretta Sanchez, Adam Schiff, Mike Honda and Lois Capps, along with Ohio representatives Mary Jo Kilroy and Dennis Kucinich. Northern Virginia Congressman James Moran joined the group. Moran serves on the House Appropriations Committee subcommittee on defense. Schiff and Honda serve on the House Appropriations Subcommittee on Commerce, Justice, Science, and Related Agencies. Kilroy sits on the House Homeland Security Committee.

These issues have been pushed by radical Islamist groups for months. The letter's close tracking of the interest groups' positions indicates that their officials dictated its terms for the members of Congress to sign. In fact, the nine entities all are listed in exactly the same sequence in this release from CAIR. The April 2009 release also cites two of the same issues as in the letter to Holder.

As I wrote in my piece, many of the representatives who signed this letter have a history of supporting CAIR. For example, Kucinich sent a video message praising the organization to the CAIR-Chicago 4th Annual Banquet on February 23, 2008:

"As the Council on American-Islamic Relations meets I want to pledge to you. I continue to pledge for your efforts to make sure that the powerful message of Islam, a message of peace and reconciliation reverberates. I want to make sure that you know that you have a friend in the United States Congress."

Sanchez has repeatedly attended annual CAIR banquets in Anaheim. Likewise, Honda spoke at CAIR's 2006 national banquet in Virginia, where called his hosts "the civil rights group that will speak on behalf of the community." Capps is included on a page of laudatory statements about CAIR, saying "I applaud CAIR for its important role in advocating for civil liberties, enhancing the understanding of Islam, and condemning acts of terrorism."

Moran is included on the same page, saying "It is through the activities of groups like CAIR that cooperation—rather than competition—between the various faiths can be achieved." Honda is quoted saying "CAIR's commitment to social justice and civil rights for all Americans will help our country to ensure that respect and tolerance exists for people of all religions and ethnicities."

In their letter, the representatives accept the claims of defendants in two criminal cases unquestioningly, despite sworn testimony to the contrary.

FP: Well we obviously see the *unholy alliance* at work here, the Left and radical Islam holding hands in solidarity. Can you talk about that alliance a bit and how it is working?

Emerson: This phenomenon is part of the Grand Deception, when radical Islam wittingly and unwittingly convinces the American government and the media that radical Islamists have no other agenda than to play pluralist politics when the real (and demonstrably unconcealed goal) is to infiltrate the American government and media and ultimately take over. The documents released from the Holy Land Foundation trial were shockingly clear: the Muslim Brotherhood in this country secretly aspires to a "civilizational-jihadist process" in which the Islamist groups will infiltrate the institutions of power and American society. No one can argue with hundreds of such documents that were released at the HLF trial. They were shocking and had never been seen before.

Their aim is simple: infiltrate the corridors of power (Congress and the government), the media, Hollywood, the intelligentsia and even law enforcement. Eighteen years after the documents were written, we can see the Muslim Brotherhood game plan has succeeded beyond its wildest dreams. Hollywood, for example the likes of Howard Gordon, executive producer of the series "24" has already been conned into legitimizing radical Islamic groups that espouse anti-Semitism, defend Hezbollah, denigrate the Holocaust, tell their members not to cooperate with the FBI, etc.

The Hollywood-based Writers Guild of America is about to hold a special seminar for CAIR, a front group for Hamas that has defended the killing of Jews and has sponsored as speakers Holocaust deniers. When was the last time the Writer's Guild held a seminar for the KKK or, for that, matter evangelical Christians? That members of the Writer's Guild are allowing this to happen is one of the most scandalous indicators of the pact between the left and the Islamic fascists. Where are the voices of the Guild protesting this outrageous seminar? Does the Guild endorse the notion of suicide bombers and also undermining the prosecution of Islamic terrorists? Does the Guild support Hezbollah and Hamas? Does the Guild support raw anti-Semitism? And the Muslim Public Affair Committee (MPAC), a radical group that has supported Hezbollah, claimed Israel was behind 9/11, and has made derogatory comments about the Holocaust. Now it has established a Hollywood liaison bureau where, believe it or not, studios submit their scripts *in advance* for approval.

The Left's Faustian alliance with radical Islamists is a pact with the devil that will ultimately behead the same leaders of the Left. Melissa Etheridge, avowedly gay, played in a concert for an annual conference for the MPAC, a group that believes homosexuality is a sin and that has claimed that Islamic law protects women, when the undeniable truth is that Sharia treats women as cattle and second class citizens, not to mention how it treats Jews and Christians. What does that tell us about the sheer stupidity of Etheridge, willing to sacrifice her own bedrock principles for the sake of collaborating with a group that defends Hezbollah, the group that has killed the second largest number of Americans next to Al Qaeda? And what do you think will happen to gays like Melissa Etheridge when Sharia law is imposed? Why would she lend her support to a group that has made pro-terrorist comments, published anti-Semitic cartoons and supported Hezbollah, as well as condemned her own gay lifestyle as evil?

These are not the only groups and individuals that have signed up to work with radical Islamic organizations. Fairness for Accuracy in Reporting, FAIR, the ultra left wing group that defends Venezuala's anti-Semitic President Hugo Chavez, works closely with CAIR. FAIR and CAIR share the public relations firm and work so closely that

FAIR is considered by many to be an extension of the terrorist front group CAIR. FAIR is so much in the pocket of CAIR that the IRS should immediately launch an investigation into the financial and other ties between the two groups to determine their abuse of the tax laws governing non profits. I know with 100% certainty that CAIR has violated the tax laws for example.

J Street, the ultra left wing Jewish group, has also secretly worked with CAIR. The ACLU, founded on the notion of the need for separation of church and state, actually collaborates with CAIR—a group whose officials want to impose blasphemy laws in this country-- to the point that it has appointed members of CAIR to local ACLU boards around the country. In terms of the media, NPR and PBS have actively colluded with CAIR and other radical Islamic groups to dishonestly portray them simply as "civil rights" or advocacy groups, when in fact these groups have actively championed terrorism. We have emails showing that CAIR actually "owns" reporters at various newspapers, which suggests the degree of penetration by CAIR and other Muslim Brotherhood groups into the media is far more extensive and far more frightening than anyone has known to this point.

FP: And the Congressmen who signed the letter?

Emerson: Either they are thinking in terms of votes and donations or they actually believe the fascist propaganda put forth by the groups on whose behalf they signed the letter. But above all else, it demonstrates the frighteningly enormous political strides that radical Islamic groups—those that purposefully undermine the security of this great nation by attacking law enforcement's prosecution of Islamic terrorists and also support violent jihad and who defend Hamas and Hezbollah—have succeed in getting the support of 7 Congressmen, 6 if you believe that Congressman Schiff actually made a "mistake" as he claims in signing the letter.

Finally and most disturbing is the fact that the seven congressmen actually accepted CAIR's views of a particular Al Qaeda case in Irvine when in fact the reality is that CAIR actively colluded with the suspected terrorist to obstruct justice. When the alleged terrorist, a member of Al Qaeda, began to suspect he had been recorded by an informant calling for bombings in the US and for praising Osama bin Laden, the terrorist conspired with CAIR's LA official Hussam Ayloush to deliberately lie and pin the blame for the terrorist rantings on the informant. This was such a blatant obstruction of justice by CAIR that Justice Department officials have considered charging CAIR's Ayloush with obstruction of justice and lying to federal officials. But the seven Congressmen actually accepted Ayloush's point of view and endorsed the notion that CAIR dutifully reported the informant as a terrorist suspect in the manner of a good citizen. That they accepted this version shows that the congressmen are in the pocket of CAIR.

All of this means that the secret Muslim Brotherhood plan to infiltrate the US has succeeded beyond the MB's wildest dreams.

FP: One of the Congressman, U.S. Rep. Adam Schiff, is actually denying that he ever had a role in this. How can this be possible and what does it tell us about him?

Emerson: Something smells to high heaven here.

An aide to U.S. Rep. Adam Schiff (D-Burbank) contacted the Investigative Project on Terrorism to report that Schiff's name and signature appear erroneously on the letter to Attorney General Eric Holder. After reading about the letter in this story, Schiff wrote his own letter to Holder in which he said "I never saw or approved the letter and my signature should not have appeared on the correspondence."

According to the aide, a staffer from U.S. Rep. Loretta Sanchez's office brought the letter to Schiff's office and said Schiff approved having his signature added to it. Schiff, the aide said, never agreed to that. The aide said he did not know whether Schiff participated in any earlier discussions about the letter and could not explain why Sanchez's office had the impression that he was on board.

None of this makes any sense, suggesting that Congressman Schiff got embarrassed when his name was disclosed as one of the signatories and simply sought a way out of it. Our sources tell us that the Congressman actually read the letter and approved signing it personally, something his aides deny.

FP: What does this Schiff affair say about Schiff?

Emerson: Schiff is a Congressmen who has long befriended MPAC, a group whose anti-Semitic cartoons published in their magazine, the *Minaret*, make the Danish cartoons look like child's play. Schiff has been befriending radical Islamic groups for years ever since his election. That he suddenly decided to concoct a story claiming that he signed on to the letter by mistake—without explaining how that mistake could have occurred—shows that some members of Congress are not exactly profiles in courage.

On the other hand, Congressmen like Frank Wolf, Pete Hoekstra and Sue Myrick have shown a backbone that is unparalleled in Congress in courageously tackling the Muslim Brotherhood, CAIR, and radical Islamic groups. So it shows there are brave Congressmen as well. The FBI should be noted for standing tall and courageous in making the decision last year to sever its relations with CAIR because of its ties to Hamas. Yet, various members of Congress—like the seven who signed the letter—have deliberately flouted the FBI intelligence and policies in such an egregious way that these Congressmen are actually endangering the security of the United States.

FP: So what lessons do we draw here?

Emerson: The chief lesson here is that the Islamist plan to infiltrate American society—Congress, law enforcement, the administration (the vast extent of Obama's willing acceptance of radical Islamic groups and leaders into key positions into his government including CAIR which I have not yet divulged), think tanks, public relations firms, academia, et—has succeeded in ways that are truly endangering our security. Yet, the stealth jihad—which is what this is—has gone unreported by the mainstream media because of factors such as laziness, the "useful idiot" syndrome, and active collaboration between these groups and reporters as well as collaboration with other influential sectors of society.

In fact, the stealth jihad is in many ways more dangerous than acts of terrorism, which seems the only time that the American public and media wake up. The American public would be absolutely shocked to witness the degree of the radical Islamic deception perpetuated, wittingly and unwittingly, across society including law enforcement, journalism, Hollywood, Congress, think-tanks, the left, and the intelligentsia. I am not talking about an unproven conspiracy. This deception—what I call Militant Islam's Grand Deception--is the subject of my upcoming documentary and book. It will shock viewers to their core.

FP: What can the average citizen do to counter-act these developments?

Emerson: They have to start bombarding Congress and the Obama administration with protests every day. They need to be protesting the one-sided coverage of these Islamic groups with their local newspapers who have been assiduously involved in a campaign to legitimize these groups and suppress the real evidence about them. Our organization, the *Investigative Project on Terrorism*, has been collecting intelligence on these groups for more than 15 years. I urge your readers to go to our site and learn about the secret Muslim Brotherhood plan to infiltrate and subvert this country, to find out more about the pro terrorist agenda of these so called "civil rights" groups. And yet, I fear that only when a violent attack occurs will the American public wake up. In his darkest hours before the war that he so courageously predicted, the great Winston Churchill said presciently that "Democracies only act when there is blood in the streets." I fear he is right.

FP: Steve Emerson, thank you for joining Frontpage Interview.

[Jamie Glazov, "The Islamist Lobby in the House,"
Frontpagemag.com, August 4, 2009.]

11. Jimmy Carter and the Middle East – Rep. Howard Berman

Frontpage Interview's guest today is Rep. Howard Berman (D-Calif), the new chairman of the House Foreign Affairs Committee.

FP: Rep. Howard Berman, welcome to Frontpage Interview.

Berman: Thank you.

FP: You have criticized fellow Democrat, and former president, Jimmy Carter for his recent meetings with Hamas. Update for us the form your criticism has taken.

Berman: President Carter has come under bipartisan criticism – from Republicans as well as Democrats -- for meeting with the leaders of Hamas, which is a terrorist group. Gary Ackerman, the chairman of our Subcommittee on the Middle East and South Asia, and I urged President Carter in a letter to cancel his plans to meet with Khaled Mashaal and other members of Hamas during his visit to Syria . We wrote, "We believe this visit will undermine the Middle East peace process and damage the credibility of Palestinian moderates, including Palestinian Authority President Mahmoud Abbas. We also believe it falls far short of the high moral standards you have set as a champion of human rights." I stand by that view.

FP: Expand for us on the bipartisan criticism of Carter on his Hamas odyssey.

Berman: In the same week that Gary Ackerman and I sent our letter, more than four dozen Republicans and Democrats together signed a letter to President Carter asking him not to press forward with his plans to meet Khaled Mashaal, and they released it to the media. Senators Hillary Clinton and Barack Obama also criticized President Carter's plans to meet the Hamas leadership.

FP: Hamas is a terrorist organization that wants to wipe Israel off the map. What exactly is Carter thinking in this effort of his? Why is he extending an olive branch to Hamas and how and why does he believe in its potential goodness? He has, after all, engaged in a one-man lobbying campaign on behalf of Hamas – despite its terror on its own population and against Israel.

Berman: In recent days, President Carter made use of several opportunities to explain his thinking to the media, including just after his meeting in Syria. He also has an op-ed this week in the Washington Post. He was not persuasive.

FP: What are your thoughts in general on Carter's view of the Middle East? What do you think of him referring to Israel as an apartheid state? Why his malice toward Israel?

Berman: Comparing Israel with Apartheid South Africa is deliberately provocative and demonstrates a very loose grasp on the details of both situations; it is a poor analogy. As to President Carter's views of the Middle East in general, his concept of the forces at work in the region – who is to blame, who is to be held accountable – is way off the mark, and this undermines any initiative he may undertake there. Unfortunately, it also undermines the very people we want to help in the Middle East – President Abbas and his supporters, on the one hand, and the Israelis on the other.

FP: What policy should Israel and the U.S. pursue toward Hamas?

Berman: Israel can make its own policies, but in my opinion it has made the right choices given the circumstances. Hamas is a terrorist organization that denies Israel's right to exist and shows no sign of changing. In fact, Israel is fully in synch with the United States and the broader international community in demanding that Hamas recognize Israel, renounce violence, and accept past Israeli-Palestinian agreements. I hope there will be no compromises on this approach; to do so would make a mockery of those Palestinians who reject violence and choose the path of negotiations. The last thing we would want is for terrorists to get the message that violence pays.

Of course, Iran is the number-one problem in the region, and we should keep in mind that Hamas is strongly backed by Iran, which provides training, funding, and probably arms to Hamas, as it does to Hezbollah. The United States needs to push for the strongest possible sanctions against Iran – and if the Security Council won't go along, we should press our European and other allies at least to join with us in a tough sanctions regime. Our top priority should be to deprive Iran of the funds it uses for its nuclear weapons program, but a successful sanctions regime hopefully would have the additional benefit of reducing Iran's material support for terrorists.

FP: Rep. Howard Berman, thank you for joining Frontpage Interview.

Berman: You're quite welcome.

[Jamie Glazov, "Why Is Jimmy Carter So Disastrously Wrong on the Middle East?" Frontpagemag.com, May 5, 2008.]

12. The Death of Feminism – Phyllis Chesler

Frontpage Interview's guest today is Phyllis Chesler, the author of classic works, including the bestseller *Women and Madness* (1972) and *The New Anti-Semitism* (2003). She is the author of the new book *The Death of Feminism: What's Next in the Struggle for Women's Freedom*. Her website is phyllis-chesler.com.

FP: Dr. Chesler, welcome to Frontpage Interview.

Chesler: As ever, it's my pleasure to be with you.

FP: What inspired you to write this book?

Chesler: I had been saddened for a long time by the failure of academics, including feminists, to celebrate, not merely tolerate, "difference." I am not talking about class, gender, race, or sexual preference diversity but about intellectual and ideological diversity which is sorely lacking in the western academy--which has been thoroughly Palestinianized.

I have also been wrestling with anti-Semitism on the left since the late 1960s. What compelled me to write this book at this time was the western intelligentsia's refusal to acknowledge the dangers of anti-Semitism and Israel-bashing even post the 2000 Intifada; and their refusal to re-evaluate their own obsessive hatred for America, post 9/11.

Finally, based on my own captivity in Afghanistan long ago, I understood that the lessons I learned at such perilous cost to myself were lessons that I now needed to share with others. Primarily, neither America nor Israel, not even Europe, are responsible for Islamic or Third World barbarism--especially Islamic gender Apartheid; that we cannot abandon women and dissidents living under Islamist tyrannies because we cherish our ideas about cultural relativity more than we cherish our obligation to try and bring more justice and freedom into the world.

FP: So how and why did leftist feminists end up sacrificing the plight of their sisters under Islamic gender apartheid?

Chesler: In the beginning, feminists were not anti-activist isolationists. We saw the plight of women world-wide as a common plight. As feminists became more colonized by left and postcolonial ways of thinking, they revised their original vision of universal rights for all to a culturally relativist and *mea culpa* way of thinking. Who are we to judge others, there is CIA blood on our hands, we, who believe in the rights of victims everywhere must therefore support the victims rising everywhere.

Thus, left feminists came to support, romanticize, or not think clearly about Third World tyrants whom they sometimes confused with liberators. They also had one very high standard for America and Israel and another much lower standard for Muslim countries. I view this as both racist and sexist but in turn, saying so has rendered me vulnerable to charges of my being a racist. Many left feminists confuse my stand against multi-cultural relativity and its attendant isolationism with a stand against multi-cultural diversity. Often, in the battle of ideas, one's great opponents include groupthink, rigidity, stupidity, as well as evil.

To be fair, feminists did rail against the Taliban, female genital mutilation, honor killings, etc. but they did not manage to forge a feminist foreign policy that would incorporate these concerns--mainly because they refused to work with a Republican administration. I hope this can change. I begin to spell out what a feminist foreign policy might be like in the last chapter of the book.

FP: H-mm. My experience is a little different I am afraid. Not one leftist feminist I know or have read anywhere has ever mouthed a criticism of FGM, the Taliban or honor killings, etc. And if they have, it has always been in some reluctant passing reference to a bitter condemnation of America and its foreign policy. The main theme is always about how no matter what injustice occurs anywhere in the world it is because of us and we are worse.

In any case, let me get back to your own life experience for a moment. Even after your own captivity in Afghanistan you remained a member of the Left and held on to many of its principles and assumptions. How did you rationalize this?

Chesler: At the time, both civil rights and left anti-Vietnam war activists espoused principles of social justice that I believed would surely apply to the disenfranchised and wretched of the earth. But I underestimated the possibility of Jew-hatred among some Christian and Muslim African-Americans and among Caucasian leftists as well as misogyny among leftists.

I did not think that conservative libertarians were a philosophical option at that time since political and religious conservatives strongly opposed feminist ideas. (This has changed to some extent today). But also: I was so busy teaching, lecturing, researching, publishing, testifying in court cases and working as a part time therapist that I was simply too busy to properly note and did not study the long-term consequences of left and gender-neutral thinking among feminists, especially in the academic and activist worlds.

Although I had not studied the history of colonialism, imperialism, or capitalism, I assumed that such systems were antithetical to freedom, especially to women's freedom. This was the cultural "sea" in which I swam and which eventually drowned freedom of thinking among intellectuals. And only feminists really cared about women both at home and world-wide; only we raised the issues of incest, rape, domestic battering, and the issues of poverty and disease and tribal barbarism (female genital mutilation, arranged marriage, polygamy, etc.) that afflicted women in the Third World. Leftists insisted that America was primarily to blame for this. I never did. I already knew too much. But I also knew that western values and civilization had not and would not, ipso facto, end misogyny either.

I did not feel I had to rationalize anything. I held an honorable minority position on many feminist issues e.g. religion, motherhood, pornography, prostitution, surrogacy, etc. And, when it came to the arts, music, literature, painting, I admit I have always been an elitist i.e. appreciative of excellence. This meant that I was never a Natural Born Leftist. And, I also believed that feminism's cause was just--I still do--and I did not break with a movement that was still vital, still evolving, still activist, and still under siege.

Also, leftists (and anthropologists) did not take over academic feminism immediately. Many pitched battles had to be fought. To some extent, America has harmed people in our pursuit of our own interests; to some extent, local governments have harmed their own people even more. Viewing the spread of western culture as a disease-- as opposed to a cure--is a serious academic failing. Second wave feminism was born in the USA and to deny or minimize this would be foolish.

FP: So why do you think the Left is so totalitarian in its thinking and so hopelessly incapable of accepting intellectual pluralism and diversity?

Chesler: From a psychological point of view, perhaps the kind of person most attracted to both Left ideology and Islamism is someone who needs their ideology to function as a Total Institution, as a way of life which will provide community, employment, and answers to the most perplexing questions, even if the answers are wrong or do not work.

Also, many leftists, like Islamists, view themselves as "good" people who are trying to help others. Even if it means slandering, ostracizing, exiling, or killing others it is "for their own good," and for the good of the world.

Many extremists exist on both the right and left--designations and polarities which may no longer serve us well. Academic leftists simply cannot stop blaming America as an evil empire and demonizing President Bush as more dangerous that Al-Qaeda. How is one to reason with those who are not acting rationally but emotionally and in a very primitive way?

FP: The Left is vicious with those who think outside of its permitted intellectual boundaries. It is especially malicious toward a former comrade who has had second thoughts and chooses to think differently. Can you tell us some of your own personal experiences at the hands of the Left?

Chesler: Oh dear, I might have to write another book to answer this question, my own personal Darkness at Noon or 1984.

It is important to note that some feminists have strongly and courageously supported what I am saying in The Death of Feminism. They have interviewed me on radio shows knowing that they would come under friendly fire themselves for having done so. Most recently, Marcia Pappas, the President of NOW-New York State stood up to the bullying and intimidation that Katha Pollitt of Nation magazine and her ally, Pam Martens visited upon her for having invited me (someone who voted for President Bush and who supported the war in Afghanistan and Iraq) to speak. Since then, Pappas has written a good review of Death which I believe she has been circulating among NOW officials. Pollitt et al persuaded WBAI to tape my lecture which they then spliced-and-diced for a one hour program in which they denounced me on-air as a "racist." They described me as "the Christopher Hitchens of the women's movement"--and then proceeded to denounce me.

Privately, the feminists who are behind this persuaded a television producer to pull an interview with me on another subject entirely; she did, but she is fighting back. A while ago, Women's E-News interviewed me about David Horowitz's Bill for Academic Freedom. They did not allow one word I said to surface in print but they did run my photo next to one of David's to position me as "the conservative feminist whom left feminists must learn to hate." Very Orwellian.

And, while Women's E-News does run important pieces about Islamic gender Apartheid, so far they have not reviewed The Death of Feminism or called to interview me. The temporarily defunct but now returned Women's Review of Books did not review The New anti-

Semitism and when I called and suggested that they might consider interviewing me about the issues raised by the book the editor said: "No thanks."

Like everyone who has dared tell the truth about Israel, who is an American patriot, and who opposes the hypocrisy and double standards of the political correckniks, one must endure very strange looks, unexpected and ferocious confrontations, turned backs, heavy silences, and the ending of political friendships.

So far, my books about anti-Semitism and about Islamic gender Apartheid, in both Muslim countries and in the West, which is what Death is about, has not been reviewed nor have I been interviewed in most mainstream media venues where once I was more than warmly welcomed, nor have I been invited to speak by Women's Studies programs on campuses.

However, both books have been praised in important conservative venues. But such mainstream/liberal/left censoring or silencing is a small price to pay for telling the truth. It is also a measure of one's power. One makes new friends and allies. One keeps learning and evolving. For me, it is very important and sustaining that my feminist beliefs are respected in conservative libertarian circles where I now share other overriding beliefs about national security and jihad.

FP: Let us suppose that your book helps change the climate within feminism. Let us suppose that within 10 years you write a book called The Resurrection of Feminism. What would be the state of the feminism at that time to merit this title?

Chesler: I am surprised that you are such an optimist. But, assuming you are right: I would hope that feminists, both men and women, would learn how to disagree in civil ways and to respect intellectual differences. I would hope that "right-wingers" and "left-wingers," who share a vision of freedom and dignity for women would work together.

Finally, I would hope that feminists would work with the American government, no matter who is in office, on feminist foreign policies. For example, we must peg every peace treaty and trade agreement to women's rights. We must peg every micro-lending program to a promise not to genitally mutilate the girls in the village, to educate them, and not to force them into arranged marriages, etc. And, we must consider the use of military force when all else has failed. Feminists understand that you have to call the police when a man is beating his wife to death or when a rape is in process; it is contradictory for feminists to resist the use of military force when women are being stoned to death, hung, jailed and tortured--repeatedly gang-raped both in Iran and Sudan (and of course, in the past in Bosnia and Rwanda). Terrorists, jihadists, torturers, and tyrants are not open to reasonable "dialogue."

I expect to be working with Muslim feminists even more in the future. For example, I was recently on a panel together with Iranian and Afghan women and managed to quiet a fairly anti-American audience afflicted with "Third Worldism" by talking about the stoning of a particular Iranian woman whose tragic fate had absolutely nothing to do with American Empire.

A few weeks ago, Iranian feminists recently invited me to testify about Islamic gender Apartheid in the Senate in a briefing which was beamed up live via satellite into the Middle East and central Asia and translated into Persian, Arabic, and Kurdish. The Committee for Democracy in the Middle East co-ordinated this impressive event at which nine Senators were represented. Ramesh Sepehrrad, a leader in the National Committee of Women for a Democratic Iran said of my speech: "Finally, an American feminist leader who will not abandon us to her theory of cultural relativity."

FP: Well, I am not really an optimist. I said "suppose" to crystallize what would have to change in feminism. Although it would be great if it happened -- thanks to people like you.

Dr. Chesler, thank you for joining us today.

I would just like to end by saying that you are an amazing person and a true courageous warrior. Thank you for giving us hope. I will tell you that as the son of Soviet dissidents, what I learned from many of those who were persecuted is that nothing is as demoralizing and depressing than thinking that, while in your own captivity, you have been abandoned by free peoples. The victims of Islam's gender apartheid have a sparkle of hope because of heroes and soldiers like you.

Thank you for setting this noble standard and dignified example not only for Western feminism but for all humanity.

Chesler: Thank you Jamie.

[Jamie Glazov, "The Death of Feminism," Frontpagemag.com, January 4, 2006.]

Part III: Islam: The Religion of Peace?

Introduction:

Since the United States was attacked on 9/11, one theme has been pounded into our collective consciousness by elites ranging from George W. Bush on the Right to Barack Obama on the Left: Islam is a Religion of Peace, akin to Christianity and Judaism. The Koran is basically the Bible. The core teachings of Islam are no different than any other faith. The 9/11 hijackers have perverted a noble religion, misinterpreting passages and reading verses out of context.

If only that were so.

The painful reality is that while Jesus of Nazareth was a radical pacifist who taught a philosophy of absolute love, Muhammad was a warmonger. Christians who use their faith to justify violence – the rare abortion clinic bomber – depart widely from their religion's teachings and can find no justification for their acts in the verses of their texts. But is Osama bin Laden that fundamentally different than Muhammad? While the Inquisition was an anomaly among Christianity, Islamic thuggery – convert or die – has been the standard means of spreading Islam for the whole of the religion's history.

The interviews collected here are the beginning of digging into the Koran and learning that the dire threat that confronts free societies today are rooted in the teachings of Islamic texts. -- David Swindle

13. Defeating Radical Islam - Brigitte Gabriel

Frontpage Interview's guest today is Brigitte Gabriel, who started her career as an anchor for *World News*, an evening Arabic news program in the Middle East. As a terrorism expert and the founder of the nonprofit organization *ACT! for America*, Brigitte Gabriel travels widely and speaks regularly on topics related to the Middle East. She has addressed audiences at the FBI, the United States Special Operations Command, the Parliament of the United Kingdom of Great Britain, and the Joint Forces Staff College, among others. She is the author of the new book, *They Must Be Stopped: Why We Must Defeat Radical Islam and How We Can Do It.*

FP: Brigitte Gabriel, welcome back to Frontpage Interview.

Gabriel: Thank you Jamie. I am delighted to be back with you again.

FP: What inspired this book?

Gabriel: After writing my first book, "Because They Hate," which tells my personal experiences facing Islamic terror and is a warning to people in the West, I realized that I must go even further defining the threat we face and follow up the warning with solutions and a call to action. "Because They Hate" paved the way and prepared readers for me to take the gloves off and really define in outright terms what we and all non-Muslims are really facing. Events following the first book dramatically enabled me substantiate the underlying motivation behind Islamic terror and Islamic goals and aspirations. I felt that the additional dearth of historically proven implications of these goals can be ignored only at our own peril. Everyone must become informed and mobilized to stop them before it is too late.

FP: You title one of your chapters, Purists Drink Their Islam Straight. Tell us a little bit about what this means.

Gabriel: This is a straightforward inside look at a devout enemy motivated by religion who is willing to destroy the whole world in order to achieve our complete submission under Islam. I do not mince words. What we are calling radical Muslims are nothing more than devout purists. I quote the Koran verse after verse using the same words these terrorists use in their speeches and their videos. We have turned a deaf ear and pretend that this couldn't be true for too long. I use a publicly suppressed and potentially volatile Pentagon intelligence study on the source of Islamic extremism to substantiate the fact that it is the Koran, the holy Islamic book, that is driving them. It is the religion itself, straight from the mouth of the Prophet Mohammed, the perfect man, according to Muslims. It is not yet politically correct to talk about a religious war. But this is exactly what we are facing: a religious war declared by devout Muslims. The Islam of Mohammed is back. It's not radical Islam. It is not Wahhabi Islam, it's Mohammed's original Islam. We are committing cultural suicide by turning a blind eye to the danger Islam continually spells out.

FP: What exactly is a moderate Muslim?

Gabriel: A moderate Muslim is a non-practicing Muslim. A non-practicing or non-devout Muslim is a man who doesn't pray 5 times a day, does drink alcohol, doesn't attend a mosque regularly, believes he is equal to all other people and God's creation. Does not believe that Apostates should be killed. He believes that people have the freedom to chose what religion they want to belong to. He does not believe that Jihad should be declared on non Muslims until they convert or pay the Jizya. He believes that gays should not be killed according to Sharia Law even if he disagrees with their lifestyle. He believes that his wife is his equal and is entitled to the same respect and education as any other man; that she is not his property according to the Koran; that she should not be covered from head to toe or even wear a hijab; that he does not have the right to beat her just because he is a man and she is a woman, that Jews are his equals in the eyes of God.

Most moderate Muslims do not know the real teaching of the Koran and many of them have never read it. In debates between the moderates and the radicals about the Koran, the radical always win the arguments because Islamic law is on their side. They can quote you chapter and verse from the Koran to support their arguments while the moderates just sit speechless not knowing how to respond.

FP: What is the Muslim Brotherhood project for North America?

Gabriel: The Muslim Brotherhood project for North America is a detailed document found in Switzerland in 2001. It details a 100 year plan for radical Islam to infiltrate and dominate the West. This document became known in the Intelligence circles as "The Project". The plan was conceived and written by the Muslim Brotherhood which is the world's oldest and most sophisticated Islamic terrorist group created in Egypt in 1928. The Muslim Brotherhood boasts seventy off shoot terrorist organizations operating throughout the world.

The project was dated 1982 and it details strategies and tactics by which Islamists can gradually infiltrate nations and ultimately dominate the world with Islamic political and religious ideology. Some of the most alarming ideas outlined are: incitement to hate and commit violent acts against Jewish, Christian and other non-Muslim entities; using methods other than violence to implement cultural Jihad, and establishing a rapport with western communities until trust is won and Islam is established. The project's intentions have been implemented throughout the world since its creation.

FP: You discuss an emerging Islamonazi army all around the world. Tell us about this frightening phenomenon.

Gabriel: The world now faces a new generation of students being indoctrinated into hatred, violence and jihad. Madrassas (Islamic schools) all over the world have paved the way and set the standards for such radical education. From Saudi Arabia to Spain, Britain to Bahrain, America to Australia, Islamic madrassas now operating in nineteen world capitals preaching intolerance and fostering an environment of hate, loathing and resentment toward Western culture, Christians, Jews, Shiites, secular Muslims and non-Muslims.

Since 1973, wealth from oil revenues has allowed the Saudis to spread the strict original Islam of Mohammad throughout the world by financing Islamic madrassas. Saudi textbooks frequently quote verses from the Koran or Hadith that condemn non-Muslims, especially Christians and Jews. In many instances, the verse will direct the reader to commit murder in the name of Allah. There are roughly 225 Islamic madrassas registered in the United States. This is what is contributing to the radicalization of Muslims born and bread in England, Canada, America and Australia who want to kill their follow countrymen in the name of Islam.

FP: There are Madrassas and Islamic schools in America that are actually using Americans' tax money to teach their pedagogy. This is quite incredible. What is happening here and why?

Gabriel: Radical Islamic influence in America's educational system reaches beyond the university level into grade schools and high schools, both public and private. Islamic schools in America teach almost 50,000 students per year. Many of them are breeding grounds for Jihad and are financed with American Taxpayer's money. I give many examples in the book about such schools. One is the Islamic Academy of Florida, a private school for grades one through twelve in Tampa Bay. In 2003 the academy received more than $350,000 worth of tax-payer-funded school vouchers to help underprivileged children attend their school. In the same year a federal grand jury in Tampa issued a fifty-count indictment against the academy for being an affiliate of the Muslim Brotherhood organization Palestinian Islamic Jihad. The indictment claimed the academy was helping support the Palestinian Islamic Jihad and its mission of murder and violence by raising funds through school vouchers and fundraisers.

Another Islamic day school, the American Youth Academy was awarded in 2005, $325,000 of taxpayer money for its elementary/secondary school program. In addition, $2,500 was awarded to the school for each child enrolled in their pre-kindergarten programs.

The Islamic Academy of Florida and the American Youth Academy are prime examples of Islamic terrorists and their associates operating right under our noses. The amazing thing is that taxpayers were unintentionally funding the overseas murders of innocent citizens, including Americans.

FP: You talk about Jihad Camps in America. What are they and how are we allowing this to happen on our own shores?

Gabriel: The Muslim Brotherhood in America is creative and far reaching in its attempts to spread the world of Allah and hatred for infidels. They are now indoctrinating young Muslim children into radicalism in boy scouts and summer camps. At some of those "Summer Camps" children spend their afternoons sitting indoors, listening to speakers that preach "the way of Jihad" for true believers of Islam. Speakers usually are well known in the field of radical Islam and instruct Muslim youth on the mission of Jihad. Before 9/11, administrators and campers would refer to these camps as "jihad camps." In the post 9/11 atmosphere, ICNA, MAS, MSA, YM, and YMS are much more cautious about making any references to jihad. The camps are now touted as retreats for Muslim children to learn about their heritage. Some speakers have prepared Muslim youth for their deaths with presentations such as "Preparation for Death," by Dr. Nouman Ali Khan, "The Life in the Grave," by Imam Badawi, and "Do You Want Paradise?" by Br. Jawad Ahmad. Ahmad began his lecture with the words, "This should be our goal in life, I want to go to Jannah [paradise]." They are using our laws and freedoms in preparing a new generation of martyrs and we are allowing it to happen in the name of multiculturalism and diversity.

FP: Are we winning or losing the fight against Islamic Jihad?

Gabriel: Right now we are in the middle of this fight militarily, socially and psychologically. Jamie, history and Viet Cong generals tell us that we were winning the war in Vietnam in the 60's, but because leftists, communist sympathizers and the media told us we were loosing, we ended up loosing. Now we are seeing the same dynamics all over again with Islamic jihad. We are winning on the battle field in Iraq and being defeated here at home. Because of our lack of national solidarity here in America we are giving the enemy confidence and strengthening their resolve making things drag on and loosing more soldiers in the field. This political and ideological division along with our apathy, ignorance, materialism and short sightedness are working against us. We must match our enemy's religious resolve for subjugation with a united secular resolve for freedom.

FP: How can we stop this threat to our western societies? What can the average individual do?

Gabriel: History reveals very clearly that the apathetic give way to the passionate and the complacent are subdued by the committed. This is why I founded ACT! for America, *www.actforamerica.org*. ACT! For America is mobilizing people all over the country and giving them the tools to resist the Islamic infiltration in our society on every level: schools, government, universities, and corporations. We now have 200 chapters across America and tens of thousands or members.

We are now conducting "citizens Action training" seminars all over the country to give people the tools and knowledge to mobilize effectively.

Organized power at the grass-roots level will trump the voices of political correctness and be more powerful than the establishment media. A good example of this is the demise of the immigration reform legislation in the U.S. Congress in 2007. In spite of support from the media, the political left, and even some on the political right, the proposed legislation was shelved due to the outcry of citizens across America. In short, the voice of grass-roots America triumphed over the voice of the elite.

We are not waiting for this phenomenon to occur in the war against Islamofascism. We are not simply hoping for a spontaneous grass-roots eruption that may or may not come. We are *making it occur* by organizing ACT! for America chapters and supporters across America. We will force elected representatives to choose – align themselves with the voice of grass-roots America or the voice of political correctness. We just launched our Congressional score cards and voter education project. We keep tabs on bills we consider important to our national security and the threat of Islamofascism. We research how each congressman and senator votes on these bills. People can download the scorecards from our website or obtain hard copies from ACT! for America chapter activists. We make it easy for every voter in America to know exactly how their congressmen and senators voted. I encourage every person reading this interview to join us by going to www.actforamerica.org. We have now launched ACT! Australia, ACT! Canada, ACT! Nigeria, and in the process of establishing chapters in Britain, France, Israel, The Netherlands, and Spain.

FP: Do you ever fear for your own personal safety? From where do you get your courage?

Gabriel: I wouldn't be human if I didn't fear for my safety especially when I receive threats and have Al-Qaida discussing me on their Internet website saying I'm fighting Islam. Talk like that tends to fire up the die-hard Islamists. And I don't want to be an easy target for their wrath. I take the security measures required to insure my safety and that of my family. I go to great length organizing security when I speak or travel publicly. However I know what is at stake and why it is so important to speak out boldly and loudly right now before it is too late. As to where I get my courage? My parents taught me to stand up for that which is right even though sometimes the right thing to do wasn't the most popular. I reflect back on talks around the dinner table about things my father was doing as a government official and the flack he was getting for doing them even though they were the right things to do. I vividly remember my childhood and the suffering I went through as my parents and I lived in a bomb shelter for 7 years. Those memories give me the courage to continue on and insure this will never happen again to me or to my children. I know what is at stake. I *do not* want history repeating itself. I lost my country of birth, Lebanon, to radical Islam, I do not want to lose my adopted country America.

FP: Who are your heroes in the world today?

Gabriel: My parents will always be my number one heroes. Having grown up in a country that did nothing for my security, I would say my next heroes are our military generals like David Petraeus, Thomas McInerney, Paul Vallely and the many others like them and those who serve under them and on whose shoulders America's freedom has been preserved. Other heroes as well are the few Muslims and former Muslims speaking out laying their life on the line to do so like Ayan Hirsi Ali, Zuhdi Jasser and others.

FP: Brigitte Gabriel, that you for joining us.

Gabriel: Thank you Jamie.

[Jamie Glazov, "Defeating Radical Islam," Frontpagemag.com,
September 5, 2008.]

14. Sex in the Islamic City - Mohammad Asghar

Frontpage Interview's guest today is Mohammad Asghar, an ex-Muslim who came out of Islam after discovering its true teachings. Together with studying the Qur'an for over twenty-five years, he has also been writing his commentary on its verses - an endeavor, he hopes, that will help non-Muslim leaders, as well as ordinary citizens, understand the true messages they convey to Muslims.

FP: Mohammad Asghar, welcome to Frontpage Interview.

Asghar: Thank you.

FP: Today I would like to discuss with you Islam's theology on Heaven and Hell and who goes there and why. What is the best way to start this discussion?

Asghar: One way to begin is to focus on the subject of prayer – considered by all Muslims to be one of the five Pillars of Islam. I think it is very important to make clear a fact about it that is not known to many students and observers of Islam.

After standing up for their daily prayers, all Muslims must say either in Arabic or in their mother tongues that they are offering their *Fajr* (morning), *Zuhr* (early afternoon), *Asr* (late afternoon) *Maghrib* (sunset) or *Isha* (early night) *Fardh* (obligatory) or *Sunnah* (non-obligatory) prayer to Allah. A sincere and honest declaration before Allah by the supplicants in the language they understand and speak completes the essential part of their prayer.

After this is done, they proceed to complete the remaining part of their prayer in a very well defined manner that requires them, among others, to recite their selected Suras or Chapters of the Quran only in Arabic. They cannot recite them in their mother tongues, or in other tongues, which they may know or be familiar with.

Sura Fatiha or the Exordium is the first Sura they must recite at the beginning of each unit of their prayer. Though it is supposed to have been revealed to Muhammad by Allah, but its content does not indicate so. Rather, the words "Praise be to Allah," without the word "Qul" (say) preceding them, indicate that it was the brainchild of a human being.

The whole Sura reads:

"Praise be to Allah, the Cherisher and Sustainer of the Worlds; Most Gracious, Most Merciful; Master of the Day of Judgment. Thee do we worship, and thine aid we seek. Show us the straight way; the way of those on whom thou hast bestowed thy Grace, Those whose [portion] is not wrath, and who go astray."

After Sura Fatiha, one of the short Suras that many Muslims recite is Sura Lahab, or The Father of) Flame. It reads:

"Perish the hands of the Father of Flame! Perish he! No profit for him from all his wealth, and all his gains! Burnt soon will he be in a Fire of blazing Flame! His wife shall carry the (crackling) wood – as fuel! – A twisted rope of palm-leaf fibre round her (own) neck!"

This Sura also appears to be the work of a human being, as it does not begin with the word "Qul" or (Say), but if it was from Allah, then I must say He cursed one of the uncles (Abu Lahab) and aunts of Prophet Muhammad in a despicable language. A vast number of Muslims repeat this curse in their daily prayers without knowing, or realizing that it is a curse, and that they have been subjecting to it a man and woman, who passed away over fourteen hundred years ago.

Muslims have constantly been cursing long-dead humans in their prayer to Allah and, yet they claim they are a kind and forgiving people.

Pleased with Muslims for repeating to Him the words or messages He Himself had revealed to Muhammad, Allah will grant them berths in Heaven -- called "the Gardens" -- on the Day of Judgment. Those humans and Jinns who failed to earn His pleasure will find themselves in the fire of Hell.

FP: Sounds quite scary. Allah seems pretty angry and very much disposed towards punishing people. What's with all the rage? What's he so angry about?

Asghar: Not only that, Allah is also very revengeful. He was in the past, and He still remains, angry at those men and women, Jinns and, perhaps, animals as well, for not believing only in Him and also for not taking Him to be their lone Master. His anger reached its extreme limit, when the Pagans of the Arabian Peninsula refused to accept Muhammad's claim on his prophethood and also for denying Allah the right to treat them as His slaves.

For the insolence of the Pagans, Allah personally fought them in the Battle of Badr and slew many of them with His own hand (the Quran; 8:17), as they were "worst of beasts in {His sight}" (the Quran; 8:55).

Despite the fact that Allah personally massacred the Pagans and destroyed an entire race of mankind for hamstringing a she-camel He had sent to it as a miracle from Him in the time of prophet Salih (the Quran; 26:157), Allah is still believed by Muslims to be kind, merciful and magnanimous to His creations.

FP: What is Hell like according to Islam and why does Allah send souls there?

Asghar: The Quran says that it is the soul of man that commits the sins. But on the Day of Judgment, it is the body of man, woman and Jinn that will be sent to Hell to burn in its fire. Why Allah would do such an illogical thing is beyond my knowledge.

FP: Before we move on, who are the Jinns?

Asghar: Jinn in Arabic mythology is a supernatural spirit below the level of angels. 'Ifrit' (diabolic, evil spirit) and 'Sila' (treacherous spirit of invariable form) constitute the classes of Jinns. They are capable of assuming human or animal form. Muslims believe that they dwell in the midst of humans and in all conceivable inanimate objects

– stones, trees and ruins – underneath the earth, in the air and in fire. They can also enter into human bodies and turn their victims into abnormal beings.

Jinns possess the bodily needs of human beings and produce children. They can even be driven away or killed, but they are free from all physical restraints.

Allah created them in the Garden with fire before creating Adam with clay or dust, and his wife (unlike the Bible, the Quran identifies Eve as the wife of Adam).

FP: Ok, let's continue with the rewards and punishments humans will receive on the Day of Judgment.

Asghar: Burning of human bodies with fire is understandable, but how about burning fire with fire? Jinns are made of fire and the Quran says that those of them who sinned on earth will burn forever in the fire of Hell.

Here is the procedure Allah will follow before sending humans and the Jinns to the Gardens or to the fire of Hell:

In keeping with His perennial policy of not using the power He posses - the immensity of which no human will ever be able to fathom - to instantly create things and to cause events to take place in no time, Allah will one day order an angel to sound the Trumpet (he has been waiting, with the Trumpet in his hand, for Allah's order from the day He created the Universe), to raise the dead humans with bleared eyes (the Quran; 20:102) from their graves and to make them face Him in the trial of all Trials. How and from where the Jinns, animals and the idols will be raised is not mentioned in the Quran.

At the sound of the Trumpet, all humans, dead or alive, on earth or in the Gardens and in the heavens as well as all the animals and Jinns, and the angels who will be living with Allah in Paradise, will faint with terror, except as such as He will be pleased to exempt from it (the Quran; 39:68), and all of them will come to Him as beings conscious of their lowliness. Simultaneously, the whole earth will become His handful, with the heavens rolled up in His right hand (the Quran; 39:67). But before letting the earth become His handful and the heavens rolled up in His right hand, Allah will give another chance to His creations to correct their ways by producing a Beast from the earth. This He will do, because men refused to believe in His Signs, which He had sent to them before through His prophets and apostles (the Quran; 27:82).

FP: What will this Beast be doing?

Asghar: It will speak to humans, animals and Jinns in their languages and try to persuade them to believe in all of Allah's Signs, including the Quran. Whether it will also be speaking to those people who passed away before the Quran came to Muhammad is not known, but the Quran indicates that the Beast will fail in its efforts whence Allah will ask the angel to sound the Trumpet for the second time, following which, He will squeeze the earth into one of His two hands.

But even after becoming a tiny thing in His hand, the earth will shine with Allah's glory (the Quran; 39:69), illuminating the path that will lead all men, Jinns and animals to His Throne.

While rushing to the venue of trial, the resurrected beings will curse themselves for waking up, on hearing the sound of the Trumpet, from their deep sleep. What will be the reaction of the animals and Jinns is not mentioned in the Quran. An unidentified voice will appear from nowhere and tell the cursing men: you have been awakened because that was what *ar-Rahman* (a deity the Pagans of Mecca did not know) had promised you when you lived on earth. It will also tell them that what the apostles had told them were true.

The second sound of the Trumpet (the Quran; 39:68), followed by a blast, will make the resurrected people hasten, like a troop, to Allah's presence, with their hearts having come right up to their throats to "choke them"(the Quran; 40:18). How the Jinns, animals and idols will approach Him is not stated in the Quran.

Sitting on the Throne of the Chief Judge (the Quran; 36:75) and the Executioner, and carried by eight angels (the Quran; 69:17), while other angels, after taking their position around Him, will sing His glory and praise (the Quran; 39:75), Allah will vow not to do any wrong to any one of the assembled beings; rather, He will take steps to justly repay them whatever they had done on earth (the Quran; 40:17). All the idols that humans had worshipped on earth will become alive, and they will face the same fate as that of their worshippers. Allah will also bring forward all the prophets, Imams and other witnesses from within the assembled crowd to make sure that the decisions He was going to make were just and fair to all of His creations (the Quran; 39:69).

Allah will subject all humans, Jinns and animals to trial, despite the fact that "not a single thing on earth and in the heavens remain hidden from Him" (cf. the Quran; 40:16). He is "aware of the treachery of the eyes and even of the secrets that the breasts keep hidden (the Quran; 40:19) from human eyes.

FP: Animals will be tried by Allah? Like dogs, cats, monkeys? Animals have souls? Some cats, for example, will go to hell and others will go to heaven? What kind of criteria will be used?

Asghar: Allah says in the Quran:

"Seest thou not that to Allah bow down in worship all things that are in the heavens and on earth,- the sun, the moon, the stars; the hills, the trees, the animals; and a great number among mankind? But a great number are (also) such as are fit for Punishment: and such as Allah shall disgrace,- None can raise to honor: for Allah carries out all that He wills (22:18].

This verse infers that all things that are in the heavens and earths, including animals, worship Him to go to the Garden. Those of them who do not worship Him are fit for Punishment of Hell.

So the answer to your question is yes; animals, too, have souls; they have been created to worship Allah and those among them who do not do this will go to Hell on the Day of Judgment.

FP: Let's move on. After the second blast?

Asghar: After the second blast, a voice from nowhere will announce: *"This is the Day of sorting out, whose truth (ye) denied"* (the Quran;37:21).

I suspect it will be the Prophet Muhammad's voice that will resonant the horizon, making the resurrected people and the idols shiver in extreme fear. He will use the Dooms Day to settle his disputes with his opponents (the Quran; 39:31).

In order to ensure a fair trial to all the people, Allah will set a seal upon their mouths and then let their hands speak to Him. Their feet will bear witness to what they had earned (the Quran; 36:65) during their stay on earth. Their ears, eyes and skins will also bear witness against them (the Quran; 41:20).

Asked by the under-trial people why they are testifying against them, the skins will tell them:

"Allah hath given us the speech, - (He) Who giveth speech to everything: He created you for the first time, and unto Him were ye to return. Ye did not seek to hide yourselves, lest your hearing, your sight, and your skins should bear witness against you! But ye did think that Allah knew not many of the things that ye used to do! But this thought of yours which ye did entertain concerning your Lord, hath brought you to destruction, and (now) have ye become of those utterly lost!"(The Quran; 41:21 to 23).

But alas. The sycophancy of the skins will not save them from Allah's wrath; they, too, will be scalded together with what will be within the bodies of the condemned sinners (the Quran; 22:20). Those of the guilty persons who lied against Allah will find their faces turned black (the Quran; 39:60).

FP: Why will Allah place seals on the mouths of the under trial people?

Asghar: There is only one plausible answer to the question: it is the fear of truth coming out of the people's mouth that will force Allah to shut them up. Feet and hands will speak in a sign language, as they have no vocal cords, thus making it difficult, if not impossible, for their owners to understand their testimonies. This will be a smart and convenient way for Allah to convict many innocent men and women to satisfy His ego.

FP: Just a second, Allah will send good innocent people to hell?

Asghar: To Allah, good people are only those who believe in His unitary existence and profess that Muhammad is (or was) His Prophet. Those humans and Jinns or, perhaps the animals, who do not believe in these two things, are neither believers nor good beings. The Jews and Christians whom Allah calls the People of the Book – a reference to the Torah (Old Testament or the Pentateuch) and the Injil (i.e. the Bible) He gave, respectively, to Moses and Issa (Jesus Christ), the son of Mary – are also bad people, as they do not believe in the prophethood of Muhammad, and as such, they, too, will find themselves in the fire of Hell- all the good deeds they performed on earth being of no value to Allah.

FP: Let's talk about the Gardens for a moment.

Asghar: Allah created seven Gardens at the time He created the Universe, which includes the seven skies. On them are located all the Gardens. Each Garden's width is equivalent to the entire width of the sky it is located on, as well as the width of the earth (the Quran; 3:133). In each Garden live various creatures like that of the earth (the Quran; 10:66). The Prophet Muhammad had seen all of them with his own eyes, when he paid a visit to Allah, whose Throne and Residences are presumably located in the Garden that is located on the seventh sky.

All the Gardens have many security gates (the Quran;13:23), manned by angels. All of them have rivers (the Quran; 54:54 et al), flowing with milk and honey (the Quran;47:15) and pure and crystal clear water and delicious wine (the Quran; 76:5 et al), the taste of all of which never changes. The inhabitants of the Gardens will drink wine from goblets (the Quran; 43:71) Allah has crafted for them.

Tall and green Lote-trees without thorns and Talh trees (the Quran; 56:28,29) not only perpetually bear cluster of delectable fruits (the Quran;76:14) and add beauty to the Gardens, they will also provide protection to their inhabitants from the non-existing sun's heat. Beneath them are laid out comfortable but throne-like benches for the Gardens' effeminate inhabitants, who will be wearing bracelets of gold, green garments of fine silk and heavy brocade (cf. the Quran; 18:31), and reclining on them, they will conduct their social intercourse among themselves (the Quran; 76:7) and thank Allah for the favors He will bestow on them (the Quran; 10:10).

Allocation of space in the Gardens by Allah will be subject to the ranks He will grant to Muslims, keeping in His mind their performance on earth (the Quran;52:20). Rank number I will go the prophets and apostles who taught and led mankind; the second to the sincere devotees of Truth, who supported His Cause in person and with all their resources; the third to the Martyrs and Witnesses who suffered and served His Cause, and the fourth to the righteous people; generally, those who led ordinary lives, but always with righteous aims.

The higher the rank the better accommodation and treatments its holder will receive in the Gardens. For instance, the residents of the higher Garden, which is also known as the Paradise, will drink their wine from Golden goblets; the residents of the lower ones will drink theirs from the silver ones (the Quran; 76:16). Despite their division into four categories, all the inhabitants of the Gardens will form one equal Brotherhood of Peace, one Society of Concord (Abdullah Yusuf Ali, the Holy Quran; vol. 2, p. 1467). This will eliminate the sense of jealousy, ill-will and competition from the Garden dwellers, thus making their lives most peaceful and dignified.

Allah will carefully control the temperature of all the Gardens. They will, therefore, be neither too cold, nor too hot (the Quran; 76:13). The vagaries of nature, which we confront on earth, will not reach them. They will be free from rain, thunderstorm, tornados, snowing and all other bad climatic effects. There will be no fear, no disappointment, nor sorrow to affect their inhabitants (the Quran; 10:25).

Because of the Gardens' pleasant and safe climatic conditions, as I have noted above, almost all of its inhabitants will live in their open space. Toilet and shower facilities will not exist in the Gardens. The grounds of the gardens on which Allah lives and walks will be holy and sacred. In order, therefore, to maintain their sanctity and holiness, humans will neither defecate, nor will they urinate on them. Allah will freeze up their wastes in their bodies.

All the residents of the Gardens will live in them without any tension or concern for their needs, health and life (the Quran; 52:19). Everything will come to them at the expression of their wish (the Quran; 16:31). If a resident, for instance, will wish to eat a particular fruit, and he will communicate his wish to Allah through a means of communication that is available only in the Gardens (the Quran; 56:12), Allah will cause a tree to spring up in front of him, bearing ripe and delicious fruit. The good resident of the Garden will not need to extend or move his hands to pluck the fruit; a simple gesture of his eye will bring it down to his silver plate (inference drawn from verse 76:14).

When he will wish to eat the meat of a rare fowl (the Quran; 56:21), it will land from nowhere on the barbeque and will cook itself into a delicious meat. Its uneaten portion will become a full bird and then fly away, waiting to fulfill at no notice the wish of another honored guest of the Gardens (cf. the Quran; 52:22).

The doors of the Gardens will be opened by Allah Himself with keys in His keeping (the Quran; 39:63). Those Muslims who will enter them will be greeted by Allah with the word "Salam," a word of salutation from "a Lord Most Merciful" (the Quran; 36:58). The Gate-

Keepers of the Gardens will also welcome them in with the words "peace be upon you" (the Quran; 39:73).

Everything in the Gardens will be for the enjoyment of their residents. In them, their male residents will have companions who will provide them with immense pleasure without feeling shame or dislike of their clients. Bashful with dark eyes and virgins, as chaste as the sheltered eggs of ostriches (the Quran; 37:48 & 49), and as young as the men themselves (the Quran; 38:52), the companions (Hurs) will provide them constant company and sex.

Those men who will not have interest in sex with the female Hurs, Allah has made arrangement for them as well: they shall be attended by boys graced with eternal youth, who to the beholder's eyes will seem like sprinkled pearls. When their clients will gaze upon that scene (what scene it will be is not known), they will behold a kingdom blissful and glorious (The Quran; 76:19-20, as translated by N. J. Dawood). Those boys will be wearing fine silk and heavy brocade, and they will be adorned with bracelets of silver. Allah will make them drunk (cf. the Quran; 76:21), so that they can serve their clients to their entire satisfaction.

FP: Just a second. So homosexual pedophiles who get to heaven will be able to have sex with young boys? This is a bit strange no? But before we even get to that, how does it make sense that a homosexual gets into heaven to have sex with boys if homosexuality is considered a sin in Islam?

Asghar: Allah made laws that suited His mission and whims. He prescribed death sentence for the lesbians (the Quran; 4:15), but requires the enforcers of His laws to set the homosexuals free, if they repent their sin, perhaps, with a pat on their wrists (the Quran; 16). This privilege is not available to the lesbians. Why?

According to Prophet Muhammad, women are an affliction and there is nothing more harmful for men than women (see Hadith in volume 7, Book 62, Number 33). He made this observation after being inspired by Allah, for he never said or did anything during his prophetic career without His consent, or permission.

Since Allah is a man, and men controlled the 7th century Arabian society (they still do), without whose conversion to Islam, it would have been impossible for Him to make it His only approved religion (the Quran; 3:85) for mankind, Allah promised boys in the Garden to those men who were homosexuals in order to win them over to His side. While making this and other promises to them and the straight guys, He did not care if what He was telling them made any sense, or if it contradicted His previous statements. Only thing that mattered to Him was His desire to succeed against the Pagans of Mecca and the Jews of Medina.

The early history of Islam tells us that Allah succeeded in His ploys – He being the best among all the "Deceivers" (3:54; the Arabic word "*almakireena*" in the verse means a deceiver). Muslims of our time take immense pride in His ability to deceive not only them, but also the rest of mankind!

FP: Let's proceed with the Gardens.

Asghar: The male residents of the Gardens and their virgin companions will be doing only one thing: sex. Those men who will be looking for privacy, they will find their beds in lofty mansions, one above another (the Quran; 39:20), which Allah has already constructed for them in an undisclosed place of an un-named Garden.

FP: So what happens to the wives of Muslim men who get to heaven?

Asghar: They will chase their husbands to satisfy their sexual needs, as Allah has created no beings, such as male Hurs, to attend to them. But their husbands will not oblige them, for they will remain busy with the beautiful and virgin Hurs all the time. Under such a situation, the good Muslim women will have to depend on each other to meet their sexual needs.

FP: There is a lot of sexual action going here. So in Islam, sexual desire obviously remains in humans when their souls get to heaven. Let me get all this straight: Muslim males will be having sex with either Hurs or little boys and since they will be busy doing this, their wives will be having sex with each other?

Asghar: Orgies will always take place in the Gardens. With their male residents' desire for sex always remaining present in them due to the presence in their midst of, perhaps, naked Hurs, they will have nothing to do, but to have sex with them with no barriers to shield their activity from the next copulating man and Hur. Fathers will be having sex with the Hurs before the eyes of their sons and daughters, and sons will be having sex before their fathers and mothers, if they entered the Gardens. The allurement of booty in their earthly life and the prospect of being able to engage in orgies in their next life brought many Pagans to Islam, thus making Allah successful in His mission against their religion.

Muslims believe in every word of the Quran, as it is from Allah. Many of them wish to die as martyrs so that they can drink and have sex with the Hurs. Not to make them wait, until the Day of Judgment, to enjoy the bliss He has promised to Muslims, Allah transports the martyrs to the Garden as soon as they lay down their lives in His cause.

Other than Muslims, no one else can believe that orgies will take place in the Gardens and that humans will live in them like beasts.

FP: So then what?

Asghar: After making sure that all pious Muslims have entered the Gardens and are comfortable there, Allah will order someone to bring to Him the wrong-doers and their wives, and the things they worshipped on earth besides Him (the Quran; 37:22). On seeing them, Allah will tell them: move away from the dwellers of the Gardens. *"Did I not tell you that you should not worship Satan; for he was to you an avowed enemy and that you should worship Me alone, for this was the Straight Way? But Satan led a multitude of you astray without* *you ever perceiving it. So, this is the Hell of which you were repeatedly warned"* (the Quran; 36:59-63). Prone on their faces, blind, dumb and deaf (the Quran; 17:97), they will move forward in terror with their necks outstretched, heads uplifted, their gaze returning towards them and their hearts a (gaping) void (the Quran; 14:43), with no hope of escaping punishment from Allah (cf. Abdullah Yusuf Ali; The Holy Quran; p. 706).

In the meantime, Hell will wait to ambush the transgressors who will live in it for ages (the Quran; 78:21-23).

FP: Ok, what happens to the sinners?

Asghar: The sinners will be "brought in front of the fire {in the} morning and evening" to hear their sentencing (the Quran; 40:46). Each Christian will come to Him singly to receive his or her punishment (cf. the Quran;19:91-95). How the Jews and the polytheists et al will approach Him is not mentioned in the Qur'an.

Seeing the terrorized sinners approaching Him slowly, Allah will order the herder:

"Bring ye up the wrong-doers and their wives, and the things they worshipped – besides Allah, and lead them to the Way to the (Fierce) Fire! But stop them, for they must be asked: "'What is the matter with you that ye help not each other?"(The Quran; 36:54).

When the sinners and their wives will find no helpers among them, and after they have demanded to 'see those among the Jinns and men who had misled them so that they can crush them under the feet' (the Quran; 41:29), Allah will place the Books of their Deeds before them that contain the details of all they had done on earth (the Quran; 18:49), and then will sentence them to the fire of Hell "to live in it forever" (the Quran; 36:64).

FP: Why do Jinns try to mislead humans?

Asghar: Jinns have a major problem with Allah, as He deceitfully expelled one of them, called Iblis, from the Gardens on the pretext that he misled Adam and his wife from His path. Since Iblis could not retaliate against Allah for His deceitful conduct, he sought His permission to mislead humans for what He had done to him. Allah acceded to his request, and as a result, he has been misleading, from the time of Adam till today, those humans who fell or are falling into his trap.

FP: There is a process of sinners entering hell?

Asghar: Yes. Hell also has seven gates; through each gate will enter separate groups of sinners (the Quran; 15:44).

After humans and their idols have been sentenced, but before the herder begins dragging them towards the Hell, Allah – like a sadist and vindictive Being- will order the herder to stop them so that He can ask them: *"What is the matter with you that ye help not each other"* (the Quran; 37:25).

When the sinners and their idols will not be able to answer Allah's question, and begin arguing among themselves on who led astray whom, Allah will ask their herder to deliver them to the Keepers of Hell. But before opening the gates of the Hell for the sinners, the Gate Keepers will ask them: *"Did not apostles come to you from among yourselves, rehearsing to you the Signs of your Lord, and warning you of the meeting of this Day of yours?* (The Quran; 39:71).

Who were the idols' apostles and what punishment they will receive from Allah on the Day of Judgment for their failure to lead their charge to His righteous path is not to be found in the Qur'an.

Hearing the idols and humans confessing their foolishness to them, the Gate Keepers of Hell, bowing to a stern command of Allah, and to the fury and raging sigh of the Fire (the Quran; 25:12), which is endowed with the faculties of seeing, thinking and judging (see Abul Ala Mududi; Tafhimul Quran; vol. 3, p. 441), will seize them and after binding them together will throw them into a constricted place, forcing them to plead with the Gate Keepers to destroy them there and then (the Quran; 25:13).

Responding to their pleading, the Gate Keepers will collect them from the constricted place and make them march in yokes and chains round their necks towards Hell – the length of the yokes being seventy cubits (the Quran; 69-31-32) - and then throw them into its "boiling fetid fluid and fire" (the Quran; 40:71-72) to be destroyed by them again and again. Inside the Hell, they will be given a 'garment of fire' to put over their heads. With their faces turned upside down in the Fire (the Quran; 33:66), 'boiling water shall continuously be pouring over their heads (the Quran; 22:19); the fetid fluid and fire shall also be performing their duties by continuously burning them. Allah will replace their burned skins with fresh ones so that they can keep on tasting the Penalty (the Quran; 4:56).

Seeing them cry out for help, Allah will have their lips displaced (the Quran; 23:104), telling them, *"were not My signs rehearsed to you, and ye did not treat them as falsehoods?"* (the Quran; 23:105). Despite having their lips displaced, the sinners will be able to tell Allah, *"Our Lord! Our misfortune overwhelmed us, and we became a people astray."*(the Quran; 23:106). They will also cry aloud, saying: *"Our Lord! Bring us out: we will live a good life and will not do as we have done"* (the Qur'an; 35:37).

Asking them not to talk to Him again, Allah will then shower them with water as hot as molten brass, which will scald their faces (the Quran; 18:29). Even with their bodies and faces completely burned out, the sinners will succeed in asking Allah to give them a "double Penalty and curse them with a very great Curse" (the Quran; 33:67-68), as they had obeyed their chiefs and great ones who misled them on earth.

Condemned men and Jinns will also have 'intimate' companions, who had made their past and present seem alluring to them (the Quran; 41:25; the word "intimate" can be found only in Yusuf Ali's translation of the verse), so that they may be able to bear their punishments with some ease.

FP: Wait a second. There is sex in hell too?

Asghar: It is not clear from the Quran, if sinners will be having sex while burning in the fire of Hell. But the use of the word "intimate" by the translator of the verse suggests such a possibility.

FP: Do all sinners suffer forever?

Asghar: No, some sinners will escape the punishments, but only after 'Allah accepts the repentance of His 'servants' and forgives them for their sins' (the Quran;39:53). He will not, however, forgive a vast number of His 'enemies' and those who joined gods with Him and will make them live in Hell forever (the Quran; 41:28).

While being continuously burned by fetid water and fire, the peccant will drink boiling water (the Quran; 14:16), and, perhaps, molten brass as well; festering blood, and other putrid things (the Quran; 38:57). They will sip putrid water without being able to swallow it. Death will assail them from every side, yet they will not die, as other harrowing punishments await them (the Quran; 14:17).

Finding the fire of Hell over them, and below them (the Quran; 39:16), and the fetid fluid making them float, the condemned sinners, in fetters and wearing garments of liquid pitch (the Quran; 14:49-50), will hold the idols they worshipped on earth as gods responsible for their plight. The idols will tell them: *"Nay, ye yourselves had no Faith. Nor had we any authority over you. Nay, it was ye who were a people in obstinate rebellion! So now has been proved true against us, the Word of our Lord that we shall indeed (have to) taste (the punishment of our sins)." "We led you astray: for truly we were ourselves astray"* (the Quran; 37:28-32).

The dwellers of Hell will be made to eat the fruit of Zaqqum tree. It springs out of the bottom of Hell-fire. The shoots of its fruit-stalks are like the heads of devil, with which they will fill their bellies (the Quran; 37:62-66).

When they will feel thirsty, they will be taken out of Hell and given a mixture of boiling water to drink. They will not be given any cool thing to drink, but a fluid that is dark, murky and intensely cold! (The Quran; 78:24-25). Their thirst over, they will be brought back to Hell's blazing fire (The Quran; 37:67-68) to live in it forever.

FP: Where is the devil in all of this? Is there any redemption for him ever?

Asghar: The devil of the Bible is known as *Shaitan* (the Quran; 7:20) to Muslims. Allah unethically used him for expelling Adam and his wife from the Garden. Living forever, he is as powerful, if not more, as Allah is, but he does not have the ability to create anything. With the help of humans, he kills many of those Muslims, who visit Ka'aba at Allah's invitation to perform their hajj; he and his progeny eavesdrop on Allah and angels to find out what they are planning for humans and the earth, at the same time, he constantly tries to mislead humans from the righteous path of Allah, who is one of their creators.

For the crimes Shaitan has been committing from the time Allah expelled him from the Gardens, Allah will never forgive him. Instead, he will burn in the fire of Hell along with Jinns and humans.

FP: Mohammad Asghar, this was quite fascinating. One almost never hears about these ingredients of Islamic theology. Thank you for enlightening us.

Asghar: Thank you Jamie.

[Jamie Glazov, "Sex in the Islamic City," Frontpagemag.com, September 19, 2008.]

15. Allah's White Faces – Abul Kasem

Frontpage Interview's guest today is Abul Kasem, an ex-Muslim who is the author of hundreds of articles and several books on Islam including, *Women in Islam.* He was a contributor to the book *Leaving Islam – Apostates Speak Out* as well as to *Beyond Jihad: Critical Views From Inside Islam.* His latest contribution is in *Why We Left Islam* published by WND Books.

FP: Abul Kasem, welcome to Frontpage Interview.

Kasem: Thank you Jamie.

FP: I would like to talk to you today about the racial apartheid that exists in Islam. How is the best way for us to begin this discussion?

Kasem: Jamie, let's begin with the incredible hypocrisy and double standard that exists on the issue of racism in general. Islamists living in the West often portray Islam as a religion free of racism. They never fail to criticize western countries of its racist attitude and contempt for people who are not of white complexion. It is quite perplexing that these Islamists never look at their own backyard, of blatant, naked racism enmeshed in the Islamic doctrine.

Any non-Arab, non-white, who has been to a Middle East Arab country will tell the story of absolute racism practiced there. It is no secret that in rich Arab countries, (such as Saudi Arabia) people of dark complexion, such those from Africa, South Asia (Pakistan, India, Bangladesh) receive much lower pay than a white person from the western country would. There is strict, unspoken, racial apartheid practiced in the rich Arab countries.

FP: And the lefties that are confronted with this reality immediately say how this has nothing to do with Islam and that it is "cultural."

Kasem: For sure, and they are completely wrong. The racism practiced in the Arab countries is solidly founded in the very doctrine of Islam.

FP: Tell us about it.

Kasem: Blatant Islamic racism is permeated in the founts of Islam, the Qur'an, ahadith, Sunna, and Sharia.

Let us start the beginning with the end in mind. What I mean is the Islamic Resurrection day.

It is an Islamic day of black and white.

Allah promises in verse 3:185 that life in this world is an illusion, that every person shall die, and every person will receive his judgment on the resurrection day. In verse 5:26, Allah vouches that all that is on earth will perish. Allah says in verse 10:26 that He will reward the doers of good with paradise and much more; their faces will be radiant-stained. They will never be humiliated.

Ibn Kathir says that there will be no blackness or darkness on their faces. In contrast, the faces of the non-believers will be stained with dust, blackness, and darkness. On the Resurrection Day Allah will remove His veil and show His face to the dwellers of paradise. He will make the believers' faces white.

Where are all the radical leftist scholars deconstructing these texts in the way they have done to Western literature?

The Islamic texts clearly reveal that Allah is a white supremacist; He does not like black faces; He likes white faces.

It is clear from the exegesis of these verses that Allah likes white people and dislikes the black people, so much so, in fact, that even when a Black Muslim is entitled to enter Islamic Paradise, he will not enter it until Allah has turned him into a white person. Verse 20:102 says that on the day the trumpet is sounded (resurrection day), the sinners will be gathered together with blue eyes and black faces. A hadith in Mishkat says that on judgment day, Muslims will have white faces, white arms, and white legs (*Mishkat al-Masabih,* Ibn Abdullah Tabrizi, Sheikh Wali-ud-Din Muahmmad, Tr. Abdul Hameed Siddiqui, Kitab Bhavan, 1784 Kalan Mahal, Daraya Ganj, New Delhi-110002, India.1990, p.1.168).

Allah's preference for light-skinned people and His disdain for dark-skinned people is repeated in verse 7:46. Ibn Abbas writes that this verse tells the joy of the believers when they know those who enter hell by their darkened faces and blue eyes and those who enter Paradise by their lightened faces: at once handsome and radiant.

Allah says in verse 86:8-9 that He will bring back life for Muhammad to commence judgment. According to ibn Kathir, on resurrection day, a banner will be raised for every deceitful person from his anus; the size of this banner will depend on the size of the perpetrator's calumny. Thus, Muhammad will have no trouble sifting the believers from the non-believers. All Muslims will be of white complexion, and all infidels will be of black complexion, with a banner on his/her anus.

In verse 18:29 Allah says that He does not care whether people believe or disbelieve in Islam. The disbelievers (non-Muslims) and the wrongdoers will be surrounded by the tent of fire; they will be given water (acid) like molten brass to shower and to scald their faces. Ibn Kathir says that this verse means the water of Hell is black, and it itself is black and its people are black.

In verse 3:107 Allah emphatically pronounces that white faces on the judgment day will receive His mercy. Jalalyn writes that, on judgment day, Muslims' faces will be white.

In Mishkat (ibid, p.1.76) we read humans were emitted as white ants from Adam; paradise is for the whites, hell is for the blacks.

Islamic Paradise will offer its white male residents unlimited, unbridled, uninterrupted sex with houris of exquisite beauty. These houris will also be of fair (read white), radiant complexion (44:54, 55:70) quite similar to the Hollywood movie actresses. Even the wine-serving boys will be white, like pearls (52:24, 76:19).

FP: How do you explain this kind of racism in Islam?

Kasem: We might wonder why Allah is such a racist—white supremacist, even on Islamic resurrection day. The answer is Muhammad was a white man. Here are a few examples:

Muhammad was white. (Sunaan Abu Dawud, 1.486)

Let us read one hadith from Sahih Bukhari (1.3.63) Narrated Anas bin Malik:

While we were sitting with the Prophet in the mosque, a man came riding on a camel. He made his camel kneel down in the mosque, tied its foreleg and then said: "Who amongst you is Muhammad?" At that time the Prophet was sitting amongst us (his companions) leaning on his arm. We replied, "This white man reclining on his arm." The man then addressed him, "O Son of 'Abdul Muttalib."

Tabari writes that Muhammad was of white complexion, reddish tinge, deep-black large eyes, long eyelashes. His breast hair was thin and he had thick beard. He had no hair in his armpit. The perspiration on his face was pearl-like (al-Tabari, Abu Ja'far Muhammad b. Jarir, *History of al-Tabari,* Translated by Ismail K. Poonwala. State University of New York Press, Albany, 1990, p.ix.157).

In Ash-Shifa, Allah, through Sharia, expresses a great disdain for the black people in this manner:

Ahmad ibn Abi Sulayman, the companion of Sahnun said, "Anyone who says that the Prophet was black should be killed. (Ibn Musa al-Yahsubi, Qadi 'Iyad. *Ash-Shifa.* Tr. Aisha Abdarrahman Bewley. Medina Press, P.O. Box 5531, Inverness IV5 7YA, Scotland, UK, fifth print 2004, p.375)

FP: So who is Allah then?

Kasem: Allah is a white Arab supremacist. Allah dearly loves the Arabs. He chose them over all other races, making them the best pedigree in the human race.

Does Allah look like an Arab, especially an Arab from Saudi Arabia and from the Quraysh stock? Let us read from ibn Sa'd, the famous biographer of Muhammad:

...Abu Damarah al–Madani Anas Ibn 'Iyad al–Laythi informed us; he said: Ja'far Ibn Muhammad Ibn 'Ali informed us on the authority of his father, Muhammad Ibn 'Ali ibn Husayn Ibn "Ali Ibn Abi Talib, who said: Verily the Prophet said: God divided the earth in two halves and placed (me) in the better of the two, then He divided the half in three parts, and I was in the best of them, then He chose the Arabs from among the people, then He chose the Quraysh from among the Arabs, then He chose the children of 'Abd al–Muttalib from among the Banu Hashim, then he chose me from among the children of 'Abd al–Muttalib (Ibn Sa'd, Abu Abd Allah Muhammad. *Kitab al-Tabaqat,* vol i. Translated in English by S. Moinul Haq, Kitab Bhavan, 1784, Kalan Mahal, Daraya Ganj, New Delhi, India, 1972, p1.2).

According to ibn Sa'd, Allah favours Arab racism—prophet is to be of Quraysh stock and of white complexion (ibid, p1. 95-96).

Here is a hadith from *Sahih Muslim* which declares Allah's special love for the white Quraysh Arabs.

Book 020, Number 4483

It has been narrated on the authority of Amir b. Sa'd b. Abu Waqqas who said: I wrote (a letter) to Jabir b. Samura and sent it to him through my servant Nafi', asking him to inform me of something he had heard from the Messenger of Allah (may peace be upon him). He wrote to me (in reply): I heard the Messenger of Allah (may peace be upon him) say on Friday evening, the day on which al-Aslami was stoned to death (for committing adultery): The Islamic religion will continue until the Hour has been established, or you have been ruled over by twelve Caliphs, all of them being from the Quraish. also heard him say: A small force of the Muslims will capture the white palace, the police of the Persian Emperor or his descendants. I also heard him say: Before the Day of Judgment there will appear (a number of) impostors. You are to guard against them. I also heard him say: When God grants wealth to any one of you, he should first spend it on himself and his family (and then give it in charity to the poor). I heard him (also) say: I will be your forerunner at the Cistern (expecting your arrival).

FP: So Arabs must rule the world?

Kasem: Yes. The ultimate goal of the Islamists is the creation of a Pan Islamic world, which must be ruled by a caliph (the Islamists call it the *Khilafat* movement) who will be responsible to enforce Islamic laws (*Sharia*) globally.

FP: What are the requirements to be a caliph?

Kasem: According to Islamic law, (*Reliance of the Traveller*, published by Amana Publications, Bettsville, Maryland, 1999, pp.640-642, law number o25.3) the mandatory qualifications of an Islamic caliph are:

1. must be a Muslim
2. must be a male
3. must be from the Quraysh tribe of the Arabs
4. must be a freeman (i.e., not a slave)
5. must be of sound mind.

This provision of Islamic law means that the world—the Pan Islamic world must be ruled by an Arab (from the Quraysh stock, probably from Saudi Arabia or Jordan) and no one else.

FP: All this racism must involve rules about marriage I assume.

Kasem: Of course.

A non-Arab Muslim cannot marry an Arab woman.

Let us refer to another law of Sharia. This law enforces the supremacy of the white Quraysh Arabs to subjugate all people on earth to their rule. The Sharia law (ibid) cited here stipulates that no other men, even when Muslims, could marry any Arab women. In some Arab countries, this is the law and there is severe punishment if a man from another Islamic country (such as a Muslim man from Bangladesh) marries a Saudi Arabian woman. If he commits such a grave crime (marrying an Arab woman) he might be subjected to harsh punishment and immediate deportation.

Let us read this racist law of Allah:

Law m4.2 The following are not suitable matches for one another:

(1) A non-Arab man for an Arab woman (O: because of the hadith that the Prophet (Allah bless him and give him peace) said: "Allah has chosen the Arabs above others"). (ibid)

Quite akin to the Nazism of Hitler, this Islamic law firmly establishes Allah's racism. Islamic law is heavily biased to establish the supremacy of the white Arabs much like the idea of Hitler's of the pure Aryan Germans, which he deemed the most supreme race on earth.

Allah made the white Quraysh Arabs the best of His creation.

Allah is adamant that they (the Arabs) are the purest, the truest, the best and the most superior of all races.

FP: Some more on Allah's racism?

Kasem: Well, Ibn Sa'd said: Abd al–wahhab Ibn 'Ata al–'Ijli informed us on the authority of Sai'd Ibn Abi 'Aribiah, he on the authority of Qatadh: he said: It has been mentioned to us that the Prophet said: When God wants to raise a prophet He chooses the best tribe of the people and then He chooses the best man (Ibn Sa'd, p.1.8).

Sahih Bukhari (4.56.704) confirms that Allah has chosen the Quraysh Arabs as His agent to rule the world (Islamic Caliphate).

Volume 4, Book 56, Number 704:

Narrated Muhammad bin Jubair bin Mut'im:

That while he was with a delegation from Quraish to Muawiya, the latter heard the news that 'Abdullah bin 'Amr bin Al-'As said that there would be a king from the tribe of Qahtan. On that Muawiya became angry, got up and then praised Allah as He deserved, and said, "Now then, I have heard that some men amongst you narrate things which are neither in the Holy Book, nor have been told by Allah's Apostle. Those men are the ignorant amongst you. Beware of such hopes as make the people go astray, for I heard Allah's Apostle saying, 'Authority of ruling will remain with Quraish, and whoever bears hostility to them, Allah will destroy him as long as they abide by the laws of the religion.'"

FP: How about some historical evidence of Islam's disdain for black people?

Kasem: Abd. Rahman b. Awf called Bilal the son of a black woman (Tabari, vii.59). Umar had a profound dislike for black people (Tabari, xii.11).

Tabari writes:

Among them, with Muawiyah b. Hudhayl, were young men of black complexion and straight hair. 'Umar turned his face away from them several times until it was said to him: "Do you have anything against these people." He said: "I am perplexed with regard to them. No Arab tribe more hateful to me than these has ever passed by me."

He then let them go, but he frequently mentioned them with hatred, and people were puzzled by 'Umar's view.

The Islamic racism is alive and well even today. Even notice the recent news report of Al Qaeda calling Obama a 'house negro'.

FP: So what do we conclude them?

Kasem: Islamic racism is endemic. It emanates straight from the Qur'an, Sunna, and Sharia. It cannot be eliminated so long the Muslims are enthused by these Holy Scriptures. The Muslims of black complexion will never be equal with the white Arabs. The concept of Islamic ummah, regardless of color and ethnic origin is simply not true.

[Jamie Glazov, "Allah's White Faces," Frontpagemag.com, December 4, 2008.]

Part IV: The Terror War

Introduction:

The interviews from the previous two parts analyze the nature of the threat facing free societies and require a question: Are we at war?

The conflict with Islamofascism is in many ways unlike the previous battles the West fought with tyranny. Both the Nazis and the Communists embraced politically-driven ideologies and could be understood as rival nation states. But with the Terror War, the soldiers do not wear uniforms. And violence is hardly the only tactic used. There is no single enemy country like Germany or the USSR. And the conflicting ideology emerges from a religion, not a political theory.

Thus, are we in a police conflict with a few terrorist criminals who happen to be Muslims? Such thinking has been the clearly articulated Democratic Party position since Senator John Kerry ran against George W. Bush in 2004. The Obama administration has since institutionalized it by dispensing with the term "war on terror" and beginning civil trials of terrorists.

Or are we dealing with a global enemy of Islamic soldiers who will use both violence and stealth jihad in pursuit of their goal of a Muslim planet?

In the interviews in this part several distinguished intellectuals give us the answer. -- David Swindle

.

16. World War IV - Norman Podhoretz

Frontpage Interview's guest today is Norman Podhoretz, the editor at large for *Commentary* magazine, of which he was editor in chief for thirty-five years. He is also an adjunct fellow of the Hudson Institute and the author of numerous bestselling books, including *Making It*, *Breaking Ranks*, *Ex-Friends*, *My Love Affair with America*, and *The Prophets*. He is the author of the new book *World War IV: The Long Struggle Against Islamofascism*.

FP: Norman Podhoretz, welcome to Frontpage Interview. It is a privilege and an honor to have you with us.

Podhoretz: Thanks very much.

FP: What inspired you to write this book?

Podhoretz: First of all, so far as I could tell, there was no other book out there that made a serious effort to set 9/11, the battles that followed it in Afghanistan and Iraq, and the war of ideas it has provoked at home into a broad historical context. This is what I set out to do. Secondly, I thought the time had come for a full-throated, wholehearted statement of the case for the Bush Doctrine. By doing this, I hoped to remind the former supporters of the Bush Doctrine who had been losing heart of how World War IV started, what the stakes are, and why we have to win.

FP: Why do you use the term "Islamofascism" to describe our enemy in this war?

Podhoretz: The term Islamofascism is as precise a characterization as I could find of the religio-political totalitarian force that we are up against. Terrorism in itself is not the enemy; it is the enemy's weapon of choice.

FP: There was a denial occurring throughout the 1990s. What was that denial and how did it hurt us?

Podhoretz: The denial that war had been declared on us by the Islamofascists goes back to the 1970's and ended only on 9/11. In my book I list a long series of terrorist attacks on American facilities all over the world that should have been recognized as acts of war demanding a military response but that were treated, by Republican and Democratic administrations alike, as random criminal acts to be handled by the cops and the courts. John Kerry still calls such attacks "nuisances" with which we can live, as we do with gambling and prostitution. The damage this attitude did was to embolden Osama bin Laden and his allies and sponsors, who decided that the US was a paper tiger that could be attacked with impunity. It seems clear that he never expected us to fight back as we did in response to 9/11.

FP: Briefly give us your defense of the Bush Doctrine.

Podhoretz: The Bush Doctrine, to simplify, sets forth a two-pronged strategy, one military and the other political, designed to confront the new kind of threat we are now facing. The military component is preemption (because, as the President has said, "if we wait for threats to fully materialize, we will have waited too long") and the political component is democratization (to "drain the swamps" in which Islamofascist terrorism breeds). What I try to show in my book is that there is no other viable way to victory over Islamofascism.

FP: One of your chapters is titled "The Radicalization of the Democrats." To be sure, it means something when, as you point out, Michael Moore sits in Jimmy Carter's box at the Democratic National Convention. (p.168)

So how and why exactly have the Democrats been radicalized? What are the key consequences?

Podhoretz: Partly for partisan political reasons and partly out of the post-Vietnam attitudes that many Democrats still harbor, they have once again been taken over by the left wing of the party, just as they were in 1972, when they nominated George McGovern. We won't know the full consequences until the results of the next presidential election. Meanwhile the Democrats have succeeded in pushing the debate over Iraq to the sorry point where the only question is how soon we can withdraw and whether to set a timetable.

FP: You leave a little bit of optimism open that perhaps a course may be set for the reform and modernization of Islam. (p.215) Can you talk a little bit about that?

Podhoretz: I believe that clearing the ground and sowing the seeds out of which new political, social, and economic conditions can grow is likely to give rise to pressures from within for religious reform. Muslim religious leaders will be faced with the demand that ways be found in the *sharia* that would make it possible to be a good Muslim while at the same time enjoying the blessings of decent government and even of political and economic liberty.

FP: Who will your book upset?

Podhoretz: The Left, the paleoconservative Right, and both the liberals and the conservatives (including some neoconservatives) who once supported the war but have now lost heart.

FP: Norman Podhoretz, thank you for joining Frontpage Interview. It was a pleasure to speak with you.

Podhoretz: Thanks very much for inviting me.

[Jamie Glazov, "World War IV," Frontpagemag.com,
September 12, 2007.]

17. The Case for Democracy - Natan Sharansky

Frontpage Interview's guest today is Natan Sharansky, a former Soviet dissident and political prisoner who is the co- author (with Ron Dermer) of the new book *The Case For Democracy: The Power of Freedom to Overcome Tyranny and Terror.* Mr. Sharansky has been awarded the Congressional Gold Medal of Freedom for his courageous fight for liberty. He currently serves as Minister for Jerusalem and Diaspora Affairs.

FP: Mr. Sharansky, welcome to Frontpage Interview. It is an honor and privilege to speak with you.

Sharansky: Thank you for giving me the opportunity to share my thoughts with your readers. I also wanted to thank you for inviting me and my co-author Ron Dermer to the Restoration weekend last month. I really enjoyed participating in your program.

FP: Thank you, but believe us, it is our whole staff that is grateful to you for accepting the invitation. We were graced by your presence.

So let's get started. What inspired you to write *The Case for Democracy*

Sharansky: I was inspired to write this book by those who are sceptical of the power of freedom to change the world. I felt that the arguments of these sceptics had to be answered. The three main sources of scepticism are first, that not every people desires freedom; second, that democracy in certain parts of the world would be dangerous; and third, that there is little the world's democracies can do to advance freedom outside their countries.

This scepticism is the same scepticism I heard a generation ago in the USSR when few thought that a democratic transformation behind the iron curtain was possible. Just as the sceptics were wrong then, I am convinced they are wrong now about the possibility of freedom spreading to the Middle East.

In this book, I explain why I believe in the power of freedom to transform our world. My optimism is not based primarily on the successful march of democracy in recent times but rather is based on the experience of having lived in a fear society and studied the mechanics of tyranny that sustain such a society. By helping readers understand these mechanics, I hope they will appreciate why freedom is for everyone, why it is essential for our security and why the free world plays a critically important role in advancing democracy around the globe.

FP: You distinguish between "fear" and "free" societies. Briefly explain to our readers what you mean by this paradigm.

Sharansky: Free societies are societies in which the right of dissent is protected. In contrast, fear societies are societies in which dissent is banned. One can determine whether a society is free by applying what we call the "town-square test." Can someone within that society walk into the town square and say what they want without fear of being punished for his or her views? If so, then that society is a free society. If not, it is a fear society.

People may believe that there can be a society where dissent is not permitted, but which is nonetheless not a fear society because everyone agrees with one another and therefore no one wants to dissent. But as we show in the book, such a monolithic society, which may occasionally emerge, will not last very long. Because of human diversity – different tastes, ambitions, interests, backgrounds, experiences, etc. - differences of opinion will be inevitable. Then the society will be confronted with the fundamental question. Will dissent be permitted? The answer to that question will determine whether the society is a free society or a fear society.

Of course, there can be serious injustices within free societies. They can have all sorts of problems and abuses of rights. But by having a right to dissent and having institutions which protect that right, free societies also have mechanisms to correct those abuses. In contrast, fear societies are always unjust and have no corrective mechanisms.

Fear societies are inevitably composed of three separate groups: True believers, dissidents and doublethinkers. True believers are those who believe in the ideology of the regime. Dissidents are those who disagree with that ideology and are prepared to say so openly. Doublethinkers are those who disagree with the ideology but who are scared to openly confront the regime.

With time, the number of doublethinkers in a fear society inevitably grows so that they represent the overwhelming majority of the population. To an outside observer, the fear society will look like a sea of true believers who demonstrate loyalty to the regime, but the reality is very different. Behind the veneer of support is an army of doublethinkers.

FP: You are critical of those who believe that democracy is suited only for certain cultures and that it is incompatible with Islam. Do you think Islam has the keys within itself to enter modernity?

Sharansky: First, as I mentioned, we can gain some optimism from history. It is important to remember that some of the most serious thinkers once thought that democracy was not compatible with the cultures of Germany, Italy, Japan, Latin America and Russia. The great historian Toynbee questioned whether democracy could ever flourish out of the Anglo-Saxon world or as he put it, in "alien soil."

Let's take Japan for a moment. Truman's advisors were very sceptical about the prospects for democracy in Japan, as were most of the "experts" of the time. And there were good reasons to be sceptical. This was a country with virtually no exposure to the West for centuries. Japan rigidly hierarchical society, and unique culture was seen as antithetical to democratic life. In fact, when the concept of rights was translated into Japan it took a compound word consisting of four characters to express it. But democracy in Japan has been a great success story. Japan is not a Western democracy. The Japanese have kept their traditions, culture and heritage, but they have joined the community of free nations.

Still, history will only get us so far. People can always argue that the "Arabs" are different -- that the sceptics may have been wrong with regard to other cultures and regions, but they will not be wrong when it comes to the Arabs and the Middle East.

And the sceptics present some weighty evidence: Twenty-two Arab countries and not a single democracy. The scenes we see on our television screens, from the celebration s that followed the 9/11 attacks to mass marches praising suicide bombers, would give even the biggest optimists pause.

But while I understand that the picture we see from the outside is very troubling, I am confident that what is really going on inside these societies is very different. Just as the 99% of Soviet citizens who supported the Soviet regime in 1985 was no indication of what the people inside the USSR really thought, the army of true believers that we think we see in the Arab world is an illusion. One only has to read the memoirs of those dissidents who have left place lake Iran and Saudi Arabia to understand that these societies are steeped in doublethink.

I have no doubt that given a real choice, the vast majority of Muslims and Arabs, like everyone else will choose a free society over a fear society. Believe me, the drug of freedom is universally potent. Once the life of doublethink and self-censorship is shed, once the brainwashing stops, once freedom is tasted, no people will ever choose to live in fear again.

FP: What were your feelings and thoughts when Arafat died?

Sharansky: First, I thought that a terrorist and murderer had left this world. Second, I thought that a new opportunity for peace could emerge if we had learned from the mistakes of the past.

Oslo failed because the democratic world, including Israel, thought that peace could be made with a dictatorship. The central premise behind Oslo was that if Arafat were given enough legitimacy, territory, weapons and money, he would use his power to fight terror and make peace with Israel.

Unfortunately, little attention was paid to *how* Arafat ruled. In fact, some saw the harsh and repressive nature of Arafat's regime as actually bolstering the prospects for peace. According to this logic, Arafat would be able to fight terror organizations without his hands tied by the constraints of democratic rule. As former Prime Minister Yitzhak Rabin chillingly put in the earliest days of Oslo, Arafat would fight terror "without a Supreme Court, without human rights organizations and without all sorts of bleeding heart liberals."

Only weeks after Oslo began, when nearly all the world and most of Israel was drunk with the idea of peace, I argued that a Palestinian society not constrained by democratic norms would be a fear society that would pose a grave threat to Israel. As Andrei Sakharov taught me, regimes that do not respect the rights of their own people will not respect the rights of their neighbors.

In the post-Arafat era, the success of the peace process will hinge on whether the world finally focuses on what goes on *inside* Palestinian controlled areas . Just as the democratic world did not care how Yasser Arafat ruled, it may not care how his successor ruled. This would repeat the mistake of Oslo and lead to the same tragic results.

On the other hand, if the free world is concerned with how a new Palestinian leader governs, then the peace process will have a real chance to succeed. By telling Palestinian leaders, whoever they may be, that the support of the free world will be made conditional on enacting real reform - from dismantling the refugee camps in which Palestinians have lived for four generations to developing private enterprise to changing the curriculum of hate in Palestinian schools - the free world can help the Palestinians rebuild a destroyed civil society and create the foundations for a genuine peace.

The message of the free world to any potential Palestinian leadership should be a simple one: Embrace democratic reform and we will embrace you. Reject democratic reform and we will reject you. By focusing once and for all on helping the Palestinians build a free society, I have no doubt that an historic compromise between Israelis and Palestinians can be reached and that peace can prevail.

FP: Why do you think Arafat rejected the incredible deal Barak offered at Camp David?

Sharansky: Arafat rejected the deal because, as a dictator who had directed all his energies toward strengthening the Palestinians hatred toward Israel, Arafat could not afford to make peace.

To understand why dictators have a problem with making peace – or at least a genuine peace - the link between the nature of a regime and its external behavior must be understood. Democratic leaders, whose power is ultimately dependent on popular support, are held accountable for failing to improve the lives of their citizens. Therefore, they have a powerful incentive to keep their societies peaceful and prosperous.

The power of dictators on the other hand is not dependent on popular will. For them, staying in power is a function not of keeping people happy but rather of keeping them under control To justify the degree of repression necessary to sustain their illegitimate rule, dictators constantly need to mobilize their people against external enemies.

It is not surprising, then, that in the decade since Oslo began, Arafat used all the resources placed at his disposal to fan the flames of hatred against Israel. The media under his control incited the current generation of Palestinians against the Jewish State and his PA run schools ensured that the next generation would be even more poisoned with hate. While negotiations were conducted and summits held, Arafat's regime was crushing Palestinian civil society and creating an autonomy of terror.

Arafat did not accept Barak's over-generous offer because Arafat's repressive rule was dependent on keeping the conflict with Israel alive. Non-democratic regimes always need to mobilize their people against external enemies in order to maintain internal stability. This is why, for example, the regime in Egypt, formally at peace with Israel, has become the sponsor of perhaps the most rabid form of anti-Semitic incitement on earth. Egypt got a lot of things from the peace process: territory, billions of dollars in aid, a modernized army, etc. But it also lost Israel as a political enemy. Its non-democratic regime cannot maintain internal stability without having an external enemy, and the only enemy that will serve as a glue that can mobilize Egyptian society is Israel. So instead of having Israel as a political enemy, Egypt has turned the Jewish religion and the Jewish people into an enemy.

Now look at Saudi Arabia. This is a country run by a tribal dictatorship. To maintain its internal stability, these dictators fund Wahabbi extremist Islam both within Saudi Arabia and all over the world. Look at almost all the areas across the world where there is terrorism. Many of the radical clerics in these places were educated at least partly in Saudi Arabia and many of the terrorists themselves were indoctrinated with Wahabbi ideology. That is why the price for stability inside Saudi Arabia has been the spread of terrorism all over the world.

The only peace that can be made with a dictator is once that must be based on deterrence. For today, the dictator may be your friend, but tomorrow he will need you as an enemy.

FP: In your book you emphasize that spreading democracy is crucial for our own security. What are some of the things that can be done to promote democracy around the world?

Sharansky: The two most important things that can be done to promote democracy in the world is first, to bring moral clarity back to world affairs and second, to link international policies to the advance of democracy around the globe.

When we are unwilling to draw clear moral lines between free societies and fear societies, when we are unwilling to call the former good and the latter evil, we will not be able to advance the cause of peace because peace cannot be disconnected from freedom.

By not understanding why freedom is so important to peace, we run the risk of trying to find "our dictator" in the hopes that he will provide security. In the end, we are likely to find ourselves supporting regimes that repress their own people and endanger us.

When Ronald Reagan called the USSR an evil empire he was fiercely criticized by many in the West who saw him as a dangerous warmonger. But when we in the Gulag heard of Reagan's statement, we were ecstatic. We knew that once there was no moral confusion between the two types of societies, once good and evil were kept separate, the Soviet Union's days were numbered. Soon, the most fearsome totalitarian empire in human history collapsed without a shot being fired and the cause of peace and security was advanced. I have no doubt that moral clarity will have the same effect today and equally serve the cause of peace, stability and security around the world.

Once we have this moral clarity then we must link our foreign policies to the expansion of freedom within non-democratic societies. The Jackson amendment, which linked most favored nation trade benefits with the US to the preservation of the right of emigration is a model of how such linkage can be created. In dealing with fear societies, the free world must have both a very big carrot and a very big stick. We should embrace leaders who embrace democratic reform and reject leaders who don't. The free world should be willing to use all its leverage – moral, political, financial, etc. – to promote freedom and democracy.

FP: You show yourself to be quite an optimist in your book, arguing that democracy can even come to places like the Arab Middle East. Some critics argue that when we look at Arab tribal culture and its intersection with Islamism, democracy for this region appears to be an almost hopeless enterprise. Give us some encouraging words. How can we bring liberty to a region where so many individuals yearn for Sharia law and despise individual freedom, Western-style entertainment, and women's rights and equality?

Sharansky: I am optimistic that peace can be achieved in the region because I believe that every society on earth can be free and that if freedom comes to the Middle East, there can be peace. Thus, the potential for peace is there.

I am often asked how I can have confidence in a democratic Middle East when there are so few dissidents in the Arab world. People ask me where are the Arab Sakharovs and the Arab Ghandis.

I would ask those sceptics to give me the names of all the famous dissidents in Stalin's Soviet Union in the 30s and 40s. Did hundreds of millions of people agree with Stalin? Of course not. There were no dissidents then in the USSR because they were all killed. Ghandi would not have had one follower, let alone millions, in Hitler's Germany. Dissent is always a function of the price of dissent. Once the price of dissent in the Soviet Union was years in prison and not death, a few hundred dissidents emerged. But they were only the tip of the iceberg. Hundreds of millions of others also wanted their freedom.

The sceptics should remember that when I became a dissident in the 1970s, I knew that I could be arrested and imprisoned, but I also believed that the free world would stand with me. That is a comfort that potential dissidents in the Arab world do not have. Not only have the regimes they are confronting treated them with impunity, the free world has also remained silent.

Once that changes, once the free world encourages democratic forces within the region, once it links its policies toward states in the region to the degree of freedom they provide their own citizens, nothing will stop the march of freedom.

What will be needed is a joint effort that crosses partisan and ideological lines. In the Cold War, security hawks and human rights activists joined forces in confronting the Soviet Union. This historic partnership was critical in ending the Cold War. Today, that partnership must be reconstituted. Security hawks must understand that security and democracy are inextricably linked. Likewise, human rights activists must understand that the struggle for human rights cannot be detached from the struggle to promote democracy around the world. I believe that by bringing these two groups together, the Bush administration can succeed in its historic task of promoting democracy in the Middle East.

If a united free world stands up for democracy, I have no doubt freedom, and ultimately peace, can prevail.

FP: Today Mr. Sharansky, once again, the world is witnessing yet another conflict between the forces of freedom and the totalitarian impulses that seek to stifle them. You are a human being that personifies that struggle in your own life, for you battled personally for freedom against one of the most ruthless and vicious despotic regimes in world history. Tell us: what made you a soldier for freedom? For instance, you could have kept your mouth shut and never taken any stands for liberty and you could have avoided the Soviet gulag. And yet, you stood up for the principles of liberty knowing full well the terrible consequences that you might have to face from a barbaric regime.

What is it sparks this instinct to do what you did? What made you put your hands up to fight a monstrous tyranny? What is the calling of a dissident? And tell us a little bit about the human qualities that you had to rely on to survive the gulag and to emerge as you did: not as a victimized prisoner, but as a invincible warrior.

Sharansky: I wrote in great detail about this subject in my first book, Fear No Evil. More broadly, I became a dissident the moment I left the world of doublethink - the moment I was willing to say what I thought. What gave me the courage to do so was the inner freedom I had found in reconnecting myself to the history and heritage of my people - a process that began for many Soviet Jews in the wake of Israel's miraculous victory in the Six Day War.

You see, a totalitarian regime is most powerful when an individual confronts it alone. But I was never alone. I was connected to thousands of years of Jewish history. I saw our struggle within the USSR as a continuation of my people's ancient journey from slavery in Egypt to our promised land. I was strengthened by so many around the world, Jews and non-Jews, who were engaged in the struggle to free Soviet Jewry and to liberate hundreds of millions of people from under the boot of Soviet tyranny. And most important, I was strengthened by the vision of being reunited again with my wife Avital in Jerusalem.

This feeling of interconnectedness is what enabled me to persevere all those years in the Gulag.

Of course, it also helps to be able to see the lighter side of life, even in the most difficult hours. I especially liked telling anti-Soviet jokes to my interrogators. I remember one time I told a joke about Brezhnev being furious when Americans succeeded at putting a man on the moon. After emergency discussions with other members of the Politburo, he assembled all the cosmonauts. "We have decided to beat the Americans by sending a man to the sun," declared Brezhnev." "But Comrade Leonid," replied one cosmonaut, "we will be burned alive." "What? You think we at the Politburo are idiots" shouted Brezhnev, "We have considered everything. You will be sent at night."

My interrogators were ready to burst from laughter, but they would not dare laugh in front of another KGB agent at such a joke, so they pounded on the table and shouted at me. I told these jokes not only to irritate my interrogators - which of course was always a source of pleasure - but also to remind myself who is really free and who is really in a prison -- the interrogator who cannot even laugh when he wants to or you, who is free to think what you want, say what you want and laugh when you want. It helps remind you why you are really there and why you will never want to return to the life of doublethink and fear.

I guess it also helps to have a hobby that is compatible with prison life, and my hobby was chess. I played thousands of games in my head and guess what - I always won.

FP: We are running out of time Mr. Sharansky. Before we finish, let me just sneak in a brief comment.

This interview has a special significance for me. I am the son of Soviet dissidents, Yuri and Marina Glazov. My dad signed *the Letter of Twelve*, which denounced Soviet human rights abuses and my mom actively typed and circulated Samizdat - the underground political literature. We were very fortunate to escape the vicious barbarity of what Soviet terror had in store for us.

You are an individual who is very close to my heart. Throughout my whole childhood I listened to your name being spoken at my family's dinner table – and it was a name that demanded respect and admiration. My dad and mom spoke very highly of you and closely followed your trials and tribulations. I remember how much we all cheered in front of our television that day when you zig-zagged walking across that bridge during the exchange that freed you from your Soviet captors and tormentors. My whole family had tears in their eyes.

And you zig-zagged because the KGB had told you to walk straight. Despite all the suffering you experienced you remained a warrior to the last second, achieving victory – a single human being against an entire totalitarian regime. That last counter-punch of resistance represented so much to all of us – it inspired and continues to inspire human hope and the unquenchable thirst for freedom and liberty that resides in the heart of man.

So this may be a little bit of a strange way to end an interview, but I would like to give you a big bear hug in emotional Russian style. And I would like to say to you that I consider you one of my personal heroes. Thank you for standing up for freedom, for sacrificing so many years of your life in the Soviet gulag for the beautiful values that you treasure, and for being the extraordinary human being that you are. The world doesn't make many people like you.

Sharansky: Thank you for your kind words. I am truly flattered. But you should never forget that I was not alone. It was precisely people like your parents, and the many people who were part of the Soviet Jewry movement within the USSR and the millions of supporters around the world who stood in solidarity with them that made it possible for an evil empire to be defeated.

When I was convicted, the KGB, the most powerful organization of the most powerful totalitarian empire in history, told me that the Soviet Jewry struggle was finished, that the human rights movement inside the USSR was over, that I had no choice but to cooperate. The KGB derided all those in the West who stood in solidarity with us as an army of students and housewives. But this army of students and housewives changed our world.

Less than twenty years later, the KGB is gone. The USSR is gone. Communism is gone. More than a million Soviet Jews have returned to their ancestral homeland. And hundreds of millions of people are now free. That should convince any sceptic of the awesome power of freedom to change our world. If we believe in that power once again then the results can be no less dramatic.

FP: Thank you, Mr. Sharansky. You are an inspiration. I hope you will visit us again soon. Take care.

[Jamie Glazov, "The Case for Democracy," Frontpagemag.com, December 17, 2004.]

18. Banquo's Ghosts - Rich Lowry

Frontpage Interview's guest today is Rich Lowry, the editor of National Review, a nationally syndicated columnist, and a Fox News political analyst. His book, *Legacy: Paying the Price for the Clinton Years*, was a New York Times bestseller. He is the co-author (with Keith Korman) of the new thriller, *Banquo's Ghosts*.

FP: Rich Lowry, welcome to Frontpage Interview. Tell us what inspired you to write this thriller.

Lowry: I originally got the idea at one of NR's editorial dinners hosted by Bill Buckley a few years ago. We were talking about Iran's nuclear program and the idea of sending an amateur assassin to Iran popped into my head and I mused "that would make a good spy novel." Keith is my literary agent (and a novelist), so we're always bouncing book ideas off one another and I lobbied him to write this one with me. We got started almost immediately and had a blast doing it.

FP: Enlighten our readers what this novel is about exactly.

Lowry: Here's the basic plot: Peter Johnson is a left-wing journalist who writes for a New York-based publication called *The Crusader*. He's a lush, a cynic, and a little corrupt. But watching the 9/11 attacks from his Brooklyn Heights apartment changes something in him. He begins to have doubts about the "hate America" pieces his editrix, Josephine von Hildebrand, constantly assigns him. Meanwhile, an old forgotten CIA spymaster, Stewart Bancroft (he works under cover of the name Banquo), has an eye on him. Banquo is old school. He's been marginalized in the new overly bureaucratic, politically correct CIA, as an anachronism who believes in aggressively and imaginatively taking the fight to the enemy. He concludes that the best possible man to send to kill Iran's top nuclear scientist is the one no one would suspect--the unreliable, famously America-hating Peter Johnson. And then, as they say, mayhem ensues.

FP: The novel is clearly a critique of the media. Can you talk a little bit about that?

Lowry: Yes, if there's a villain in the book--besides the ones coming out of Iran--it's the media. And why not? The media in this country is shallow, self-obsessed, and defeatist. If it had had its way in Iraq, we would have lost the war there, and now that the situation has stabilized, it has moved onto declaring Afghanistan--previously the "good war"--the latest Vietnam. In the struggle with radical Islam, maintaining our will and civilizational self-confidence is absolutely essential and the media undermines both.

FP: Why do you think our media is saturated with such defeatist elements? What is the best way we can counter this defeatism in our media?

Lowry: A couple of things. As James Burnham said "liberalism permits Western civilization to be reconciled to its dissolution." Also, there's a generational thing going on. For Baby-Boomer media types, whatever it is--it's always another Vietnam and always another Watergate. Ultimately, though, the truth will come out; the press, for instance, was reluctant to report on the progress forged by the surge in Iraq--with honorable exceptions, including USA Today--but when conditions had undeniably changed on the ground, that reality got out. Unfortunately, there's not much we can do about the mainstream press in the near time--all the more reason to at least have some laughs at its expense with *Banquo's Ghosts*!

FP: *Banquo's Ghosts* pokes at various people. Some of the characters appear to be based on some real people. Can you give us an insight into some of the realities here?

Lowry: We're hoping readers will enjoy trying to puzzle that out. There's a former New York Times theater critic turned op-ed columnist named Neville Poore. I'm sure people are going to think of Frank Rich. I bet Josephine is going to call to mind a couple real grande dames of left-wing journalism. But ultimately these are characters in a work of fiction, and they have lives all their own. Although we do skewer some real-life media figures by name, from Chris Matthews, to Sy Hersh, to Joy Behar. Jamie, I think you in particular will relish the scene of Keith Olbermann giving a lap-dog interview to a notorious Hezbollah symp from the Council on Islamic Peace and Tolerance, a guy named Ibrihim Mahdi.

But I don't want to give people the wrong impression. You used the phrase "poking fun," and I want to put the accent on "fun." This book is first and foremost a pot-boiler. We do everything we can to keep the pot boiling for 350 pages, with as many thrills and laughs as possible.

You'll meet Agents Smith and Wesson, the gorgeous, leggy FBI agents working the beat in New York, and all manner of other zany and--we hope--memorable characters.

FP: What are some of the joys in writing fiction that surpass the joys of writing non-fiction for you? What are some ways that fiction can make a point about the real world in a stronger way than non-fiction can?

Lowry: Obviously, just making it up is tremendously liberating--no foot-noting, no checking of sources. And it allows you to dramatize, and therefore make more vivid, certain truths.

FP: Did anything unexpected happen to your way of thinking while you wrote this novel?

Lowry: Not having done this before, I was surprised by the extent the characters take on a life of their own. We set out to make the journalist Peter Johnson a lovable rogue, which is easier said than done. Most rogues aren't particularly lovable. But by the end we really cared about the guy--it's his development that is most central to the novel as he confronts the question of whether, for the first time in his life, he will care about something enough to put himself utterly on the line for it. Josephine is not the most sympathetic character, but I found myself admiring her self-promotional moxie. And there are characters who sprang up unplanned as we wrote, like the "deliciously" named Yasmine, the young woman who is the assistant to the Iran scientist. She's one to watch.

FP: This thriller is, more than anything, a reminder to all of us of the dire threat we face from Islamic Jihad. What is the greatest threat in your view and who is posing it?

Lowry: Well, it's a hydra-headed threat obviously, but it emanates from Iran more than any other one place. That regime has a hand in practically every terrorist movement destabilizing the region from Gaza to Lebanon to Iraq. It declared war on us from its inception in 1979, and is getting closer and closer to a nuclear weapon. As Banquo says of A-Jad at one point, when he is trying to gin up Johnson for his mission, "That single man is on the verge of delivering to crazed monkeys high on Apocalyptic crack a supply of radioactive handguns, matches and gasoline -- then sending them into a kindergarten with unsupervised children and hoping for the best."

FP: Your thoughts on the behaviour of the Lib-Left in this terror war? How is the Obama administration handling it thus far in your view?

Lowry: The left's performance has been appalling, as you yourself have documented. In *Banquo's Ghosts*, we refer to the Left and the elite it has taken hostage as "the West-hating, postmodern, gender-bending, self-congratulatory super-rich and talentless mediocrities -- the whole collection of 'progressives' who, as the saying went, wouldn't take their own side in a fight, even if they knew which side they were on."

As for President Obama, I have been pleasantly surprised so far. I think he's been relatively centrist on the Iraq and the Afghan wars.

I'm not sure that's out of any great conviction--in fact, I don't trust his gut instincts in the least. But my sense is that he doesn't have any great interest in foreign affairs and just wants to reasonably manage the war, while he goes about massively expanding government at home.

There are two big questions outstanding: 1) Even though he's committed to shutting down Gitmo and limiting interrogation methods to those approved by the Army Field Manual, he's also left the door open to long-term detention of enemy combatants--although he won't call them that--and ramping up interrogation when necessary. Where does he come down on this stuff when push comes to shove? 2) What does he do about Iran's nuclear program when Tehran insists on keeping it--as it almost inevitably will--despite his diplomatic blandishments?

FP: What are the essential things we need to be doing to defend ourselves from radical Islam?

Lowry: We need to leave in place the domestic architecture-- the Patriot Act, the terrorist surveillance program, etc.--created by President Bush. We need to win in Iraq and in Afghanistan, where the future of Pakistan is also at stake. We need to do everything we can to keep the Iranians from acquiring a nuke. We need to keep from feasting on ourselves--as we did so disastrously in the 1970's--when we make mistakes. And, above all, we need to realize that this is a war and buckle down for the long haul, because will and patience are absolutely indispensable.

FP: Rich Lowry, thank you for joining us at Frontpagemag.com.

Lowry: Thanks so much, Jamie, and keep up the great work. We can work in a cameo for you in any sequel if you like!

FP: It's a deal!

[Jamie Glazov, "Banquo's Ghosts," Frontpagemag.com,
April 02, 2009.]

Part V: The Evil Empire

Introduction:

While there are significant differences between the Islamist threat of today and the Stalinist enemy of yesterday, there are crucial important lessons to be learned from the Cold War era. One of the primary lessons concerns the non-violent techniques the USSR pursued during the conflict. This was not solely a military threat waged through proxy states around the globe. The USSR attacked America from within – utilizing networks of communist spies who projected a false reality of who they really were.

The Islamist threat has pursued a similar strategy – nurturing Muslim Brotherhood front groups like the Council on American-Islamic Relations (CAIR) and the Muslim Students Association (MSA) to pursue stealth jihad strategies while "lone wolves" like Nidal Hasan pop up to commit acts of violence. The enemies of freedom are not just off in the caves of Afghanistan and the deserts of Saudi Arabia. They are in our backyards, lobbying our congressmen, and showing up as respected "civil rights" advocates on MSNBC.

If Americans could grasp the record – were the Left not so dominate in shaping the popular narrative of the Cold War – then they would be prepared to anticipate what is happening to them now. Instead, though, to point out these facts results in one being labeled a "racist" or "Islamophobe," an epithet not dissimilar to "McCarthyite" and "redbaiter."

The four important authors interviewed in this section bring decades' worth of research to demonstrating the reality of the USSR's espionage. But will the modern political culture learn from the past and apply the lessons to today's conflict? Let's not get our hopes up. -- David Swindle

19. Spies – Harvey Klehr and John Haynes

Frontpage Interview's guests today are Harvey Klehr and John Haynes. Harvey Klehr is Andrew Mellon Professor of Politics and History at Emory University. John Haynes is 20th Century manuscript historian at the Library of Congress. Their new book, written with Alexander Vassiliev, *Spies: The Rise and Fall of the KGB in America*, has received wide attention this summer. Along with positive reviews in magazines and newspaper ranging from *The Wall Street Journal* to *The New Republic* and the *New Yorker*, it has drawn angry denunciations from admirers of I.F. Stone, defenders of Alger Hiss, and left-wing bloggers unwilling to confront the legacy of American communist support for Soviet espionage.

FP: Harvey Klehr and John Haynes, welcome to Frontpage Interview.

Tell us a bit about how the Left is still denying the undeniable evidence you have revealed.

Klehr: There has been an outpouring of rage at the possibility that I.F. Stone could ever have worked for Soviet intelligence, despite abundant evidence in Vassiliev's Notebooks that he did so - evidence that gives context to earlier allegations made by General Oleg Kalugin.

Stone's defenders have taken several tacks. One is to assert, with absolutely no evidence, that the documents implicating Stone must be disinformation, cunningly inserted by Alexander Vassiliev more than a decade ago, so he and we could traduce Stone in 2009.

FP: What has been the most pathetic denial?

Klehr: Possibly the silliest one, made by a left-wing blogger and picked up by Myra McPherson, one of Stone's biographers, has been the claim that a document reporting that relations with Stone had "entered the channels of normal operational work" did not mean he was cooperating with the KGB because when you Google that phrase the only hits are from our article. Apparently, spy agencies are only supposed to use language approved by the Left!

FP: And I'm sure another tactic of denial has simply been just to ignore your findings.

Klehr: Of course. Other critics have simply just refused to deal with the evidence, asserting that because he was so independent, Stone could not have cooperated with the KGB - even though they admit that during this period - 1936-1939- he was a devoted fellow-traveler and apologized for all of Stalin's crimes.

A handful of writers like Amy Knight, who has never found a source on Soviet intelligence she trusts, have tried to minimize or deny the vast extent of Soviet espionage revealed in the Note-books. Predictably, the *Nation* magazine, *Huffington Post*, Eric Alterman, Glenn Greenwald and other reflexively deny that the Soviet Union recruited hundreds of Americans to spy. A major part of the reason, I believe, is that acknowledging these facts would require them to rethink the entire mythology of the McCarthy era. And that is something they are not prepared to do.

FP: John Haynes?

Haynes: The hard Left's reaction reinforces in my mind the fundamental contempt for historical accuracy that permeates its intellectual world. The past is treated simply as another arena of partisan polemic. The hard Left sees history as infinitely malleable and remakes it to conform to whatever are its current concerns. It can never learn from history because the past it ardently believes in is always one that ratifies its worldview.

Consequently, when historical evidence on some issue does become so heavy that even intellectual equivalent of shouting, screaming, and throwing sand in the air is no longer sufficient to obscure the facts, the hard Left just drops the issue and pretends that it doesn't exist. Call it the ostrich strategy.

Notable in the reaction to our *Spies* has been the near absence of any response to the extremely lengthy treatment of Julius Rosenberg and his network of engineer spies in the book Vassiliev's Notebooks allow us to fill-out the story of the Rosenberg ring, identify more members of it and give a better picture of the impressive quantify and quality of its military technology espionage.

Most interestingly, we identify Russell McNutt as a young engineer and secret Communist that Rosenberg recruited into espionage and urged to get a job at Kellex, a contractor for key facilities at the secret atomic project at Oak Ridge, Tennessee. McNutt got the job and provided the KGB with information on the design of the massive uranium separation plant at Oak Ridge.

Rosenberg, thus, recruited two atomic spies, not just his long-known brother-in-law David Greenglass. This fact demolishes one of the hard Left's recent fall-back positions on Rosenberg: that while he may have provided the Soviets (usually referred to in this excuse making motif as 'our wartime allies') with some innocuous information on conventional weaponry, he emphatically was *not* an atomic spy. Yet Julius Rosenberg's espionage, the subject of thousands of impassioned public protests, books, articles, public exhibits, letters-to-the-editor, and so on from the 1960s until last year, has simply dropped off the hard Left's agenda. While hard Left commentators rail away at our about six pages on I.F. Stone, the sixty-plus pages on Rosenberg and his apparatus go without significant mention. Dr. Amy Knight, for example, dismisses McNutt as not important and doesn't even note the Rosenberg connection.

FP: Why the silence on your evidence on Rosenberg?

Haynes: The hard Left's silence on the Rosenberg matter serves to avoid calling attention to an intellectual battle it has lost and avoids the necessity of explaining why it got the issue so wrong for so long.

FP: Do you feel you have accomplished what you set out to do in Spies?

Klehr: I'm delighted with the book and the attention it has gotten. We were able to highlight many of the fascinating and historically significant material in Vassiliev's Notebooks. Outside of the fever swamps of the left, I think most people recognize the new light this throws on the issue of Soviet espionage. The fact that tens of thousands of people have viewed and/or downloaded the Notebooks from the Cold War International History website is testimony to the widespread interest in the topic. And, we have been told that a significant number of the visits to the site have come from the Russian Federation - a sign that there is considerable interest in this story in Russia.

There are always disappointments and one of mine is that the New York Times decided not to review the book. That the so-called "newspaper of record" concluded that this book, which attracted enormous controversy because of its new evidence about I.F. Stone, Robert Oppenheimer, the Rosenbergs and Alger Hiss, generated hundreds of articles and links because of its revelations about Ernest Hemingway, and drew a large crowd to the Woodrow Wilson Center for a symposium on its findings, was not worthy of its attention says something sad about its willingness to confront this issue from America's past.

Haynes: Klehr and I have written a number of good books, but SPIES is our best work. It is our best not because we have gotten better, although we do understand Soviet espionage in America in the 30s and 40s much better than when we first ventured into espionage history fifteen years ago. It is our best because of the richness of the underlying source material. Vassiliev's Notebooks easily provide more documentation and more detailed records than anything that has hitherto been available and that has allowed us to provide a much more comprehensive description of Soviet espionage operations than was possible earlier.

FP: Final thoughts?

Klehr: I hope that more scholars and journalists will dig into some of the material that we were able to discuss only briefly or not at all due to space limitations. Spies raises important questions about why so many American citizens cooperated with Soviet espionage and helps us understand more about the politics and passions of the McCarthy era. It would benefit everyone if discussion of these issues was based on factual evidence and not ideological preconceptions.

Haynes: We are confident that by making the Vassiliev Notebooks easily available on the web that many other researchers will make use of them to further fill out the story of Soviet espionage by bringing out matters we did not deal with and integrating them with other source material in order to illuminate still murky issues. Despite screams by the dwindling camp of Hiss defenders (dwindling but loud) that they can keep doubt alive and the drama queen histrionics of I.F. Stone worshipers, SPIES and the Vassiliev Notebooks have turned a corner in espionage history in the Stalin era.

The story isn't finished. There is still much we do not know. We still understand very little about the WWII operations of GRU (Soviet military intelligence) in the United States. But debate is over on the basic issues of the two cases that dominated historical discussion for fifty years, the Hiss and Rosenberg cases. The broad outlines of KGB operations in the 1930s and 1940s are understood. Not all, but most of the KGB's sources are identified. The discussion and research in the field should proceed in a more normal fashion with much less of the ideological partisanship that retarded historical understanding in the past.

FP: Harvey Klehr and John Haynes, thank you for joining Frontpage Interview.

[Jamie Glazov, "Spies: The Rise and Fall of the KGB in America," Frontpagemag.com, September 11, 2009.]

20. Putin's Spies in America - Konstantin Preobrazhenskiy

Frontpage Interview's guest today is Konstantin Preobrazhenskiy, a former KGB agent who became one of the KGB's harshest critics. He is the author of seven books about the KGB and Japan. His new book is *KGB/FSB's New Trojan Horse: Americans of Russian Descent.*

FP: Konstantin Preobrazhenskiy, welcome to Frontpage Magazine.

Preobrazhensky: Thank you for giving me a chance to address the realistically minded people.

FP: Tell us about your background and the circumstances under which you came to the KGB.

Preobrazhensky: I graduated from the Institute of Asia and Africa of the Moscow University in 1976. Before that, I was an intern at the Tokai University in Japan. I am a specialist in Japan, a fluent Japanese speaker. I love Japan very much. And this love has brought me to the KGB.

FP: What do you love about Japan?

Preobrazhensky: Because it is a fairyland. In its ultra-modern society you can see the medieval society of "samurai" like through a magic telescope. This unbelievable combination makes Japan a magic fascination which cannot be expressed in words.

FP: Ok, so tell us how you ended up in Japan.

Preobrazhensky: Well, if you are a specialist in Japan, you had to travel to the country that you were studying. And that was possible only if you were working for KGB. By the way, Soviet specialists in the U.S.A. were in the same situation. They all were connected to the KGB and most of them were its officers. There was only one chance to avoid working for KGB: becoming an officer of the

Central Committee of the Communist Party, the member of the highest elite. But it was very hard to do that.

So I only had one choice: either become a KGB collaborator, whose position is very dependent, or its staff officer with shoulder-stripes and high military salary. The second variant was much better.

But it was very hard to do. In the end, my father, the Deputy Commander of the KGB Frontier Troops, "pushed" me into KGB intelligence, the most privileged and well-paid job in the USSR.

My work in Tokyo as a spy from 1980-85, was very successful. I was covered as a correspondent of the Soviet TASS Agency. But it was not a cover for me. It was my actual job, because I am a born author. My KGB colleagues in Tokyo called me, with a grin, "An author covered as a spy." And they were right.

While in the KGB, I published a couple of books on Japan: *The Sports Dressed in Kimono* (1985) and *The Bamboo Sword* (1982). Both were a success. And two of my short novels, *Karate Begins with Bows* and *Very New and Old Pagoda* were published by the Soviet Academy of Science in 1987, in the Academic Anthology, *Soviet Authors on Japan, 1917-87*.

In Tokyo, I was spying on China. I recruited a Chinese scholar there. But Japanese counterintelligence learned about it somehow and caught me in 1985 on my way to contact this new Soviet agent. It became a spy scandal. The KGB forcibly returned me to Russia and accuses me solely of this scandal, though nobody knew the real reason. It tragically interrupted my career as a Japanologist.

FP: So when did you turn on the KGB?

Preobrazhensky: My interviewers always ask me when I got disappointed in the KGB. Never. Because I came there disappointed. Contrary to most young officers, I knew about its criminal and inhumane activities from my father's colleagues. That is why I began to write a book of revelations about the KGB from my first day of serving there. It was first published in Tokyo in 1994, soon after I left the KGB in 1991. It was entitled, "The Spy Who Loved Japan." It became a best seller.

When I left the KGB in 1991, it was dissolving at that time, although under Putin it has resurged. Immediately I went to the Japanese media in Moscow and began to publish interviews, articles and even books disclosing the KGB. I became a security columnist at "Moscow Times" newspaper which made me world known. "The Spy who Loved Japan" irritated the KGB greatly, but they could not do anything against me in 1994: it was a short period of Russian democracy. But finally my anti-KGB activities forced me to run away from Russia.

FP: So under what circumstances did you come to the U.S.?

Preobrazhensky: After Putin came to power in 2000, he began the persecution of all the KGB dissidents. In 2002, Oleg Kalugin was sentenced in absentia to 15 years, being accused of disclosing the KGB secrets. I knew I was next. Unfortunately, I was not "in absentia", but in Moscow. As a professional, I got a feeling that they were going to arrest me very soon. I urgently went to the U.S. on a private visit and asked for political asylum. Now I am permanent resident in the U.S. This dramatic story has been described in my new book, *KGB/FSB's New Trojan Horse: Americans of Russian Descent.*

FP: The American media and literary culture ignored your book. How come?

Preobrazhensky: My book was ignored. Only a few religious writers have reviewed it as it is devoted to the KGB penetration of America through the Russian Orthodox Church. It tells how the KGB managed to put Russian Americans under its control by merging the Russian Orthodox Church abroad with the Kremlin-controlled Moscow Patriarchate. That is why the laymen journalists probably did not want to cover such a delicate topic. How is possible to speak about the Church as a tool of espionage? It would not be "politically correct." So political correctness has helped Putin to keep his espionage in America secret. Moreover, it is helping him facilitate it. Putin knows very well about American political correctness and about the fact that American counter-intelligence is not eligible to monitor clergymen. The KGB is doing it in Russia very aggressively in spite of the fact that Church and State are separate there too.

So we have a situation that Putin is openly spying in the U.S. and Americans are afraid of writing about it. This idiotic paradox is a symbol of current American-Russian relations. They bring profit only to Russia.

Just recently, the wall of silence about my book was finally broken. My book was reviewed by Professor Clare Lopez, published by Gerard Group International:

Professor Clare Lopez has come to a conclusion which is very important for me: "For those who think the Cold War ended in 1991, this book will have you thinking again. Konstantin Preobrazhensky wants Americans to wake up to the ongoing agenda of the Russian regime, which he says under the rule of Vladimir Putin and the KGB has reverted to the intelligence-dominated repressive state of the 20th century."

FP: Can you talk a bit about the growth of leftism in America and the KGB influence on it?

Preobrazhensky: Well, the KGB has no special need to influence American leftists any more. Their ancestors in Stalin's time have done it for them. They have seeded leftism among the American intellectuals, and today's KGB is only gathering their crop.

On the other hand, a lot of American leftists were recruited by the KGB in the Soviet period. They are still working for the Russians. There are many KGB collaborators in this country.

Also, a lot of Americans have been educated as leftists at the leftist universities in America. Their professors were contacting the KGB in the 1930s, or were "useful idiots," as Lenin has cynically called the Western intellectuals devotedly working for Russia. Their successors are teaching there now. The graduates of such universities are joining the most important governmental offices, and it might very well affect the American political course.

But there is one more reason for the growth of leftism. Many people get disappointed in capitalism. A lot of Americans are still sure that socialism is better. When I tell them that socialism inevitably brings the GULAG they do not believe me.

Russian intellectuals of 19th century made the same mistake, but they were severely punished for it by the 70-years of horrible Communist rule. Americans have not suffered such a disappointment yet.

Leftism brings a specific damage to America. Let's not forget that Julius and Ethel Rosenberg delivered American atomic bomb secrets to Russia not for money, but because of being leftists.

And the wide spread of leftism in the U.S. alleviates Russian influence here as Russia is a leftist country.

FP: What is the extent of Russia influence in the U.S.?

Preobrazhensky: It is very strong. The Russian mechanism of misinformation and manipulation includes the utilization of some American think-tanks and political scientists.

Democratic states are much more vulnerable than authoritarian ones. That is why Putin's machine of lies not only deceives America, but creates an inadequate and adorned image of Russia, provoking America to make wrong decisions about this country.

One example is provided by the decision to close Russian Service of the Voice of America in 2007. Maybe Americans consider Russian Service to be a mere relic of the Cold War, unnecessary in free Russia, but in fact it has been one of the last sources of independent information for Russians. It has irritated Russian authorities. Putin has managed to close it with the Americans' hands.

But the Russian propagandist TV channel, "Russia Today," is very active in America. Nobody is going to close it or transfer to Internet!

The clear one-sidedness of American-Russian relations is also exposed by the Russian lobbyism here. There are the opened Russian lobbyists in America like Ketchum Company and others. But are there any American lobbyists in Russia? Oh, no.

Any Russian that agrees to become an American lobbyist would be declared a national traitor. Putin calls such people "the jackals at foreign embassies". Mikhail Khodorkovsky, a Russian tycoon and the former President of the YUKOS Company, was said to be a sort of American lobbyist. Where is he now? In prison, from where he will hardly ever get out. In Russia, it is considered non-patriotic to be an American lobbyist.

"Do not criticize Russia because it will strengthen the position of the opponents of its pro-Western course there." Such a phrase is very much used by both Russian and American authors. It is a very sophisticated piece of misinformation. It postulates that still not all the people in the Russian elite are anti-American and they all have a freedom of arguing against Russian anti-Americanism. Such a notion is very well understood by Americans. But in fact, there are no pro-American people in the Kremlin. Hatred of America is symbol of loyalty there. If you love America, you cannot work in the Russian government.

Sometimes this myth is pronounced in another version:" Oh, do not criticize Russia or they will make friends with China." But they are friends already. It is too late to caution about it. This is the misinformation thesis invented by Directorate "A" of SVR, that the Russian Foreign Intelligence Service Directorate "A" is tasked to misinform American and Western public opinion about. Many journalists are reproducing this false thesis, not knowing where it was invented. But recently some American politicians began to pronounce a far more dangerous thesis: "Let's yield Georgia and Ukraine to Russia, and Russians will help us in Iran."

FP: The chance of Putin helping the U.S. in Iran?

Preobrazhensky: Zero. The Russians will never do so. They will never help the U.S. in any Islamic country. They have developed their own, very special relations with the Islamic World, based on anti-Americanism.

Russia has a four-centuries experience of tolerating Islam and does not want to share it with America. Moreover, Russia's strategic goal is to display the U.S. to militant Islam as a scapegoat instead of itself.

FP: What are the methods of Russian influence

Preobrazhensky: In 2004, Putin revived Stalin's practice of inviting Western writers directly to Moscow and charming them personally. He has founded the "Valdai Discussion Club" for them. The club meetings are held at Golitsyno, one of Putin's residences in Moscow suburbs, and also in other places of Russia. There Putin is hosting luxurious receptions at which he is fascinates American intellectuals.

Putin is a good actor. He presents himself as a sole liberal captured by the conservative KGB surrounding. He portrays this picture: they are urging him to deviate from democracy, so the West should not criticize him too much or he will yield to the KGB completely.

Dr. Andrei Piontkovsky of the Hudson Institute has called members of Valdai Club "a collective Feuchtwanger".

Leon Feuchtwanger was a famous German writer of the 1930s who admired Stalin's regime. Today, the "collective Feuchtwanger" is propagating an adorned image of Russia, which affects American policy towards Russia. All this mechanism of Russian influence in America will be disclosed in my forthcoming book, "How Russian Federation is Ruling United States".

FP: What can Americans do to protect themselves from these Russian threats on their own territory? And what U.S. policy do you recommend toward Putin?

Preobrazhensky: America should stop the current abnormal situation which finds Russian intelligence working here manifestly, being sure that Americans now cannot afford a spy scandal against its supposed "ally" in fighting terrorism.

America should stop tolerating Russia by concessions and apologies which cause nothing but laughter from Russians. Americans should understand that Putin and other Russian leaders have a criminal psychology as they are building criminal capitalism. From the point of view of the mafia, those who make concessions are losers and fools. They deserve only further pressing, which Russia is demonstrating. America should be hard with Russians. Only after that Russians will respect America.

America should get rid of false expectations about Russia, the most dangerous of which is the following: "We need each other to oppose China and militant Islam". Russia does not need America at all in this. Russia tolerates both China and Islam in a way of betrothal, behind the back of America and in spite of it.

America should finally comprehend that Russia does not share American values. That it is not a democracy. America should treat it like it is treating China and other non-democratic countries.

FP: Konstantin Preobrazhenskiy, thank you for joining Frontpage Magazine.

[Jamie Glazov, "Putin's Spies in America," Frontpagemag.com, June 19, 2009.]

21. Ted Kennedy and the KGB - Paul Kengor

Frontpage Interview's guest today is Paul Kengor, the author of the New York Times extended-list bestseller *God and Ronald Reagan* as well as *God and George W. Bush* and *The Crusader: Ronald Reagan and the Fall of Communism.* He is also the author of the first spiritual biography of the former first lady, *God and Hillary Clinton: A Spiritual Life.* He is a professor of political science and director of the Center for Vision and Values at Grove City College.

FP: Paul Kengor, welcome back to Frontpage Interview.

Kengor: Always great to be back, Jamie.

FP: We're here today to revisit Ted Kennedy's reaching out to the KGB during the Reagan period. Refresh our readers' memories a bit.

Kengor: The episode is based on a document produced 25 years ago this week. I discussed it with you in our earlier interview back in November 2006. In my book, *The Crusader: Ronald Reagan and the Fall of Communism*, I presented a rather eye-opening May 14, 1983 KGB document on Ted Kennedy. The entire document, unedited, unabridged, is printed in the book, as well as all the documentation affirming its authenticity. Even with that, today, almost 25 years later, it seems to have largely remained a secret.

FP: Tell us about this document.

Kengor: It was a May 14, 1983 letter from the head of the KGB, Viktor Chebrikov, to the head of the USSR, the odious Yuri Andropov, with the highest level of classification. Chebrikov relayed to Andropov an offer from Senator Ted Kennedy, presented by Kennedy's old friend and law-school buddy, John Tunney, a former Democratic senator from California, to reach out to the Soviet leadership at the height of a very hot time in the Cold War. According to Chebrikov, Kennedy was deeply troubled by the deteriorating relationship between the United States and the Soviet Union, which he believed was bringing us perilously close to nuclear confrontation. Kennedy, according to Chebrikov, blamed this situation not on the Soviet leadership but on the American president---Ronald Reagan. Not only was the USSR not to blame, but, said Chebrikov, Kennedy was, quite the contrary, "very impressed" with Andropov.

The thrust of the letter is that Reagan had to be stopped, meaning his alleged aggressive defense policies, which then ranged from the Pershing IIs to the MX to SDI, and even his re-election bid, needed to be stopped. It was Ronald Reagan who was the hindrance to peace. That view of Reagan is consistent with things that Kennedy said and wrote at the time, including articles in sources like Rolling Stone (March 1984) and in a speeches like his March 24, 1983 remarks on the Senate floor the day after Reagan's SDI speech, which he lambasted as "misleading Red-Scare tactics and reckless Star Wars schemes."

Even more interesting than Kennedy's diagnosis was the prescription: According to Chebrikov, Kennedy suggested a number of PR moves to help the Soviets in terms of their public image with the American public. He reportedly believed that the Soviet problem was a communication problem, resulting from an inability to counter Reagan's (not the USSR's) "propaganda." If only Americans could get through Reagan's smokescreen and hear the Soviets' peaceful intentions.

So, there was a plan, or at least a suggested plan, to hook up Andropov and other senior apparatchiks with the American media, where they could better present their message and make their case. Specifically, the names of Walter Cronkite and Barbara Walters are mentioned in the document. Also, Kennedy himself would travel to Moscow to meet with the dictator.

Time was of the essence, since Reagan, as the document privately acknowledged, was flying high en route to easy re-election in 1984.

FP: Did you have the document vetted?

Kengor: Of course. It comes from the Central Committee archives of the former USSR. Once Boris Yeltsin took over Russia in 1991, he immediately began opening the Soviet archives, which led to a rush on the archives by Western researchers. One of them, Tim Sebastian of the London Times and BBC, found the Kennedy document and reported it in the February 2, 1992 edition of the Times, in an article titled, "Teddy, the KGB and the top secret file."

But this electrifying revelation stopped there; it went no further. Never made it across the Atlantic. Not a single American news organization, from what I can tell, picked up the story. Apparently, it just wasn't interesting enough, nor newsworthy.

Western scholars, however, had more integrity, and responded: they went to the archives to procure their own copy. So, several copies have circulated for a decade and a half.

I got my copy when a reader of Frontpage Magazine, named Marko Suprun, whose father survived Stalin's 1930s genocide in the Ukraine, alerted me to the document. He apparently had spent years trying to get the American media to take a look at the document, but, again, our journalists simply weren't intrigued. He knew I was researching Reagan and the Cold War. He sent me a copy. I first authenticated it through Herb Romerstein, the Venona researcher and widely respected expert who knows more about the Communist Party and archival research beyond the former Iron Curtain than anyone. I also had a number of scholars read the original and the translation, including Harvard's Richard Pipes.

Of course, all of those steps were extra, extra, extra precautions, since the reporter for the London Times had done all that work in the first place. He went into the archive, pulled it off the shelf, and the Times ran with the story. This wasn't rocket science. I simply wanted to be extra careful, especially since our media did not cover it at all. I now understand that that blackout by the American media was the result of liberal bias. At first I didn't think our media could be that bad, even though I knew from studies and anecdotal experience that our press is largely liberal, but now I've learned firsthand that the bias is truly breathtaking.

FP: So what shockwaves did your exposure of this document set off in the media?

Kengor: Well, I thought it would be a bombshell, which it was, but only within the conservative media.

I prepared myself to be pilloried by the liberal mainstream media, figuring I'd be badgered with all kinds of hostile questions from defenders of Ted Kennedy. I still, at this very moment, carry photocopies and the documentation with me in my briefcase, ready for access at a moment's notice. I've done that for two years now. The pages may soon begin to yellow.

I need not have bothered with any of this prep, since the media entirely ignored the revelation. In fact, the major reviewers didn't even review the book. It was the most remarkable case of media bias I've ever personally experienced.

I couldn't get a single major news source to do a story on it. CNN, MSNBC, ABC, CBS, NBC. Not one covered it.

The only cable source was Fox News, Brit Hume's "Grapevine," and even then it was only a snippet in the round-up. In fact, I was frustrated by the occasional conservative who didn't run with it. I did a taping with Hannity & Colmes but they never used it, apparently because they were so focused on the mid-term elections, to the exclusion of almost any other story or issue. The Hannity & Colmes thing was a major blow; it could've propelled this onto the national scene, forcing the larger media to take note.

That was the single greatest disappointment. I think Sean Hannity might have felt that I wasn't hard enough on Senator Kennedy during the interview. He asked me, for instance, if what Kennedy did could be classified as treason. I told him honestly, as a scholar, that I really couldn't answer that question. I honestly don't know the answer to that; I'm not a constitutional scholar. I don't have the legal background to accuse someone of being a traitor. I was trying to be as fair as possible.

Rush Limbaugh, God bless him, appreciated it. He talked about it at least twice. So did blogs like Michelle Malkin's HotAir. Web sources like FrontPage hit it hard. But without the mainstream news coverage, the story never made the dent I expected it would.

I should note that Ed Klein of Parade magazine recently contacted me. He himself got a rude awakening on the media's liberal bias when he wrote a negative book on Hillary Clinton. I've not heard back from him. But he's a rare case of journalistic objectivity.

If I may vent just a little more on the mainstream press, Jamie: There's a bias there that really is incredibly troubling. Over and over again, I've written and submitted the most careful op-eds, trying to remove any partisan edge, on issues like Reagan and Gorbachev privately debating the removal of the Berlin Wall (I have de-classified documents on this in *The Crusader* as well), on Reagan's fascinating relationship with RFK, on various aspects of the Cold War that are completely new, based on entirely new evidence from interviews and archives. When I submit these op-ed to the major newspapers, they almost always turn them down. The first conservative source that I send them to always jump at them. The liberals, however, are very close-minded. Nothing is allowed to alter the template. You can construct the most fair, iron-tight case, and they turn it down. This is not true for everything I write on the Cold War era, but no doubt for most of it. And certainly for the case of Senator Kennedy and this KGB document.

FP: How about trying to place some op-eds on the Kennedy document?

Kengor: Here again, all the mainstream sources turned me down. I had no alternative but to place the op-eds in the conservative outlets. Liberal editors blacklisted the piece. I began by sending a piece to the New York Times, where the editor is David Shipley, who's extremely fair, and in fact has published me before, including a defense I wrote on the faith of George W. Bush. This one, however, he turned down. He liked it. It certainly had his intention. But he said he wouldn't be able to get it into the page.

I sent it to the Boston Globe, three or four times, actually. I got no response or even the courtesy of an acknowledgment. It was as if the piece was dispatched to the howling wilderness of Siberia—right into the gulag—airbrushed from history.

The most interesting response I got was from the editorial page editor of the San Francisco Chronicle, another very fair liberal, a great guy, who since then has retired. He published me several times. We went back and forth on this one. Finally, he said something to the effect, "I just can't believe that Ted Kennedy would do something this stupid." My reply was, "Well, he apparently did." I told the editor that if he was that incredulous, then he or someone on his staff should simply call Kennedy's office and get a response. Hey, let's do journalism and make news! It never happened.

For the record, one news source, a regional cable outlet in the Philadelphia area, called CN8, took the time to call Kennedy's office. The official response from his office was not to deny the document but to argue with the interpretation. Which interpretation? Mine or Chebrikov's? Kennedy's office wasn't clear on that. My interpretation was not an interpretation. I simply tried to report what Chebrikov reported to Andropov. So, I guess Kennedy's office was disputing Chebrikov's interpretation, which is quite convenient, since Chebrikov is dead, as is Andropov. Alas, the perfect defense—made more perfect by an American media that will not ask the senator from Massachusetts a single question (hard or soft) on this remarkable incident.

FP: So, Kennedy's office/staff did not deny the document?

Kengor: That's correct. They have not denied it. That's important. Because if none of this had ever happened, and if the document was a fraud, Kennedy's office would simply say so, and that would be the end of it.

FP: Tell us about the success the book has had in the recent past and the coverage it has received outside of the U.S.

Kengor: The paperback rights were picked up by the prestigious HarperPerennial in 2007, which I'm touting not to pat myself on the back but to affirm my point on why our mainstream press should take the book and the document seriously. The book has also been or is in the process of being translated into several foreign-language editions, including Poland, where it was released last November. It is literally true that more Polish journalists have paid attention to the Kennedy revelation than American journalists. I've probably sold about 20 times more copies of the book in Poland, where they understand communism and moral equivalency, than in Massachusetts.

FP: One can just imagine finding a document like this on an American Republican senator having made a similar offer to the Nazis. Kennedy has gotten away with this. What do you think this says about our culture, the parameters of debate and who controls the boundaries of discourse?

Kengor: History is determined by those who write it. There are the gatekeepers: editors, journalists, publishers. The left's ideologues are guarding the gate, swords brandished, crusaders, not open to other points of view. The result is a total distortion of "history," as the faithful and the chosen trumpet their belief in tolerance and diversity, awarding prizes to one another, disdainful and dismissive of the unwashed barbarians outside the gate.

You can produce a 550-page manuscript with 150-pages of single-space, 9-point footnotes, and it won't matter. They could care less.

FP: So, this historical revelation is not a revelation?

Kengor: That's right, because it is not impacting history— because gatekeepers are ignoring it.

Another reason why the mainstream media may be ignoring this: as I make clear in the book, this KGB document could be the tip of the iceberg, not just with Kennedy but other Democrats. John Tunney himself alluded to this in an interview with the London Times reporter. That article reported that Tunney had made many such trips to Moscow, with additional overtures, and on behalf of yet more Democratic senators. Given that reality, I suppose we should expect liberal journalists to flee this story like the plague—at least those too biased to do their jobs.

For the record, I've been hard on liberal journalists in this article, and rightly so. But there are many good liberal journalists who do real research and real reporting. And it's those that need to follow up on this. I'm a conservative, and so I'm not allowed into the club. Someone from inside the boys' club needs to step up to the plate.

FP: All of this is in sync with David Horowitz's and Ben Johnson's new book, *Party of Defeat*, isn't it? As the book demonstrates, many Democrats are engaging in willful sabotage in terms of our security vis-à-vis Islamo-Fascism today. And as the Kennedy-KGB romance indicates, a good portion of Democrats have always had a problem in reaching out to our enemies, rather than protecting our national security. Your thoughts?

Kengor: Obviously, as you know and suggest, this does not apply to all Democrats, needless to say. But there are many liberal Democrats who were dupes during the Cold War and now are assuming that role once again in the War on Terror. President Carter comes to mind, as does John Kerry, as does Ted Kennedy, to name only a few. When I read President Carter's recent thoughts on Hamas, it transported me back to 1977 and his stunning statements on the Iranian revolution, or to 1979 and his remarks on the Soviets and Afghanistan. Many of these liberals and their supporters on the left literally see the conservative Republican in the Oval Office as a greater threat to the world than the insane dictators overseas that the likes of Reagan and George W. Bush were/are trying to stop. That's not an exaggeration. Just ask them.

History is repeating itself, which can happen easily when those tasked to report and record it fail to do so because of their political biases.

FP: Paul Kengor, thank you for joining us.

Kengor: Thank you Jamie.

[Jamie Glazov, "Ted Kennedy and the KGB," Frontpagemag.com, May 15, 2008.]

VI: Leaving the Faith

Introduction:

As the previous sections in this collection have demonstrated, the West is currently engaged in a war to defend itself from Islamic aggressors aided by leftist apologists.

As is evident, this is not a conflict that can be won only on military grounds. It's a war of ideas as well -- where the naïve captives of anti-Americanism have to be liberated from their intellectual prisons. In pursuing this task, it's vital to understand how one makes the transition from an enemy of America to an ally. The testimonies of ex-believers throughout history are certainly useful – Whittaker Chambers' *Witness*, David Horowitz's *Radical Son*, Ron Radosh's *Commies* – but more modern narratives are important too. The interviews in the following section shine light on three individuals who had the courage to abandon their destructive ideological addictions.

Curing a hatred of freedom is not as easy as locking a heroin addict in a padded room for a cold turkey treatment. As these three testimonies demonstrate, in most cases the only person who can change a radical mind is the believer himself. -- David Swindle

22. My Way Into and Out of the Left - Andrew Klavan

Frontpage Interview's guest today is Andrew Klavan, the author of such internationally bestselling crime novels as *True Crime*, filmed by Clint Eastwood, and *Don't Say A Word*, filmed starring Michael Douglas. He has been nominated for the Mystery Writers of America's Edgar Award five times and has won twice. His last novel for adults, *Empire of Lies*, topped Amazon.com's thriller list. His new novel series for young adults continues in February with *The Long Way Home*. Andrew is a contributing editor to *City Journal*, the magazine of the Manhattan Institute. His essays on politics, religion, movies and literature have appeared in the *Wall Street Journal*, the *New York Times*, *The Washington Post*, the *LA Times*, and elsewhere. As a screenwriter, he wrote the screenplays for 1990's *A Shock to the System*, starring Michael Caine, and 2008's *One Missed Call*. His *Klavan on the Culture* videos appear at PJTV.com. His website is *AndrewKlavan.com*.

FP: Andrew Klavan, welcome to Frontpage Interview.

I'd like to talk to you today about your journey into and out of the Left.

How did you at first become a member of the political faith? Tell us about the beginnings of your intellectual journey.

Klavan: Well, I was always a dissatisfied liberal. I just never knew there was anything else to be. I was born Jewish to a mother who worshipped FDR and a father who thought that any Republican victory prefigured the return of Adolf Hitler. That's not an exaggeration: he thought Republicans were all just Hitler in disguise. So going from that family into the arts, where everyone mouths this elitist, pseudo-sophisticated left-wing bushwa without any real understanding of the underlying issues: leftism was simply the water I swam in. Conservatives were the bad guys. Everyone knew that.

FP: So how did your second thoughts begin? Tell us about your journey out of the Left.

Klavan: It was an experience that very much mirrored the pattern of the famous paradigm shift described in Thomas Kuhn's "Structure of Scientific Revolutions." Anomalies started to occur, things that didn't fit into what I thought of as a "liberal" world view. The Bakke case, in which the Supreme Court supported affirmative action – that was a big one: I thought it was a clear sign that the left – my side – had signed on to racism. Feminism, political correctness, the disaster of welfare, the appeasement of the Soviet Union – I kept saying, "Well, that's no good," but I thought they were anomalies. I still didn't realize there was an alternative philosophy that described the world more accurately. Then the Berlin Wall fell down – everything Reagan predicted – stupid Reagan, cowboy Reagan, dumb old movie actor Reagan – every single thing he said would happen, happened. And it finally began to dawn on me, "Oh, I get it: it's not this and this and this that's wrong. It's ALL wrong." And I started the long, difficult process of changing my mind.

FP: As you began changing your mind, what happened to your relationships? The leftist milieu does not allow dissent and will banish a heretic into "non-person" status. Did something of this nature begin happening to you? Tell us a bit about how your second thoughts affected your friendships and social life.

Klavan: A lot of friends dropped away and a lot of business opportunities disappeared. Working in Hollywood became much, much more difficult. The worst time, I think, was during the Bush/Kerry election when passions were running so terribly high. Liberals would say things to me, like, "I hope the war goes badly so Kerry wins." When I would point out that they were essentially wishing Americans dead so that their candidate would win, they felt I was being cruel and uncivil. The left is fine with calling you racist, sexist, a pig, a Nazi – but if you point out the simple inarguable consequences of their words and actions, they feel you've just gone way too far!

FP: A leftist is also part of the political faith very much because of his own vision of himself being a social redeemer and there is much self-satisfaction that comes with seeing oneself in this way. Can you share a bit how you had to shed yourself of some ways you saw yourself and also what it meant to you to become someone who your dad had demonized? This must have been very difficult.

Klavan: It's a lot like the Matrix, you know: once you take the red pill, once you see that leftist virtue is an illusion created by an ideologically driven media and academy, once you see what leftist policies have *really* done to black people in this country, how they've appeased and encouraged tyranny, destroyed cities, ruined economies, blasted cultures it's just impossible to re-submerge yourself in the left's self-righteous illusion. Was it difficult to have people I liked or even loved reel back in moral horror and disgust when they learned I was a conservative? Sometimes, I guess. But I'm a hard guy about stuff like that. There's so much true love in my life – the love of God, my wife, my kids, my friends – it's an embarrassment of riches. That hasn't changed.

FP: What are your thoughts on the position the Left has taken in our conflict with radical Islam?

Klavan: If I were still capable of being appalled by them, I'd be appalled, but as it is… well, I don't know how you shrug in print but picture me shrugging. So desperate are they to display their tolerance, to claim virtue and open-mindedness for themselves, so secretly ashamed and guilt-ridden and self-hating are they, I guess, that they will give aid and comfort to a philosophy that turns everything they're supposed to stand for on its head. Anti-female, anti-gay, anti-religious liberty, anti-humanity, radical Islam is a cancer on the face of the earth. Ignoring it, pretending it isn't there, moral equivalence, relativism – all the various forms of false piety in which the left specializes – are as helpful with radical Islam as they are with other cancers. It's like having your doctor say, "Yes, there's a spot on your x-ray, but let's not do anything about it, in case we make it angry or seem biased!" Academics, entertainers, wealthy elites like Michael Moore who think Islamists are going to like them, spare them and their limousines and their millions, because they're such ever-so-good people… well, they're like the intellectuals who lined the streets of Vienna to welcome Hitler. The next day, they were gone.

FP: What is it in your character that made it impossible for you to remain a leftist?

Klavan: I think that question should be answered by whoever delivers my eulogy. Personally, I'm hoping he uses phrases like "an undying love of truth," and "an uncompromising commitment to authenticity." Then a little something about my sparkling smile, my lambent wit and my kindness to widows and orphans. Some praise for my sexual prowess wouldn't go amiss. But perhaps I've gotten off the subject.

FP: You mentioned that leftists are "secretly ashamed and guilt-ridden and self-hating." Can you expand a bit on this? What is it, in the end, that is at the core of the leftist mindset and belief system?

Klavan: Shame and guilt and self-hatred are universal. Whether you chalk it up to original sin or to Oedipus or call it Jewish guilt or Catholic guilt or white guilt or black guilt, every single one of us knows he is not the person he was made to be. There are honest ways to confront that. You can kneel before God and pray for forgiveness and live in the joy of his love. Or you can drink heavily and make sardonic remarks until you destroy everyone you care about and then keel over dead – that's honest too. But what a lot of people do is try to escape their sense of shame dishonestly by constructing elaborate moral frameworks that allow them to parade their virtue and their lavish repentance without any real inconvenience to themselves while simultaneously indulging in self-righteousness by condemning others for their impenitent evil. That's the bad version of religion – the sort of religion Jesus came to dismantle. And that's exactly the sort of religion leftism is: an elaborate system for hiding shame behind a cheap mask of virtue. That's why they demonize any opposition. To them, we're not just disagreeing with them, we're threatening to tear off the mask of their virtue and reveal them to themselves. Which, without God or sufficient whiskey, would be unbearable.

FP: You mentioned your love of God. Is your faith connected to, or influence, your view of the limitations of the leftist vision? How if so?

Klavan: I was an atheist and an agnostic for a long time. Finding God, or perhaps accepting the God I always knew was there, was transformative in too many ways to describe. But one of the most important things God did was make a realist of me. There's a great joke for you. The atheists preen themselves on their realism and accuse the faithful of wishful thinking, but for me, God freed me to develop a full, honorable and tragic sense of life, to perceive both the nobility and the sinfulness of every individual, and to understand why no system will make us good or fair but that there are systems that can keep us free so that we can choose whether or not to be good or fair. That understanding – plus a sense of peace in the face of the left's slavering insults and hatred – were gifts of God to me and it turns out they're very helpful in maintaining my conservatism.

FP: Radical Islam is gaining much strength on myriad realms and the Left has disabled us from even being able to name the enemy, let alone fight him properly. Are you optimistic or pessimistic that our civilization has the will and capacity to defend itself?

Klavan: Radical Islam is sort of like an opportunistic virus, you know. If it's the final cause of the West's death, it will only be because we weakened ourselves so badly that we gave it a chance to take hold. And listen, death comes eventually to us all, right? Countries die, civilizations die, nothing made by man's hands lasts forever. Conservatives are sort of like the doctors who are trying to keep America alive as long as we can and the question is: how long? My own feeling is that the country right now is in some danger from radical Islam, but that the real and present and terrible danger is to our republic, our system of individual liberty under limited government – and that danger comes from within. Bread and circuses – or as we call them today, entitlements and the mainstream media – are being employed to poison our will and moral seriousness. I foresee many years of American power yet to come, maybe more American power than ever before – but will it be republican power, the power of a free people over themselves, or will it be imperial power, the bloated strength of a slave state on the march? We'll see.

FP: You mentioned Michael Moore. Who are some leftists that you think are especially pathetic sad cases?

Klavan: Al Gore is quite hilarious. Global warming! I love that. I seriously think the man had a nervous breakdown and decided to parlay it into an industry. Why go nuts for free when you can make a fortune at it? Going around in his fume-spewing jets preaching to us about our carbon footprints, he reminds me of some ancient Pope with mistresses and catamites and palaces condemning the sinfulness of the poor. Then there's that knucklehead Evan Thomas. He's the guy who practically lynched the Duke University Boys on the cover of Newsweek and then said, "Oh, we had the narrative right we just got the facts wrong." In my business – writing novels – you can get the narrative right and the facts wrong. In his business, the facts *are* the narrative. He's lucky there's a Keith Olbermann, or he'd be the poster boy for our corrupt idiot news media.

FP: Who do you admire in our political theater today in terms of warriors for freedom?

Klavan: Rudy Giuliani is a great man in terms of his accomplishments but he may have played out his political string. We have all the good writers and thinkers, every single one: Horowitz, Krauthammer, Fouad Ajami, Jonah Goldberg, Mark Steyn, on and on - who has the left got to touch the hems of their garments? Our entertainer-slash-commentators are great. El Rush-bo is a radio genius. Coulter, Beck, Hannity. It makes me crazy the way right wingers are always nervously edging away from them, while the left embraces their John Stewarts and Michael Moores. Andrew Breitbart is terrific; he's building an empire of truth to defeat the msm's empire of lies – and he'll do it too. And we've got some good pols, especially the babes: Michelle Bachman, Sarah Palin, Liz Cheney. What we're missing is a towering figure to take the presidential helm but, you know, cometh the hour, cometh the man. And the hour is sure enough cometh-ing.

FP: Were you always a man of humor? Why humor to fight our enemies and fight for the truth? What is especially meaningful and powerful about humor? Interestingly enough, humor is not something that the Left and radical Islam particularly excel in, to say the least.

Klavan: LOL, no, the funniest Muslim right now is Achmed the Dead Terrorist, that Jeff Dunham puppet who's always screaming, "I'll kill you!" But you know, my Dad was a radio comedian so I guess I inherited a certain sense of hilarity. But it's not a weapon to me. I mean, in comedians, humor is frequently an expression of anger or hostility. In me, it's something different. I know this sounds silly when you say it flat-out, but the truth is: I'm very fond of the human race. Too fond of them, I sometimes think. And when you see how small we are, how brief our lives are, what gifts of creation these fingersnaps of consciousness are in God's great scheme... and then you see what we do to one another: the holocausts and the little cruelties, the elaborate lies and self-deceptions... gassing a child to death because his name ends in *itz* instead of *er,* betraying and abusing the spouses who love us, hurting our own kids, all the ways we spend our little moment when we could be loving each other and making funny faces.... well, it's absurd, isn't it? And the absurdity either makes your heart explode with pity, or you have to laugh. Or both. For me, it's both.

FP: Andrew Klavan, thank you for joining us. It was an honor to speak with you.

[Jamie Glazov, "Andrew Klavan: My Way Into and Out of the Left," Frontpagemag.com, December 11, 2009.]

23. Gay and Leaving the Left – Charles Winecoff

Frontpage Interview's guest today is Charles Winecoff, a TV writer, entertainment journalist, and author of *Anthony Perkins: Split Image*, the definitive biography of the *Psycho* star. A native New Yorker and avowed, lifelong Democrat, Winecoff never lived anywhere besides Manhattan and L.A. But like many people, 9/11 sent him on what he has termed "an inner journey that was by turns painful, scary, and eye-opening." Recently, he came out as a non-Leftist on Andrew Breitbart's new website, Big Hollywood, with the essay *The Awakening of a Dumb (Gay) American*. Winecoff compares his experience coming out of the conservative closet in the 21st century with coming out as a gay man in the 1970s.

FP: Charles Winecoff, welcome to Frontpage Interview.

We're here today to talk about your intellectual journey from Left to, well, I guess we could say "non-Left." Tell us about your youth and how you became a member of the political faith.

Winecoff: Thanks, Jamie.

I always like to say I was raised by a television set, as many Americans are. Not because my parents were not good parents, but since the atomic age, the TV has become a convenient babysitter for a lot of people. And the TV was certainly always a comfort to me. When the TV was on, I never felt alone. And I grew up not just believing what I was fed by the major networks - this was before we had 300 channels on cable - but really having no other alternative for my information about the world.

I was not unlike the character in Jerzy Kosinski's novel *Being There* - and not unlike many immigrants, who learn English and American customs from TV series as ridiculous as *The Love Boat*. So there's an up side to the influence of TV. But for me, it served more as a primer on how to distrust my own country. I learned about America from Walter Cronkite and Jane Fonda – their anti-war stances, that America was imperialistic and culturally arrogant - before I even took an American History class in school. So that really set the tone for my own naive belief system. This was also the era of Watergate, which saturated the news, and as time went on, I came to believe the media image of Republicans as evil and backward, of America as a rigid, conformist, Puritanical nation of religious fanatics – this was a typical urban American upbringing. And especially in the 1970s, in New York City, there was a lot of paranoia about venturing beyond the island of Manhattan, what with crazy Manson types on the loose and rednecks as portrayed in *Deliverance*. Never mind real people, this was the culture we absorbed. It's amazing how little the climate has changed since then. In fact, it's even more stifling.

FP: Tell us about the book you wrote, what you wrote about and why.

Winecoff: Having been raised by a television set, naturally I was obsessed with Hollywood films and stars. After all, they are America's royalty, unfortunately. I even went to film school at UC-LA. Anyway, I was especially fond of horror films, and Anthony Perkins, who played Norman Bates in *Psycho*, happened to live about two blocks from where I grew up in New York.

He was probably the first movie star I actually saw in the flesh, on the street - and his performance in *Psycho* really struck a chord with me. You can read all about it in the book. Flash forward a couple decades: Perkins dies of AIDS in 1992, and through a series of serendipitous events, I get a contract to write his biography. Remember: at this time, "outing" of closeted homosexuals was all the rage, and AIDS still had a huge stigma attached to it - it was like leprosy. So this was touchy stuff, especially given the fact that Perkins had a wife and two sons who were still alive.

I felt enormous pressure to go along with this trend of outing, and I looked up to other gay writers, one in particular who was a bona fide activist and Communist "sympathizer" - in the sense that he viewed American Communists as harmless, misunderstood, counter-culture underdogs. So I felt that in order to be taken seriously, I had to attack or criticize American society as well, and present it as the most hypocritical and oppressive society on earth. Not realizing, of course, that in many countries, criticism of one's own country is verboten. Suffice it to say, I editorialized in the text - not very well, I might add - to appease that faction of the gay community who I imagined would be my readers and my champions. To gain their approval. And in my opinion that aspect of the book pretty much backfired. The rest of the book - the life story - was fine, and that's why the book is still in print, but the editorializing stood out like a sore thumb.

FP: Just a second, what exactly did you editorialize about in the text of your book? What themes were you stressing to appease that faction of the gay community who you imagined would be your readers? What were you saying and why? And why were you trying to appease this group? How did it all backfire?

Winecoff: Because the story of Tony Perkins is largely the story of a gay man making a big name for himself at a time when gay people were not really supposed to exist in America - homosexuality was considered a mental illness, or merely a "phase" that some folks hadn't outgrown yet, the result of having a domineering mother and an absent father - naturally, there was a lot of social and psychiatric history that had to be weaved into the narrative of his life.

There's no way to write about being gay in the 1950s without being legitimately critical of the era. But in my research of gay history in the US, usually in quite slanted chronicles, there was often a parallel drawn between the McCarthy "witchhunt" of Communists and the oppression of gay men. This is because McCarthy did want homosexuals purged from the federal government as they were seen as potential risks for blackmail, etc. Be that as it may, the writers generally failed to make much of a distinction between the "commies" and the gays - they're all just presented in these books as victims of rightwing American tyranny.

So for an uninformed reader, such as myself at the time, it's easy to draw the blanket conclusion that America has long been a rightwing fascist paradise where anyone who didn't drive a Chrysler and live in a suburban house with a white picket fence and two kids was a target. I thought Communists were just nonconformists, people who thought differently from rightwing American Puritans - and who, like gays, were punished for their difference.

I knew nothing of the very real history of famine and mass murder in Communist countries around the world. I had no concept of totalitarianism - why would I? - except for a very narcissistic, mythical idea revolving around an imperialistic America that could not tolerate any thought or lifestyle that threatened its healthy, wealthy, post-War image. Unfortunately, this lack of education about world history - and American history - is still very prevalent today. So in the text, I editorialized far too much about "witchhunts" and US intolerance of anyone outside the mainstream - i.e. commies and gays - because that was the narrow focus of the gay history books I turned to.

So basically, I learned my American history from books about identity politics, which again, is still very common today. In the 1960s, Perkins spent several years working exclusively in France - so naturally, I romanticized the European attitude toward homosexuality, and parroted the idea that Europe was some kind of welcoming haven for gays. One of Perkins's friends, however, set me straight on that, explaining to me that the French were just as provincial and bigoted as anyone else, if not more so.

In retrospect, Perkins probably felt freer being gay in France simply because he was so far away from home base and from the studios. Hollywood is certainly no barometer for America as a whole. But just look at how far the American gay community has come since then. I'm not saying it was great to be gay in 1950s America. What I'm trying to say is, my book was saturated with an underlying attitude that America was the most hypocritical, stifling country in the world - the oppressor of the weak - an attitude that was really a product of my own ignorance and media saturation. An attitude that is, sadly, very prevalent today among young urban Americans. Of course, my motivation for expressing this negative point of view was to appear "smart." Yet in reality, America is a country of incredible, rapid change.

Meanwhile, with regard to Perkins the man, I was also torn between two opposing perspectives. Upon initial publication of my book in 1996, there was much outrage that I had dared to illuminate the first 40 years of Perkins's life, which he had lived as a gay man - since he had spent the last 20 years of his life married with kids (before his death from AIDS). The longevity of his marriage - this was no "Hollywood marriage" - belied the common notion that he had turned straight in order to have a "beard" to guard his career, which was pretty much the party line among gays.

By the time Perkins married, his career was on the wane. He wanted to have a traditional family with kids at a time when it was next to impossible for gay people to adopt or anything. So while I wanted to cater to the activists in the gay community, like my friend, and claim Perkins as a gay icon - a figure of gay victimhood - I also had to be fair. The fact that I did not trash Perkins's marriage disappointed some in the gay community. So I realized I really couldn't win. You have to be true to yourself, and forget about the group.

FP: Let's go back to a crucial time when something could have been done to stop the spread of AIDS in the United States but wasn't -- because of radical politics. Your perspective on this, as a former gay leftist, would be very interesting and important.

Back in the early 1980s, when the AIDS epidemic was just starting to break out in the three gay communities (San Francisco, Los Angeles and New York), David Horowitz was one of the few individuals who stood up and publicly opposed gay leaders' efforts to subvert the public health system and conceal the nature of the epidemic. Specifically, in the name of "gay liberation," gay leaders denied that sexually transmitted AIDS was almost exclusively caused by promiscuous anal sex, refused to close sexual "bathhouses" which were the breeding grounds of AIDS, opposed testing and contact tracing which were the traditional and proven public health methods for containing epidemics, and promoted the false idea that AIDS was an "equal opportunity virus" when in fact it was a virus threatening very specific communities -- gays and intravenous drug users.

For speaking truth to gay power, Horowitz was widely condemned by radical activists who demonized him and caricatured his warnings as, among other things, homophobic prejudice. As Horowitz has written in these pages, the success of the gay radicals resulted in a ballooning epidemic that has killed some 300,000 Americans, the majority of them young gay men. The AIDS catastrophe, as he wrote in "A Radical Holocaust," a chapter in *The Politics of Bad Faith*, is "a metaphor for all the catastrophes that utopians have created."

It is interesting that the most basic facts that Horowitz articulated at that tragic time, and for which he was so viciously demonized by radicals, are today considered to be just standard truths about HIV and AIDS. And yet, there has not been one *mea culpa* targeted in his direction by those who pointed accusatory fingers at him, but who sacrificed countless lives for the idea. Nor have the traditional public health methods that would have contained the epidemic – testing, contact tracing etc. – been restored. Instead, drugs have been substituted for behavioral changes.

One of the reasons that there is no apology or admission of guilt by the radicals is because they continue to dominate the media culture, which is why the lies continue, along with the needless deaths. Somehow it is all the fault of Ronald Reagan, etc.

Could you kindly comment on this phenomenon and give your perspective on some of the themes I have raised?

Winecoff: Yes, and if I'm not mistaken, Mr. Horowitz is in good company because even Randy Shilts, who wrote the groundbreaking *And the Band Played On*, his chronicle of the AIDS epidemic, addressed the issue of the gay community not closing the bathhouses simply out of political correctness - and he, like AIDS activists Michael Callen and Richard Berkowitz, took a lot of flack for it.

I recall visiting a friend in San Francisco in the early '80s, when AIDS was a rapidly spreading menace no one knew much about yet, and seeing posters all over the place to keep the bath houses open

- or risk being thrown into a concentration camp by the Reagan regime. This was the kind of leftwing fantasy that was, and is, so typical. Watch out, or those evil Republicans are going to get you. But again, as a young gay man, I deferred to this fear-mongering - even though, in my gut, the rationale not to close the bathhouses struck me as strange, wrong - even kind of crazy. But what did I know? I wasn't a political or community leader. So mentally, I bowed to the greater gay community, which I assumed must know better than I, and went along with the fantasy logic of persecution, which I assumed muct be correct.

I figured they knew something about Ronald Reagan that I didn't know. And again, in the popular culture, "conservative" equals "bad." On the other hand, the gay community also took it upon itself to educate people about the disease and to raise awareness, while the government moved at a snail's pace. So that was a huge effort - and a necessity. It's just sad to think that some gay leaders thought anonymous sex and bathhouses were the "gay culture" that had to be protected from the "rightwing nuts" - to quote Peggy Lee, "Is that all there is?" - as opposed to protecting the actual gay *people*, who were put even more at risk by their choice.

I hope we have come to like ourselves a little more than that by now. The gay community has come a very long way very fast. Just in my lifetime alone, America has done a real 180 in how it perceives and accepts gay people. It's generally much easier today for a gay person to come out, and there are plenty of examples in the popular culture of healthy gay couples with children, etc. So there's a lot to be proud of.

That said, I do think the gay community in America is kind of stuck. They still rely on an old way of doing things - militant tactics leftover from the '70s and '80s, as seen in the recent fracas over Proposition 8 here in California - that perpetuates an awful lot of animus. It's almost as if the gay community, which is generally affluent, doesn't know how to do anything but play victim. We're way past that. People say, "But there always needs to be a vanguard." Well, the vanguard has to adapt too, to different circumstances. What worked in 1977 doesn't necessarily work in 2009.

Also, the gay community rarely gives society at large any credit for how far it has come in accepting us. Some gay activists I know continue to treat their straight friends and acquaintances as if they're a bunch of backward, knuckle-dragging ingrates. It's very patronizing. Personally, I think it's time for the gays to take stock of how much they have gained over the past forty years - which is to say almost all the same rights as heterosexuals - and try a new tack.

An effort needs to be made at this point to make friends with our fellow Americans, stop the us-against-them attitude, and show some mutual respect. Because we all need to work together. Yes, gay couples in The Netherlands may have full marriage rights already - but they also have hostile Islamic immigrants to contend with, who, from what I have read, are starting to destroy what was once considered a gay paradise. So if we are to keep advancing, and living the lives we want, we need allies here at home. I'm tired of the complaining. I want to see gays show a little more generosity towards their fellow Americans. Because they - we - are not the enemy. And this no time for confusion about that. There are imams in mosques all over the place - in Nigeria, in the UK, even in Canada - who regularly call for the death and beheading of homosexuals. But for whatever reason, the gay community here in America seems to take no offense. This is a growing problem that really needs to be addressed, because everyday it gets a little closer.

FP: Let's talk about 9/11, it would change you forever.

Winecoff: Okay, deep breath. I had just left New York for LA when we were attacked. LA felt like a ghost town that day - nobody was driving, no cars on the street, dead. It was very eerie. And like everybody else, I was glued to the news, trying to make sense of what was happening. As it turned out, Anthony Perkins's widow, Berry Berenson, was on board American Flight 11, the first plane to hit the WTC. I was stunned, and very saddened. That was the first victim I learned of who I had some sort of connection with - I learned of others later - and I was overwhelmed by the cruelty of her death. It seemed so incredibly unfair. I couldn't stop speculating what the last 45 minutes or so of her life might have been like.

Meanwhile, right away, friends began forwarding me emails from MoveOn.org, urging Americans to look at ourselves and ask ourselves why we were objects of such hate. So no sooner had we been attacked, and were all trying to process what had happened, than the indoctrination began. A very well-organized, well-orchestrated indoctrination. It struck me very clearly that groups like MoveOn.org were making a concerted effort to undermine Americans' natural grieving process - in essence, to remove the emotion from our response to the attack, and thereby defuse our power. Because there is power in emotion. And there's knowledge to be had from grief.

Understand, I had never heard of MoveOn.org before. Under normal circumstances, because my friends belonged to this group, I probably would have signed up myself. Because they were against Bush and against Republicans and against all the things the gay community was against. But suddenly, for the first time in my life, I saw how the Left operates - in this telling, well-organized response to 9/11. It was quite chilling to realize that these believers, the kind of people I had been raised to trust, were actually not on my side. They were not treating me, or any other American, with respect. They were simply trying to make us doubt ourselves, second guess ourselves, with an email campaign intended to "correct" our thinking immediately after the attack - grieving process be damned.

That's when I realized something was rotten in Denmark. I don't like being told how to think. I don't think too many people do. A couple years after that, my book was republished - and I had the opportunity to add an epilogue about Mrs. Perkins's murder, which I very much wanted to do. I very much wanted to try to recreate, as best I could, what that terrible, last flight must have been like. I felt I owed it to her, and at the time it felt to me like a hugely political thing to write about - because by 2005, after the re-election of Bush, it was already a big no-no to talk about 9/11 anymore. It was considered "fear-mongering" to bring it up in conversation. 9/11 had fallen into the category of Neo-Con Conspiracy and was being buried under all the complaints about the war in Iraq and how our civil liberties were being taken away. I just wanted to remind people that someone's *life* had been taken away, never mind the alleged civil liberties abuses. Civil liberties don't mean anything if you are not alive to enjoy them. It was amazing to me how quickly people were forgetting that, in all the politically correct hysteria. And the fact of who had done this was also getting blurred, with conspracy theories and self-hatred. I wanted to remind people who had done this. Radical Islam had done it. And radical Islam wasn't done with us yet. It still wanted gay people dead.

So I wrote the new epilogue - and I also got to revise the rest of the text, which proved to be a real eye-opener. Re-reading the whole book after several years, I was really shocked by the overall tone of the book. My own knee-jerk editorializing was very snide and venal - in many asides about the "hypocrisy" of my own country and our supposedly rigid society, and of course towards conservatives. Now, don't get me wrong, when Tony Perkins was a young gay man in the 1950s, homosexuality was considered a mental illness and gay men were routinely baited and jailed, bars were raided, and so on. It was a dark time in American gay life. So a certain amount of criticism was appropriate.

However, I felt I had really overdone it - and without any real understanding or perspective. So I took the opportunity to cut much of that out, and try to make the text more balanced. Because I was so shocked at my own mindless anti-Americanism. And I never even considered myself anti-American! But I saw how indoctrinated I had been, mostly by television - it had simply become second nature to me. Is America perfect? No, of course not - what place is? But we do have the ability to change - and we have changed, with regard to minorities (just look at our President) and gays - whereas all kinds of truly horrific physical abuses, not theoretical ones, are still systematically perpetrated today against gays and other minorities in places like Iran, Gaza, and so on.

FP: Indeed, leaving the Left is torture for a believer. Membership in the political faith is very much a need to belong. It's not about the facts. It's about a social life and also about the terror of losing that social life – losing one's reputation and standing in the eyes of one's comrades and so-called "friends." Can you identify with that as you are describing the "need to feel included"?

Winecoff: Sure. When everyone around you, and all of your friends, do nothing but complain about what they don't have - as opposed to reminding themselves of all the things they do have - you go along with it. It's peer pressure. And when there's never any alternative to that, you believe it's totally justified and normal. I used to believe the popular adage that a gay person voting for a Republican is like a Jew voting for a Nazi. Mind you, I never met any Republicans - except my grandfather, who always described himself as a "skeptic." But now, having recently befriended a number of "conservatives," I realize that's most definitely *not* the reality. Most Republicans and conservatives are actually just kind of normal - middle of the road, and not homophobic at all. They are not religious fanatics. Rather, they believe in individual freedom, without government intervention or meddling. They believe in personal choice and personal responsibility. Many of them actually consider themselves socially "liberal," like me, but are very concerned about national security - an issue which has, sadly, been tainted as "rightwing." The picture you get from watching television is that conservatives are corrupt, hypocritical, bigoted Evangelical Christians. Newsflash: conservatives are a lot more diverse than that.

FP: So for many years after 9/11 you kept your opinions to yourself?

Winecoff: Well, after 9/11 I really began to view things differently, I started evolving. You could call it growing up. I could no longer just spout the party line that everything was America's fault, and leave it at that. That's a convenient excuse people use to dismiss unpleasant reality and get on with their day. That just didn't cut it for me anymore. Meanwhile, the attitude among most people I knew was increasingly self-hating - terrorism was entirely our fault, Bush's fault, and the jihad was somehow justified. Friends would make gloating jokes when Americans were beheaded, as if to say, "See what an idiot

Bush is." But no one seemed to care about the people whose heads were actually sawed off.

As for the myopic view that all this was just Bush's fault: In 1989, I worked at a book publishing company in New York in that distributed Salman Rushdie's *The Satanic Verses*, and we were targeted in the Ayatollah Khomeini's fatwa. You could not imagine a more harmless, old-fashioned workplace - and yet the FBI had contacted our Editor-in-Chief, we had to hire an armed guard, and the company name had to be removed from the lobby directory. This was 20 years ago. None of us knew what a fatwa was then. Today, everyone in America knows what a fatwa is - and we shouldn't. That kind of barbarity should not be part of our culture. Yet here we are, absorbing it - accepting it.

My point is: the jihad against us did not start in 2000. It had been building for a long time. But by 2005, I didn't know anyone who could have a civil discussion about this - everyone always flew off the handle about the Iraq War - so I kept my thoughts to myself and just watched as everyone around me became more and more obsessed with Bush-bashing and less and less concerned with the fanatics who had actually slaughtered 3000 innocent people in my hometown - and were still calling for our heads. It was very, very frustrating.

FP: You took a scary step in December 2008. Tell us what happened and the reaction of the community that witnessed your thought crime. Give us the details of what happened and how the events unfolded. Your own psychological and intellectual state as well.

Winecoff: Well, after eight years of more and more stifling political correctness - eight years during which people I knew had basically forgotten all about 9/11 and no longer felt any need to be vigilant - because they were far more focused on getting George Bush out of office than anything else - I really began to feel isolated. I felt like I was the only person in all of Los Angeles who was concerned about national security. I felt completely isolated, completely alone, helpless. So I read a lot of books to try to understand what was happening in the world out there.

Finally, I picked up a copy of Brigitte Gabriel's book, *They Must Be Stopped* - and learned about her grassroots organization, ActforAmerica.org. I was thrilled to think there was a group out there still keeping its eye on the ball, and giving a voice to people like me who wanted to support legislation, etc. to combat the jihad. So at Christmas time last year, in lieu of presents, I gave gift donations to Act for America. Well, the silence was deafening. You would have thought I'd made donations to the KKK. Not one friend or family member acknowledged the gift - and one friend actually wrote me a rather angry email.

I doubt very much that donations to the Human Rights Campaign or GLAAD would have been met with the same response. And the irony is that Islamic supremacism is one of the biggest enemies of the gay community. You would think other gay people would be supportive. But no. In some weird way, I think political correctness has made many gays and lesbians mistake Islamic supremacists for fellow victims in the fight against oppression - rather than recognizing them as the actual oppressors who believe gays should be annihilated.

Anyway, needless to say, I was a little shook up, and hurt by the reaction. So I sat down for several very long hours and wrote a letter to my friends and family explaining to them why I had made the donations, why I thought the organization was important, why I was still concerned about terrorism, what I had learned about radical Islam over the past eight years, how I had evolved politically, why I thought we still needed to be vigilant - I just got it all off my chest. It was really like coming out of the closet for the second time, but even more difficult.

Coincidentally, I also heard that Andrew Breitbart was launching Big Hollywood, a website to give the silent, conservative underground in LA a voice. So, since I was fired up and fed up with being silent, I mailed him a copy of the letter and asked if he thought it could be turned into something. Long story short: the letter became my debut blog, *The Awakening of a Dumb (Gay) American* - and I'm happy to say the response was terrific. People really responded positively, and supportively. So that was a great way to kick off the New Year.

FP: So are you now, for the second time of your life, "out" and trying to be proud?

Winecoff: Yes, I am "out" now, I have continued to blog - and I am trying to be proud. It's really important for like-minded, "conservative" people to know that they are not alone. There are a lot of people in LA who secretly still have common sense, but are muzzled by the political correctness that is so overwhelming in this town and elsewhere. You learn to suffer in silence. I really have come to believe we have a serious problem with free speech now, because a good percentage of the population has been bullied into self-censorship. This isn't right. I shouldn't feel afraid for expressing an opinion, not in America. And yet I do feel afraid, even still. Everytime I post a blog, I panic. Then it passes. People, particularly younger people, really need to re-learn the meaning of tolerance and how to reach across the aisle in civil debate. Diversity isn't just skin color. It's ideas too. But once you have spoken up, and have met other people in the same silent boat, you can't go back to hiding and pretending. We need to be able to celebrate our freedom of speech, not be frightened of it. Also celebrate our pluralistic society, flaws and all. So yes, I am out and trying to be proud. Just like everyone else.

FP: Were you hurt by the friends who abandoned you because of your political differences? Tell us about some of the friends that abandoned you. By the way the community treated you. Many leftists had to go down this path of being made into a non-person by their communities once they abandoned the faith (David Horowitz, Phyllis Chesler, Ronald Radosh, Eugene Genovese etc.).

Winecoff: Well, like I said, the silence is most deafening. It's as if people - so-called "liberal" people - don't want alternative points of view to exist, so they don't acknowledge the difference. Very much the way gay people were forced to live in the shadows in the 1950s. Suffice it to say, it's just become a little strained with some people. My father did thank me for the letter and for explaining myself. But at a certain point you can't keep living your life to please other people. You have to be honest with yourself and learn to trust yourself. And you make new friends.

FP: Sorry for asking this question, but it seems essential that, in this interview to get to know you and to get a grasp of how your experience affected your life, it be asked: How has becoming an anti-Left gay person affected the personal side of your life in the context of relationships etc? Can you talk a bit about this area of your life in a way that is comfortable for you and which reveals the personal obstacles, if they exist for you, of being a gay anti-leftist or conservative, or whatnot?

Winecoff: Let me clarify: I consider myself an Independent - socially liberal, except when it comes to national security. And I've discovered that, if you actually talk to them instead of relying on MSNBC for your information, this is how a lot of "conservatives" really feel, certainly in Los Angeles. I've only been "out" as a "conservative" for a few months, so it's still new to me - I was "passing" for a very long time, nearly a decade. But so far, so good. There has been the odd kerfuffle.

I'm fortunate in that I have been with the same partner for several years now - a Democrat who has common sense and who has allowed me, and even encouraged me, to be myself. That is a great gift, let me tell you. I understand dating in this town can be quite tough for gay Republicans. And judging from what I overhear at parties, etc. I have no doubt that's true.

The gay community as a whole really needs more of my partner's attitude - we need to be able to agree to disagree. This is America, nobody should feel pressured into silence. That's just wrong. And gay conservatives need to speak out, now more than ever. It's been tougher for me "coming out" to friends - many of whom first knew me when I was totally in the dark or still "passing" as a good Leftie. Honestly, I hate all the labels. I am, as Debra Burlingame puts it, evolving. We need to be allowed to evolve.

But I also think it's a natural progression in life to become more "conservative" (for lack of a better word) as you get older. So why fight it? Embrace it! Contrary to popular belief, there *are* Republicans and conservatives and moderates within the gay community, but many of them are silent - the Democrats and Leftists have co-opted the gay community, which normally prides itself on its diversity. Gays and lesbians need to rethink diversity - and realize it does not just apply to the color of your skin or what's between your legs. It should also apply to what is inside your head.

No one should be afraid to express an opinion or an idea. No one should be ostracized or called names for that - and no one should understand this better than gay people. The American gay community needs to stop pretending that it is oppressed - and start reaching out to its fellow Americans, straight and Christian and Mormon and everything else. Just in my lifetime, I've seen Americans come a long way in changing their attitudes. Heterosexuals are not as backward as many in the gay community insist upon treating them. There is common ground. And with the enemies we face abroad - and even within - this is no time to be self-segregated. I really wish the gay community here would get over itself and use its energy to help gays and lesbians in the Middle East, where there is real oppression, wiretapping, torture, and very often death. We don't realize how lucky we are.

FP: What are you future plans?

Winecoff: Well, because of my blogging, 2009 has been an exciting year so far. I feel like I can breath again. And I've met a lot of new and very interesting people. I intend to keep writing and I am hoping to organize an event for the gay community here in Hollywood - to give them a chance to hear Brigitte Gabriel speak about the treatment of LGBT (lesbian, gay, bisexual, transgender) people in Lebanon, Iran, Gaza. She's on board, we are just working on a date. In addition to being a powerful speaker, Ms. Gabriel is gay-friendly, a lot of fun, smart, open - and I have no doubt the boys will love her when they meet her. Time to bust some stereotypes. Plus I think it will be eye-opening for a lot of people. The gay community in the US has won so many great and heartbreaking battles. We really need to find it in our hearts to show some gratitude - as we continue to press for full rights here at home (we're not far off) - and share our wealth and freedoms with the LGBT communities is less fortunate countries.

FP: Charles Winecoff, thank you for joining Frontpage Interview.

[Jamie Glazov, "Gay and Leaving the Left," Frontpagemag.com, May 13, 2009.]

24. A Terrorist Who Turned to Love - Walid Shoebat

Frontpage Interview's guest today is Walid Shoebat, a former PLO terrorist who has become an ardent Zionist and evangelical Christian.

FP: Mr. Shoebat, it is a privilege to have you as a guest. Welcome to Frontpage Interview.

Shoebat: Thank you

FP: Tell us a bit about the violent culture you come from.

Shoebat: This question requires an entire book to respond to fully, but simply put, one must never forget Nazi Germany. Nazism was the process of robbing the religious institutions, arts, media, and the social fabric of the German society. Likewise, in the Middle East, one can find the same elements as Nazi Germany, with a crucial difference:

1 - This form has a religious twist to it – Islamic fundamentalism.

2 - This goes beyond one country as Germany. Islamic fundamentalism is attempting to spread itself throughout 55 Muslim states.

But like Nazism and Communism, it has no respect for national borders and the end justifies the means.

Now, what type of a child can a system like this produce? So I was taught day-in-and-day-out: Jew-Hatred. In the mosque, songs, social life.

Hatred develops like drug addiction, from stone throwing to Molotov cocktails to ending up planting a bomb.

FP: Why is it so vital for Palestinians to hate Jews?

Shoebat: Once the disease has been identified in my lines above (Islamo-Nazism), it would be easy to respond to your question with a question - why do Muslim fanatics behead Americans on TV?

Well... they hate Americans, but is it only Americans? Koreans die as well as even other Muslims.

The response to this question has been well documented in history - why did Nazis destroy 6,000,000 Jews by public shooting and extermination camps? And even Germans who didn't agree were exterminated as well.

Cult-like hatred. Nazism is a cult, a process to brainwash an entire society to believe that Nazi Germans are more special then others. The Arian special race in Nazism was one of these methods. In other words, an unhealthy dose of extreme national pride can go too far. Evil in Nazism didn't have to outwardly say "kill Jews" right from the start, but simply made Germans think in such pride to say "you are a special people, better then anyone else". From that point, the rest was history.

Similarly Islamism, the process of saying that Muslims are better then others, that we need to Islamize the world by the sword. This cult has gone as far as to kill and behead people in front of a camera, carry body parts in Ramallah and praise Allah in public view for the whole world to see.

It is one thing if a private cult practiced some sick idea, but when the entire city of Ramallah openly carries body parts and praises Allah for the death of Jews?

The difference is that the first is condemned by the others. Yet this is not the case in "Palestine" and much of the Arab world who paraded the death of almost 3,000 Americans who died in 9/11.

Very few dare to object (besides public officials for the media's sake), they would be branded as traitors and publicly lynched.

One can see several photos of public lynchings in "Palestine" and they are done openly with the blessings of entire populations.

What were the crimes of the victims?

They didn't follow the party line. Period. These are the things you rarely hear or see in the media today.

FP: Do you agree that the yearning for murder and suicide in Palestinian culture - and in Islamic-Arab culture in general -- would not disappear even if Israel and all Jews disappeared from the face of the earth?

Shoebat: I agree. Even if every Jew is dead it would make no difference. As I responded previously, they kill anyone who is not like them. The goal is "Islam to the world." This is the banner you see them carry all over their demonstrations.

Palestine and its cause is hardly a secular one, it is far from being multi-ethnic or multi-religious.

The Palestinian charter is calling for an Arab state (with no Jews allowed) and Islam as a the official state religion. It is crucial to ask ourselves: why? Why are Jews not allowed to exist in this state? Why Islam a state religion? I had thought that we are living in a world of tolerance. Not so in the Arab world with a culture that has a short fuse.

Arafat was always kissing Sheikh Yassin for his own survival. He knew that if he diverted too much from the main line of Islamism that he would die. Much of the Arab world is still calling for the destruction of the Jewish state. The only difference between Hamas and the PA is the dose of Islamofascism. If Hamas introduced 1000 mg, 500mg Sharia law (both government and secular), and 500mg Jihad, Arafat would introduce 250mg Sharia (Islamic civil law) and 500mg pure Jihad.

FP: Tell us the significant stages that led to your decision to reject your culture and its terrorism.

Shoebat: I had to go through a self-detoxification program. A daily dose of questioning everything I believed in. It started in 1993 and progressed by studying the Jewish Bible, arts, and history. It was sparked by a question my wife asked me in the process of me Islamizing her - "Show me the bad things the Jews did in the Bible?"

In the Bible, all I found was that the Jews were on self-defense mode throughout Bible history, and even until now. From Babylonians, Assyrians, Amorites, Philistines, Edomites... always in self-defense mode.

While I learned in my Islamic study that when the Jews come back to the land, that we will kill them, and the trees and stones will cry out: here is a Jew hiding behind me, come O Muslim, come and kill him.

One is on self-defense mode, and the other on the attack. Why? Then I started on the arts, songs, movies, culture.

I began with Fiddler on the Roof. This was Jewish culture 101. I watched it over 350 times.

Then came Jewish songs, with not a single song that had the words "kill", "war" or "death".

After I expressed my findings, my enemies accused me of transforming from one extreme to another. They accused me of being racist.

When I was a terrorist I was labeled "freedom fighter", but for loving Jewish culture, Jewish religion, Jewish preservation, I was called a racist.

Then I made a trip to the Holy Land, stopped with shock in Hebron when I saw Palestinians stone the Jewish bus in Qiryat Arba'a.

The taxi I was sitting in wanted to leave and I asked him to stop. I wanted to see this. The Jews took the stones without a single word of anger. Quietly entered the bus. I couldn't believe what I saw.

Why I asked?

Not why they stone Jews, but why it's making me so sad to see Arabs stoning Jews.

I had thought that we hated Zionism and not Jews. Why were Jews not allowed to exist in Arab villages, yet Arabs exist in Israel proper?

This and thousands of questions. I realized that I was being infected with all of these feelings. I concluded that if love was an "infection" I prayed to God that I get plagued with it, and that I never recover. Is this my sin? That I began to love Jews? As well as Hindus, Buddhists, and Moslems?

To love life is a sin? To want to preserve both Jewish children and Arabs is a sin?

I was so hurt when my cousin Raed was killed on his way to plant a bomb in Ben Yehuda Street, yet I also felt bad for the kids he was about to kill. I realized that he was infected with a Nazi like cult just as I was.

To love ourselves is easy. To love our children is easy, but the deepest love is to love other people's children as well. Adoption was made null and void in Islam, yet I saw in the Judeo-Christian culture that adoption is a beautiful thing.

Hatred is a cancer that spread. I know that they say that Islamism is only 15% of the Muslim world, but it's a cancer, and it's spreading. We are not winning fanatics into the fold, but loosing secular Muslims to the fanatics. We need to put on a fight. Extracting cancer is painful. The scales began to fall from my eyes a year later and documenting everything.

I decided to convert to Christianity as a result and fight for justice for Jews everywhere. It's a myth that Palestinians are the underdogs, it's not an Israeli-Palestinian war, but an Arab-Islamofascist war against Israel. Once we get the big picture, we can see who the under-dog is - the Jews. There was only one reason we called for the destruction of Israel, and one reason alone - we simply hated Jews.

FP: What do you think of Western leftists who demonize Israel and exonerate Islamic-Arab terror? What is their psychology?

Shoebat: I am not into modern psychology and at times I have clashes with "psychoanalyzing" everything. How do we psychoanalyze Hitler? Can we psychoanalyze evil? Some try. But since you asked me to do so I will try.

There are two types of "leftists". One is naive and believes in his cause out of what he thinks is love. These are a group of people who think they are dreaming of peace but view it through tunnel vision.

Peace cannot be obtained in a vacuum without using truth and justice. This group unfortunately dominates much of the Jewish community and the western world.

With the Jewish community, they allowed their enemy to put a wedge called "Palestine". Now the Jewish community is divided either pro or against a Palestinian state. I am not against such people, at least we all need to unite to SAVE Israel and Jewish existence.

At least this group should adjust and stand for a "democratic Palestine", a "multi-cultural multi-religious Palestine." Yet they are blind to what is the intention of Arafat and Hamas. This is the group who had hopes in Oslo. They condemned me for saying that Oslo will bring more dead Jews. This was in 1993. Today not one single member of the "lightly breaded lefties" say the Oslo indeed brought peace. They all realize that if Arafat had his way, they too will be deep fried.

The other type are these groups that attack Israel in their claim to love the world, yet are silent towards the real issues, silent when over a million Sudanese are butchered. Silent when Christians die in Indonesia, or Cypriots are killed by Turks. Silent regarding women's rights abuses.

You never hear a peep. But when Israel defends itself, and in the process they kill attackers. They are too quick to point their fingers in isolating Israel as the world villain.

To this group, if they saw the unprovoked stoning of Palestinians against the minority Jews in Hebron as I did, they will always conclude that the Jews must have done something to deserve this. That it takes two to tango. To these I have but a simple question – what did the Jews do to tango in Nazi Germany? The Jews of Hebron at one time were all exterminated with the men's testicles cut off, women raped, their breasts cut off, and babies slashed to death. This happened way before the so-called occupation when Haj Amin Al-Husseni called to "kill them were ever you find them and rape their women" as he collaborated with Hitler to rid the Muslim world of Jews and even organized an SS Khanzar Muslim division for the service of Adolf Hitler and literally Islamo-Nazism.

No one talks about the Hebron massacre, and everyone talks of Jenin, forgetting that many Israeli soldiers were killed in their attempt to dismantle bomb making houses. When does the world blame the law for a drug bust?

These are lead by wolves in sheep's clothing. But even wolves can be transformed into sheep. Nothing is impossible in my view. After all, I myself was once a wolf.

FP: Walid Shoebat, thank you for joining us today. You are a truly courageous man and we wish you all the best.

Shoebat: Thank you Jamie.

*[Jamie Glazov, "A Terrorist Who Turned To Love,"
Frontpagemag.com, July 9, 2004.]*

Part VII: The Titans

Introduction:

The following final five interviews are from some of the most gifted intellectuals and polemicists of our time. These five figures – conservative godfather William F. Buckley Jr., iconic contrarian journalist Christopher Hitchens, sharp polemicist and satirist Ann Coulter, Cold War diplomat Richard Pipes, and doctor and essayist Theodore Dalrymple – all produced deeply different works. But their message was ultimately the same: freedom must be defended, the individual is sovereign, tyranny and terror cannot be tolerated. The wide range of their backgrounds, experiences, and views should serve as a reminder that those who would fight together for the American Idea come from many places and should not allow their differences to divide them from standing strong against those who would annihilate us and our way of life. -- David Swindle

25. Miles Gone By - William F. Buckley Jr.

Frontpage Interview's guest today is William F. Buckley Jr., the founder of *National Review and* the father of modern American conservatism. He has just published his literary autobiography, *Miles Gone By* (available in Frontpage's bookstore for a special offer of $23.95).

FP: Mr. Buckley. It is an honor to speak with you. Welcome to *Frontpage Interview.*

Buckley: Thanks very much, Jamie. I am at your service. You're a very pleasant extortionist.

FP: I'll try to take that as a compliment.

Let's begin with your memoir. You start with how your father initiated piano lessons for you at a young age. You write very movingly about your eternal gratitude to him for this gift -- as well as to your piano instructor, Marjorie Otis ("Old Lady").

What do you think your dad's objectives and desired effects were in introducing music into your life?

Buckley: My father liked music, but was uninstructed in it. Most of his young manhood was spent in Mexico, and there he heard and reheard Mexican folk songs. He thought it appealing to hire a teacher, Mr. Pelaez, who would instruct his children in that repertory. We mastered about 12 songs, including lyrics. Father knew that there was great music there.

His choice of piano teacher was a matter of great luck, because she stayed a family friend for seventy years. Marjorie Otis would arrive at our house in northwestern Connecticut every Monday morning and stay until Wednesday afternoon. She was an inspiring figure, in part because of her mischievous and endearing personality, in part because of her extraordinary talent as a jazz pianist and as an organist.

Soon we were being taken to New York to recitals and operas and concerts of every kind. This went on for YEARS--I mean, right until college age--and left the brood of children permanently oriented to musical life. Father really accomplished what he intended, namely to root music in his children as a permanent legacy.

FP: What do you think your father had in mind in exposing you to music in this way?

Buckley: In such matters as these, my father was guided by two purposes. One of them was: It was vital for his children to engage in a discipline; the second, with his children having done so, was for us to profit from the effort.

My father was contemptuous of Americans who had the opportunity to learn a foreign language but didn't do so. He was himself bilingual in Spanish and English. Although his knowledge of French was extensive, he declined to speak it because he was a perfectionist.

In respect of music, he sensed the pleasures it brought to those who gave time to familiarizing themselves with it. His own curiosity stopped at popular music, but he knew there was an extensive world beyond that, which he wanted his children at least to know about.

We were taught piano above all, but also guitar, mandolin, ukulele, and banjo (so that we could make up our own orchestra). Father also hired a teacher to give us classes in music appreciation. She required us every afternoon to shut out other activity for one hour and listen to fine music on the great big Capehart phonograph kept in the schoolroom. The Capehart could take 78 rpm disks and turn them over, giving you 20 records without interruption.

These things never work out evenly. But eight of the ten children became pretty addicted to fine music, and two of us persevered for years with piano and harpsichord. I did 9 concerts as a soloist, playing the harpsichord, before I decided I wasn't good enough to pursue the instrument further. My younger sister was a soloist at Vassar and, before that, at Ethel Walker, though she gradually relinquished the piano, prodded by an infirm back.

FP: The essays in your book on your love of sailing and skiing are splendid. Tell us a bit about what sailing and skiing represent to you in your own life, in terms of, well, perhaps, metaphors for how we live – or should live. What is it about these activities, do you think, that brings you so much joy and satisfaction?

Buckley: The challenge here is to avoid the obvious, which cannot be avoided. What is it that constitutes a thrill? Dropping from an airplane at 3000 feet and surviving? Diving with air tanks and chasing fish at 120 feet below the surface? Yep. Add hurtling down a mountain in the snow at 60 miles per hour, and sailing with the wind at 8 knots as if the ocean decided to act for you like a skateboard. Oh, add this: skimming over frozen water on skates at 40 mph. You are both defying nature and dominating it. Okay, Glazov? Try it.

FP: Thanks, I think I'll pass. I'm scared of that stuff.

Let me get back to music for a moment. I have always been fascinated and intrigued with those individuals and regimes that detest it, wondering why and what it says about them.

We know that Lenin frowned on music, in part because he feared that it might reduce humans' rage and make them disinclined to kill in a revolution. We know that Stalin was threatened by certain music that didn't even have lyrics (e.g., Shostakovich, the Eighth Symphony of 1943). Khomeini despised music. The Taliban illegalized music. Etc.

Why do you think many despots and totalitarian regimes are so petrified and threatened by music -- or certain kinds of music?

Buckley: Hitler adored music, and so, actually, did Stalin, though he thought some music counterrevolutionary. It's probably true that music is feared insofar as it is thought capable of affecting an in-

dividual wholly, but I know of no society -- or no Orwellian society---
that has sought to simply suppress it.

FP: Fair enough. I'm just saying that Khomeini banned most
music from radio and TV. The Taliban illegalized it. I'm interested in
the utopian impulse to purify humans, which Islamism also is, and
how this interrelates with demonizing music.

But let's move on. What do you think: is militant Islam a
greater threat to us than communism was?

I come from a family of Soviet dissidents and hate communism. But I would much rather live under communism than under Islamism, and would much rather have communists as enemies than Islamic fundamentalists.

At least under communism you can see women in society and
appreciate their physical curves and beauty. You can have women as
friends, and you can have intimate relations without fearing some kind
of execution on a Friday. And you can get a bottle of vodka when you
feel like it.

With communists as enemies, at least you have people that
care about their own preservation. With what we are facing now, we
have psychopaths who want to blow the whole planet up -- and themselves along with it.

It is very depressing, and it's hard not to be pessimistic.

Your thoughts on this?

Buckley: Totalist ideologies are the enemy. In Communism,
there were gradations. Under Stalin, to quote one historian, you were
allowed to do anything that was not proscribed. Under Mao, you could
do nothing except if specially permitted. Under Pol Pot, you were
marked if you had ever learned how to read.

Anything in a totalitarian society that subtracts from the comprehensiveness of the things that are banned is welcome. If one wants to look for compensations, it would be to ask whether the proffered substitute provided substantial relief. Monks lead a spartan life, but their experience is the kind where they feel elation in other ways, which causes them to hang in there, which of course they do voluntarily. The Benthamite formula is simply inapplicable, so I'm not sure we should spend much time on it.

FP: Fair enough. So how do we fight militant Islam? What tactics will yield victory? If President Bush called you tomorrow and asked you what he should do next in Iraq specifically and in the War on Terror in general, what would you tell him?

Buckley: *Divide et impera.* We must vigorously pursue Muslim leaders who know of the sequential violations by Al Qaeda of the Islamic faith. The goal would be the honest one of charging with infidelity those who practice what Al Qaeda has been doing. Residual disputes on doctrine need to be treated as empirical challenges to co-existence as, we know from history, went on for many years among Muslims and Christians and Jews. In any such conversation with the president I would stress this point.

FP: Give us your report card on President Bush in the War on Terror.

Buckley: A grade given to Mr. Bush in the matter of the war on terrorism would require scales of performance by others in similar situations. The one tactile confrontation we all have is at airports, and I decline to believe ingenuity has been exercised there. Though that perhaps reflects my having to bare my toenails to somebody or other a couple of days ago. Another measure is a posteriori: If there are no terrorist attacks, progress is being made.

FP: The behavior of the Left in the War on Terror has really reached new pathetic and pathological lows. "Progressives" are now excusing, and even supporting, religious zealots who persecute women and gays -- and suppress all the democratic rights that are supposedly the center of progressive ideology.

This is nothing new, of course. The Left did the same with our totalitarian adversaries throughout the 20th century. But it completely boggles the mind how, for example, radical leftist feminists are now making excuses for regimes where they themselves would be executed simply for showing an ankle in public.

What is your insight into the leftist's urge to promote regimes where his/her own existence would be extinguished?

Buckley: The Left has priorities, and the priority this time around is to damage the United States. Conversely, their fear is that to support our missions overseas would undermine their whole anti-US structure--so let the gays burn and the ladies be flogged. What does give me pause is their failure even to decry the crimes you mention.

FP: Anti-Semitism has become the new mantle of the Left. Much of the international community, except for the U.S. and a handful of other countries, now condemns Israel for trying to defend itself with a fence while it turns a blind eye to the mass murderers of our time. The U.N. completely condones anti-Semitism. What do you think is behind these pathological developments in regard to the new Jew-Hatred?

Buckley: No doubt some people who oppose the fence do so because they want to be anti-Israel; and some of these individuals are motivated by anti-Semitism. But my sense of it is that most believe the fence inordinate and opportunistic. In my book *In Search of Anti-Semitism*, I quoted Norman Podhoretz: If you are anti-Israel, you may well be an anti-Semite, but not all anti-Israelis are anti-Semitic.

FP: Mr. Buckley, clearly not all anti-Israelis are anti-Semitic. But the point here is that whoever believes the fence is "inordinate" and "opportunistic" lives in a delusional fantasy world. Israeli citizens are the victims of a pathological enemy that sends its young kids to blow themselves up inside Israeli cafes and shopping malls. Israel has a right and a responsibility to defend itself. The fence is not even half finished, and suicide bombings have greatly decreased.

My question is, why is Israel not allowed to defend itself? Why does the world protest a fence meant to keep terrorists out, while it remains silent at the grotesque inhumanity of suicide bombings? This is directly connected to the fact that anti-Semitism has become the new call of the Left. Could you comment on this phenomenon? Or do you disagree with my assumptions?

Buckley: I don't disagree with your assumptions, but they are incompletely elaborated. It's correct that the Israelis should have their fence, but some critics persuasively argue that its shape is opportunistic--that it is being used to settle the settler problem. They are most definitely entitled to a fence or whatever else they deem useful to augment their safety. But they must not use the fence to close out territorial issues that are legitimately in question.

FP: What did you think of the Democratic National Convention? Carter struck me as especially pathetic. This is a President who lost two crucial allies of America's, Iran and Nicaragua, to our enemies and who stood by when the Soviets invaded Afghanistan. In many respects, the rise of militant Islam was spawned under – and because of – his incompetent presidency. And yet he is still lecturing – moralistically at that -- the Republicans on how to conduct foreign policy. What did you make of this in particular and of the DNC in general?

Buckley: Dear Jamie, you are answering my questions for me. Thanks. Carter is a lost cause, and lost causes don't get any loster. For my views on the DNC, see my last two columns.

FP: Mr. Buckley, we have run out of time. It was a great honor to speak with you. Let's close on your decision to relinquish ownership of *National Review*.

Everyone here at *FrontPage* would like to extend our immense gratitude to you for this priceless gift that you have given America – and the world -- for a half century.

Could you kindly give us a glimpse into your thoughts concerning what *National Review* has accomplished, and also your decision to depart?

Buckley: Thank you for your very kind remarks, Jamie. What I said to the *New York Times* when I retired was pretty much the whole story. Perhaps you will trouble to look at the current issue of *National Review* -- which is chock full of high-nutrient flattery. I so much appreciate your good wishes. *National Review* should continue to be interesting, readable, buoyant, and brightly aware of challenges ahead.

FP: Thank you, Mr. Buckley. We wish you the best and we are all grateful to you for who you are and what you have given us.

Buckley: Thank you very much, Jamie.

[Jamie Glazov, "Miles Gone By," Frontpagemag.com,
August 9, 2004.]

26. god is Not Great – by Christopher Hitchens

Frontpage Interview's guest today is Christopher Hitchens, one of the most prominent political and cultural essayists of our time. He is the author of the new book, *god Is Not Great. How Religion Poisons Everything.*

FP: Christopher Hitchens, welcome back to Frontpage Interview.

Hitchens: Nice of you to invite me again.

FP: I was very moved by your book -- a very profound and powerful read. A lot of what you said really needed to be said, and I guess it took someone like you to say it in the potent, wise and courageous way that you did. I say this, incidentally, as confusing as it may be to some readers, as a person of the Christian faith. I value and appreciate your slicing attack on the hypocrites and slime who have caused so much pain in the name of religion.

There is, obviously, another book that could be written on the good that religion has done. Also, of course, the existence of religious hypocrites and of those who commit evil in the name of religion does not negate the existence of God. And there remains the possibility that, as in Dante's inferno, "religious" people who abuse the faith are in hell.

But we'll get to some of this a bit later perhaps.

First, let's begin with what led to the creation of this book. It was clearly inside your head throughout much of your life. What were some of the developments/circumstances that made you realize that you had to write it *now?* For instance, the title is clearly a counterpoint to what Islamic suicide bombers yell ("Allu Akbar" -- "God is Great") before they blow themselves up. Was the image of the suicide bomber in our terror war a significant motivator for you to write the book?

Hitchens: Too kind.

Someone recently sent me an interview I gave years ago, in which I had said I wouldn't write a book advocating atheism because there was no need: the existing works were more than good enough. So my mind must have changed somewhat and, yes, I think your surmise is probably correct, it was the Islamist assault that got me off the fence.

It had done that before, in 1989, with the murder-campaign against Salman Rushdie. The crude people who were using assassins and butchers then are now about to get their hands on a nuclear weapon, so I don't apologise for my sense of urgency.

I also notice again what I noticed then, which is that "faith" leaders of other denominations tend to make excuses for Islamism. We saw it with the Vatican's recent condemnation, not of the hideous organised attack on Danish society, but of the cartoonists in Copenhagen. We see it with the softness of the so-called religious when it comes to condemning the so-called "insurgency" in Iraq. And I don't forget that the supposedly secular "Left" is actually saturated with piety and relativism - a rather sickly combination - when it comes to these matters, as well. I was very glad to launch my book-tour with a debate against the posturing figure of Al Sharpton, for example.

As to the "good" that religion has done, I state very clearly in *god Is Not Great* that many believers have done exemplary things. But I insist that they are valued for qualities and deeds that any humanist can applaud, and that supernatural authority is not required to oppose Hitler or Stalin, say, or slavery. Whereas scriptural authority WAS required, for example, to justify racism and slavery in the first place. And it is available now, to excuse the killing of apostates and infidels. We would be better off without these man-made texts, which have the effect of making normal people endorse actions and policies that only a psychopath could ordinarily be expected to approve. If you want good people to do bad things, religion is always there for you - like the rats and bacilli that lurk at the end of Camus's "La Peste" - even in periods where "faith" seems domesticated and benign. Its foundational documents are fundamentally irrational and cruel, and this tends to tell.

FP: You are right, of course, that if you want good people to do bad things, religion is always there for you. That is, unfortunately, the empirical reality of human existence.

At the same time though, my friend, our sense of morality is rooted in our conception of God and his laws. The Ten Commandments I don't think are such an awful thing. Many of the premises of our Judea-Christian religion surely keep many humans in check. Without these foundations for morality, surely there would be more pain and evil in the world, no? Look at the former communist countries where atheists eradicated religion and replaced the Ten Commandments with class hatred. This engendered mass Holocaust. Aside from all of its mass crimes, the greatest damage done by communism was moral in its removal of religion and the replacement of it with hatred.

You are right, sir, that religion, or the exploitation of it, has caused massive barbarity. But surely the removal of religion would eradicate the very concept of morality, which would lead to something even more savage amongst humans and how we treat each other.

Your thoughts?

Hitchens: One reason why I say that faith poisons everything is that it degrades our ordinary morality and solidarity. Quite apart from the fact that the Ten Commandments are not mainly concerned with morality (more with worship and abjection) and quite apart from the things that they do NOT forbid - genocide, racism, slavery, child-abuse - I decline to believe that our ancestors ever thought that murder, theft and perjury were OK. No society ever has.

In *god Is Not Great* I also point out how this same fallacy applies in the New Testament. The story of the Good Samaritan is quite unmoored from its local ethnic and confessional context: it comes to us as the tale of a man who went out of his way to help a fellow-creature. Since the parable is told by Jesus, the man in the story cannot by definition have been a Christian. We do not need supernatural license for kindness, and we most especially do not need the offer of divine reward or hellish punishment, since these pollute the well of our better instincts.

On your point about the secular nihilists and totalitarians (our common foes, along with the jihadists) again I have a whole chapter in my book. Not to compress the whole thing but just consider Russia in 1917. Millions of ignorant and superstitious people have been told for hundreds of years that the absolute head of the state - the Czar, who is also the head of the Russian Orthodox Church - is a little higher than merely human. If you are Josef Stalin, the former seminary student, you should not even be in the dictatorship business if you cannot exploit a ready-made reservoir of credulity and servility on this scale. And mark the sequel: everything from Inquisitions and heresy-hunts to "miracles" like Lysenko's pseudo-genetics and the overall worship of the supreme leader. The task of humanism is to raise the average person above the floor on which grovelling takes place. Name me a society that has degenerated into famine and misery and fear because it has adopted the teachings of Spinoza and Jefferson and Einstein. Dare you say that these and other men had no ethics because they self-consciously rejected a personal or intervening deity?

FP: I guess we return here to the question of how ethics can exist without the notion of an existing God – a notion that Dostoevsky clearly struggled with.

Let me bring up the reality of our conscience. Doesn't the existence of our conscience prove the existence of something greater than ourselves?

Isn't there something innate in all of us and in our existence that proves the existence of God?

For instance, I don't think a child is traumatized by witnessing the brutal murder of his mother because he was socially constructed to do so. He is traumatized because there is a right and wrong that transcends what humans construct it to be, and that right and wrong stems from something that is created by something greater than ourselves.

I must say that, for me, the existence of God is proven to me every day in almost everything I see. Especially the existence of love. When I see a child crave its mother's and father's love, and beg for a hug, I see God. When I see our need for love from one another, I see him. Surely our need for love, as one example, is not socially constructed or a reality that was just created by chance or fluke.

And surely evil is a spiritual force as well.

This is just my own faith and perspective of course. But what is your perspective on these things?

Hitchens: If you are a "pantheist", as the men I mentioned earlier (Spinoza and Jefferson and Einstein) probably or arguably were, you will agree with me that a god which is everywhere is just as likely to be nowhere in particular. If someone says that god is love I don't violently object. If he then says that love is god I find myself feeling uneasy. The undoubted existence of conscience - doing the right thing when nobody is looking, and even deriving satisfaction from the doing - need not posit the supernatural. I like to give blood when I can: I don't lose a pint but someone else gains one. I also hope to benefit when I need blood myself (I have a very rare blood group). Why intrude extraneous complexities here?

As for evil, I say in the book that I believe in its existence and even feel that I have felt its presence. But this does not lead me to infer the existence of Satan and, as you well know, believers in god only complicate their ontology when they try (or fail) to do the same.

FP: So do you wish there was a God? Do you believe that you have a soul and do you ever worry about where it might go in the afterlife? Or these are all just silly notions for you?

And if there is no God or afterlife and nothing afterwards, what then is the meaning of life? Can there be any meaning if there is no God?

What is the meaning of life for you?

Hitchens: I like to think that I can resist wish-thinking in all its forms, and I do not in any case wish that there was a supreme being, let alone a heaven or hell, because I do not desire an unalterable dictatorship of a celestial kind, which would subject me to permanent supervision and surveillance. I should add that dictatorship is even more repulsive to me when it presents itself as benign - its most common seduction.

So I am happy that there is no evidence for such a belief. The immortality of the soul (notice I do not say that I must be soul-less while I am still alive) is indeed a silly fable. The natural world is wonderful enough, with the beauty of science and the consolation of philosophy and literature. One's only hope of immortality lies in the rearing of one's children, for whom one must in due course make room. Their presence is the answer to the last part of your question. A feeling of the transcendent and the numinous is inseparable from a morally serious human existence, but it is not satisfied by myths which are in fact deeply and obviously self-centered.

FP: You refer, at one point, to your religious friends and how some of them say that you are a "seeker." This relates to how many religious people often try to force the non-believer, usually with bullying tactics, into their own vision of the world. But as you say, you are not a "seeker" in any sense of the way these friends try to label you.

How do you interpret the psychology of religious individuals who need to impose their views? If one believes in God, one can obviously share that belief with one's fellow man in a patient and loving way and then leave it to that individual to decide what they will do with it. That's fine obviously. But what's with the inability to allow another human their own space and views? What's with the threat, and anger and terror, that some believers feel by someone else's disbelief? In my own life experience, I have gathered that these are almost always the individuals whose own lives cannot withstand any moral scrutiny whatsoever.

In any case: if a person is so certain about God's existence, or with the justification of going to Church, or with how they are going straight to heaven, why their inability to sleep at night at the thought of someone who doesn't think and live like them?

What would be your analysis of the psychological mindset?

Hitchens: I'm interested very much by the lack of confidence that is displayed by the faithful. Why doesn't their conviction - that they are divinely supervised and loved and even saved - make them happy? Why must they insist that I have to believe it, too? I take their anxiety as a manifestation of a repressed form of doubt and fear, and their claim to know god's will as the arrogant presumption of a reinforcement for a weak case.

I also have come to the conclusion that religious belief, even in its supposedly benign form, is the clue to the origin of totalitarianism. A permanent inescapable surveillance; the abolition of the private thought; the constant guilt and fear; the irremovable and unchallengeable authority; the sado-masochism of begging for rewards and fearing punishments - this is the species at its most servile and primeval level. The wish for a Big Brother comes from the childhood of the race, and has to be outgrown in order for us to develop self-respect.

FP: You discuss the pathology in religion regarding sexuality and how the guardians of religion, while moralizing about sex, are sometimes the worst sexual offenders there are. And yet their victims, who are usually children, receive no defense while the perpetrators themselves are exonerated because they act in the name of religion. I shake your hand in standing up for the victims of these mass crimes.

The parts in your book about the mutilation of babies' genitalia, male and female, and the great damage and harm it does, is clearly instructive. It is incredible that such silence prevails in the world while this violence is perpetrated on millions upon millions of infants in the name of religion. Can you talk a bit about this?

Hitchens: Another proof that religion is not just man-made but Male-made (as I say at some length in the book) is its primitive attitude to sex and especially to female sexuality. The disgust at menstrual blood, the insistence on virgin births (common to the announcement of all prophets or god-kings), the revulsion at the genitalia and the wish for quasi-castration - all this is deeply unwholesome and has led to the infliction of misery upon countless generations.

Again, I would insist that no morally normal person would agree to inflict cruelty upon children if this were not supposedly mandated by heaven, and that is why I regard religion as a source of immorality rather than otherwise. It is not that we fail to live up to its precepts: it is that its precepts operate on a level below the recognisable moral norm.

The idea of the Apocalypse, or end of days, is another very dangerous preachment of this kind and I hope you will ask me to say a few words about that, too.

FP: Ok, say a few words, or many words, about the idea of the Apocalypse, or end of days, and why you think it is a very dangerous preachment.

Hitchens: In *god Is Not Great* I do my best to say why I think that eschatology is unwholesome, and why I think that the obsession with the "end times" is one of the creepiest aspects of the religious mentality. (Look at the poor Iranians today, bullied by a scrofulous despotism into hymning the arrival of a "Twelfth Imam" who has no more validity than the Tooth Fairy, and who lacks even the charm - and even the utility - of a nice tale for children.)

We already have a good picture of the way that the world will end: the heat-death of the universe. Through telescopes, we can already see this happening to countless other stars. This is awe-inspiring enough for anybody, and far more impressive than any Book of Revelation. It seems to me to be merely contemptible and solipsistic to contemplate such overwhelming reality, and then to mutter foolishness about an exception perhaps being made in our own case.

FP: Surely you have considered that God may not fall into any of the paradigms that you have forced him within the structures of your own thinking and understanding? Our human understanding may be a bit limited in terms of understanding God and his ways, no? After all, if we understood God, then he wouldn't be God. And if God revealed himself, then we wouldn't be free.

Surely, Mr. Hitchens, you recognize that you yourself, as all human beings, may not understand fully something about an existence that a higher power has created, no?

In other words, can you concede that perhaps human reason and the human mind might not be enough to completely understand, let alone serve as grounds to reject, the reality of God's existence and the reality of his creation?

In another sense: do you recognize that your own rejection of the possibility of God's existence is completely independent of the fact that God exists?

Hitchens: Well, you actually re-state part of the case that I make in *god Is Not Great*. Given the impossibility of disproving god's existence, one must also admit the impossibility of proving it. But religion, which does claim to possess proofs of revelation, proposes to go further, and to state that one can actually know god's mind and interpret his instructions (about diet, say, or sexual conduct, or Iranian foreign policy). Thus, given the impossibility of "knowing", the first people to eliminate from the argument are those who are vain enough to claim to "know".

I do not think that my non-conviction and the faith of the godly are on all fours: all man-made arguments for the existence of a deity have actually been examined and exploded (see Victor Stenger's excellent recent work: *God: The Failed Hypothesis*). The Einsteinian pantheist concession, which allows that there may well be more to the wonder of the universe than we think (or even than we *can* think) explicitly repudiates the idea of a personal god, or a force that responds to human demands or intervenes in human affairs. It thus leaves religion behind, in the infancy of our species.

As I mentioned earlier, I do not wish for a benign celestial dictatorship anyway. Nor do I attribute my presence here to a divine plan instead of the laws and workings of biology. Above all, though, I refuse to submit to dictates from other mere mammals, who claim to know what they cannot know and who seem principally interested in wielding power in the here and now.

One last point if I may: a question I meant to pose earlier. Can you, or any of the readers of FP, give an instance of a morally right action, or morally rounded statement, taken or made by a religious person, that could not have been performed or uttered by a non-religious one?

FP: Your point is a strong one. Yes, a non-believer can be as equally moral as a religious person and a person can be moral without being religious.

There remains the question of where the notion of "morality" comes from that the non-religious person may engage in. Isn't it only because of religion that morality exists in the first place? If there is no God, and if there is no belief in God, then does morality even have any meaning?

But perhaps these questions are just a reflection of my own personal faith.

In any case, our time is almost up my friend.

Christopher Hitchens, thank you kindly for joining us. Your book is a valuable intellectual gift.

It is appreciated that you expose the savagery that has been perpetrated in the name of religion and that you stand up for the victims – many of whom have been forced into invisibility by those who seek to enforce historical amnesia on this phenomenon. As you point out, when Hasidic fundamentalist mohels (appointed circumcisers) put baby boys' penises into their mouths and give these babies genital herpes -- and then, in some cases, cause death to these babies (pp.49-

50), and nothing is done or said about it, something seems, well, a little bit wrong. As you note, if any citizen did such a thing to a baby *outside of* religious window dressing, he would immediately and legitimately be seen as evil and be charged and prosecuted by the law. But for some reason, when it comes to grotesque abuses such as these that prevail in many quarters of the earth's religions, if the perpetrator acts in the name of religion then the abuse is considered to be everything but what it is – and no cops show up and no prison sentences are dished out.

So thank you, Mr. Hitchens, for standing up for the victims.

In this light, and perhaps to answer your last question in a round-about-way, your anti-religious book is, on several levels, a powerful moral and humanitarian statement.

And I say this as a believer in God.

Thanks for joining us sir.

It was an honor and privilege to speak with you.

Hitchens: Thank you again for the hospitality of your pages.

[Jamie Glazov, "god Is Not Great," Frontpagemag.com,
June 5, 2007.]

27. Treason – Ann Coulter

Frontpage Interview's guest today is Ann Coulter, America's renowned political and social commentator, author and syndicated columnist. Her new book is *Treason.*

FP: Hi Ms. Coulter, welcome to Frontpage Interview. We really appreciate you taking the time out of your schedule to chat with us.

Coulter: My pleasure Jamie.

FP: Saddam's capture is still, naturally, the big news. What do you think about it? Tell us how you found out and what your reaction was.

Coulter: Well, when the story first broke I had the TV on with the sound off. I saw the footage of that filthy, hairy, unshaven creature looking dazed and out of it and I thought: "My God, they've arrested Nick Nolte again!"

FP: Um, ok. . . well, were you happy when you realized it wasn't Nolte but Saddam himself?

Coulter: I had mixed feelings about it - sort of a combination of unbridled joy and hysterical elation. Pity it wasn't a week or so earlier, though. Hussein might have made the cut as one of Barbara Walters' "10 most fascinating people of 2003."

FP: And what do you think are the implications and significance of us succeeding in capturing this scoundrel?

Coulter: It's really no more significant than the arrest of, say, Adolf Hitler would have been in 1945. It's great because it's separated the Democratic Party into two distinct camps: Your garden-variety losers and your genuine nut-bar conspiracy theorists like Madeline Albright.

FP: I think you are right about the state of the Democratic Party. They don't have a prayer in hell to beat Bush in 2004, right?

Coulter: If they have a prayer, it will be answered by someone whose kingdom is not heaven.

FP: Let's talk about your latest book, *Treason*. It caused quite a stir. You were certainly right to attack liberals on many fronts. But what do you say to those Conservatives who argue that you went overboard by defending McCarthy and that you should have also pointed out that many liberals, especially during the Cold War, like Lyndon Johnson and John F. Kennedy, were solid anti-communists and patriotic Americans? What do you say to those who charge that you undermined your case with these arguments?

Coulter: I'm still waiting for my detractors (of any stripe) to identify the inaccuracies in my book that would lead them to conclude that I went "overboard." However, I am no longer holding my breath.

JFK, as I note in my book, was -- in theory -- as ferocious an anti-communist as the great Joe McCarthy. But Kennedy was a Democrat and thus an utter incompetent when it came to execution. (Johnson is not your strongest case. He had all of JFK's incompetence without the good heart.)

To summarize a subject explored in lascivious detail in my book: JFK refused to provide air cover for the Cubans at the Bay of Pigs leading to their slaughter and imprisonment -- and to the Cuban missile crisis. He started the Vietnam war but would not fight to win. Democrats love taking the nation to war, they just have a phobia about winning. As a consequence, the world's greatest Super Power seems to get involved in "unwinnable wars" only when a Democrat is president.

I'm not a psycho-biographer. I'll leave it to others to explore why even those Democrats who appear to be genuinely patriotic - and we don't see so many of those anymore - still manage to screw up foreign policy every bit as much as Howard Dean would. (I would imagine their deeply-felt need for approval from the French would figure into any psychological profile.) Besides JFK, I believe the only other Democratic presidential candidates in the past half century anyone would dare cite as hawks on national defense are Scoop Jackson and Joe Lieberman. You can see how well they fared within their own Party. What is one to say about a Party like that?

FP: Let's move on to discuss your own personal background. Tell us, what influenced you to become a Conservative? Were there some people or events that molded your views in your childhood, youth, etc?

Coulter: There was an absence of the sort of trauma that would deprive me of normal, instinctual reactions to things. I had happily married parents, a warm and loving family, and a happy childhood with lots of friends. Thus, there were no neurotic incidents to turn me into a liberal.

FP: No neurotic incidents to turn you into a liberal? Would you, then, argue that leftism/liberalism is ultimately, in most cases, the depersonalization and politicization of personal neuroses?

Coulter: Pause for a moment to consider the probable mental state of Howard Dean and then ask me that question again. Yes, of course liberalism is a mental defect. Liberals are wracked by self-loathing as the result of some traumatic incident -- say, driving drunk off a bridge with your mistress passed out in the back seat and letting the poor girl drown because you're a married man and a U.S. senator, just to take one utterly random, hypothetical example off the top of my head.

FP: I'm not even gonna bother playing the devil's advocate on this one -- it's a losing battle. So speaking of the Left, what do you think its behavior during Iraq's liberation revealed about it?

Coulter: I don't think there was much left to reveal.

FP: Ok, let's get back to your intellectual journey: what led to your interest in law?

Coulter: Inertia.

FP: Did the study of law influence your political views?

Coulter: No. I do hate trial lawyers, but then again I hated them before I began the study of law.

FP: Why do you hate trial lawyers? And if you don't mind, could you name a few prominent ones that you are not extremely fond of?

Coulter: You mean besides John Edwards? Before I answer that question I'll need you to initial this waiver here, here, and here, and then sign it here at the bottom and have it notarized. I'll also need you to post a small cash bond so as to indemnify me against any legal action which might result from my response. Thanks.

Everything you do -- from driving to earning a living to making a cup of coffee to owning a home to getting medical care -- is more expensive and difficult simply because of trial lawyers, who, at the same time, contribute absolutely nothing of any value to society. You can't buy as simple a device as a telephone without having to wade through a 50-page manual to locate information you actually need, like what your new security code is. (How about adding a one-page short list of instructions for consumers who already know not to place their phones in a microwave oven?) But other than the fact that trial lawyers have made every single facet of life worse, I can't think of a single good reason to dislike them.

FP: What is it that you would say inspires you?

Coulter: Love of God and country.

FP: Why do you think you do what you do?

Coulter: Love of God and country (and it's a great gig).

FP: If you wouldn't mind, I'd like to talk a little bit about your September 13, 2001 column over at National Review and your subsequent departure from that magazine. Could you tell us a bit about what you think happened? What does it say about the contemporary nature of "conservative" journalism?

Coulter: In this one instance, the idiot Clintonheads are worth quoting: Let's move on. (I note that the incident did lead to my syndicated column being picked up by the great David Horowitz at frontpagemag.com!)

FP: Ok. Let's move on, then, to your personal views on some subjects. Tell us a few figures that you admire in the 20th century. That you despise?

Coulter: Admire: Joe McCarthy, Ronald Reagan, J Edgar Hoover, Winston Churchill and the *young* Richard Nixon.

As for the other category, perhaps "detest" is not the right word. Just this once, I would borrow from Madeline Albright to say these are my "people of concern": Justices Sandra Day O'Connor, David Hackett Souter, Stephen Breyer, Anthony Kennedy, Ruth Bader Ginsberg and John Paul Stevens.

FP: Ms. Coulter, I completely agree with you on Ronald Reagan but, with all due respect, how could you possibly admire Joe McCarthy? He was a hideous character. I don't think you can find many individuals more anti-communist than myself, but I detest McCarthy for how he discredited anti-communism. I can't think of anyone else in America that did so much damage to the anti-communist cause. What exactly do you see in McCarthy? Yes, he fought the right enemy, but the way that he fought it was extremely counterproductive. He armed our liberal enemies with powerful ammunition against us. What is your thinking here?

Coulter: I notice that you have just reeled off a slew of insults without a bare hint of a fact. And for good reason -- actually for no good reason. You're interviewing me, you should have read my book.

Until Treason, that's all it ever was with McCarthy. Portraits of Kathy Boudin, Che Guevara, Ted Bundy, and Joe Stalin are more nuanced than portraits of McCarthy. He is the only person in history for whom, apparently, there is absolutely nothing good that we can say. No nuance, no good side -- just invective, fake facts, myth, and anger. It's amazing that guy ever got elected to anything! I wrote my book, I made my case, and people decided not to argue with me on the merits. So now I guess we're back to fact-free invective against McCarthy. When you start to sound like Molly Ivins talking about George Bush, you might want to entertain the possibility that you are a few tweaks away from the dispassionate truth.

FP: I would never disagree that McCarthy has been demonized to the ultimate degree in a very absurd manner, especially in proportion to the real villains of our times. I am just wary of seeing him as some kind of hero, especially since he did a lot of damage to anti-communism.

In any case, let's save it for a future debate. Tell us, what is your favorite book?

Coulter: Apart from the Holy Bible, I don't have a favorite. But among the books I am especially fond of are:

Witness by Whittaker Chambers,

Mere Christianity by C.S. Lewis,

Modern Times by Paul Johnson,

The Bell Curve by Charles Murray and Richard Hernstein,

Radical Son by David Horowitz,

Hustler by Joe Sobran,

Takings by Richard Epstein,

Economic Analysis of the Law by Richard Posner,

Brain Storm by Richard Dooling,

Anna Karenina, Jane Eyre, Wuthering Heights, anything by Dave Barry, and almost any true crime story about a serial killer.

FP: Very interesting. And what three books do you consider essential reading?

Coulter: The Old Testament, the New Testament, and *Treason*.

FP: Goodness. . .your book right after the Bible? Sounds about right to me I guess.

Let's move to the War on Terror. If President Bush called you today and asked you for your advice on the next moves he should take in our battle with militant Islam, what would you advise?

Coulter: Fire U.S. Transportation Secretary Norman Mineta. Keep excluding the New York Times from all exclusive press briefings.

FP: Could you kindly briefly highlight the reasons why you want Mineta fired? Is it mostly for his failure to implement tough "profiling" at airports after 9/11?

Coulter: Take out the word "mostly" and you're getting warm.

FP: What do you think about the idea of American President Ann Coulter? Have you ever considered this?

Coulter: I like the ring of it, but no.

FP: Hypothetically, if you did become president, what are two or three things you would immediately pursue?

AC: 1) Fire Norman Mineta.

2) Pack the Supreme Court.

3) Demand that Congress present me with a bill eliminating the withholding tax. Apart from killing terrorists, there is no more important political issue. People need to pay taxes in one lump sum every year in order to fully appreciate all those wonderful services the government provides.

FP: And where would you appoint this interviewer in your administration?

Coulter: You would be put on retainer with the assignment of eliminating the withholding tax. If you succeeded, something more permanent might be arranged.

FP: I am very grateful for this honor you would bestow on me. In any case, we are running out of time, so let me ask you this question to end the interview:

If you were asked to give a report card on President Bush's performance as our leader overall, and this involved a letter grade and short comment, what would you say?

Coulter: War on Terrorism: A-. His perfect grade was reduced on account of the continuing presence of Norman Mineta.

War on Democrats: B-. Problem areas: creating enormous new government entitlement programs, placing limits on political speech per the campaign finance reform bill, delivering an annual Kwanzaa message in honor of a phony holiday no one celebrates except white public school teachers, and the continuing presence of Norman Mineta.

FP: I don't think you have left any ambiguity for our readers about how you feel regarding Noman Mineta. Well, we are done. Thank you Ms. Coulter, it was an honor to speak with you - and also very enjoyable. I hope you will come back to join us again.

AC: Thank you Jamie, I would love to. Perhaps we can have a drink together at Norman Mineta's retirement party.

[Jamie Glazov, "Treason," Frontpagemag.com, January 12, 2004.]

28. Vixi: Memoirs of a Non-Belonger – Richard Pipes

Frontpage Interview's guest today is Richard Pipes, a Professor Emeritus at Harvard who is one of the world's leading authorities on Soviet history. He is the author of 19 books, the most recent being his new autobiography, *Vixi: Memoirs of a Non-Belonger.*

FP: Dr. Pipes, welcome to Frontpage Interview. It is an honor to speak with you.

Let's begin with your own personal role in the defeat of the Soviet Empire.

You served in the National Security Council in the Reagan administration, during which you pursued a touch approach toward the Soviet regime. Your assumption was that U.S. pressure would crack the communist system. I guess it is undeniable that history has vindicated your approach.

Could you talk a little bit about the strategy you pursued and what you think history now says about? And also comment on what it feels like to have been personally responsible for helping destroy one of the most evil regimes in history.

Pipes: I am proud to have played a part in bringing down the Soviet regime. Although at the time I was almost universally condemned for my views of the USSR and for the strategy which I recommended to deal with it. The situation has dramatically changed in the past several years and now praise greatly outnumbers criticism.

FP: But what is the situation that has changed and why do you think this change has occurred?

Pipes: Undoubtedly, I get more praise than criticism for my views on the USSR and Russia today because I have been proven largely right. What in the 1970's and 1980's were controversial speculations are now facts.

FP: Let's turn to the War on Terror. Do you think some of the same tactics that worked in defeating communism can succeed in our present war with Islamism? Does the present threat outweigh that posed by the Soviet Empire? What strategy do you think is crucial now?

Pipes: The threat of Islamism is quite different from that posed by the USSR -- both less menacing in that its adherents are much weaker, and more so in that they are fanatics with whom it is impossible to negotiate. History indicates, however, that in the long run all terrorist movements are defeated by firm action and police penetration of their structures.

FP: Expand a bit on what you mean by "police penetration" and how this would work with a terror group like al Qaeda.

Pipes: By "police penetration" I mean planting agents in the terrorist organizations. They can forestall terrorist acts. Their presence also sows suspicions and demoralizes. The Israelis have developed excellent methods to this end and have a lot to teach us.

FP: Let's talk about your memoir and your personal journey. Your subtitle of being a "non-belonger" is in reference to you having been an outsider as a Soviet historian among your academic colleagues, most whom, as we know, were – and remain – sympathetic to the Soviet regime and to communism.

It is interesting that your son, Daniel, has followed in your tradition, and remains an "outsider" in his profession as well -- in Mideast scholarship. Like his father, he refuses to follow the favorite Party Line in academia: to toe the anti-American line and to sympathize with the tyrannical entities in his field of study.

Why do so many academics who flock to their professions admire the most despotic creatures and regimes of their studies? What made the Pipes scholars different?

Pipes: I have never been able to understand the penchant of US academics for totalitarian regimes. This is a matter for psychologists and psychiatrists.

FP: Ok, now in your memoir, you discuss how Harvard reminded you of the early Soviet educational experiments, where institutions of learning were used for learning, but as political instruments for social change. Why do you think the Left has been so successful in dominating -- and suffocating -- academia? And what do you think of the potential of David Horowitz's manifesto, the Academic Bill of Rights, which calls for universities to function without discriminating against political or religious beliefs?

Pipes: The predilection not only of academics but intellectuals in general for left-wing causes is a complicated matter that does not lend itself to quick analysis. I have dealt with it to some extent in my *Russian Revolution*. Russian experience from the nineteenth and early twentieth centuries is, in this respect, not irrelevant to us.

FP: In your memoir, you give a powerful and moving account of your Jewish family's escape from the Nazis in Poland after the outbreak of the Second World War. Could you talk a bit about how your brush with the evil of Nazism nurtured your spider sense vis-à-vis tyranny and how, in turn, this influenced your interest in Russian history and your view of communism in general and the Soviet regime in particular?

Pipes: Since I left Poland after the outbreak of World War II, I experienced the siege of Warsaw and lived one month under German occupation. As I write in the book, my knowledge of Nazi totalitarianism has conditioned me to feel extreme hostility toward its Soviet variant.

FP: In your scholarship, you have emphasized the traditional authoritarian character within Russian political culture and how, therefore, communist tyranny was in continuity with the Russian past, rather than an aberration or break from it. Why has Russia historically been so addicted to authoritarianism and so reflexively opposed to liberal Western notions?

* I come from Russia and I have always been mesmerized by my people's peculiar inability to think in terms of individualism. The boundaries between what is your business and others' business are extremely blurry. And there is a very eerie need to believe that some kind of stern father figure is in charge out there somewhere, and that he is thinking of you. It was not just communism that created these instincts and characteristics.

Could you give an insight here?

Pipes: The Russian penchant for authoritarianism is also too complicated a subject to be discussed in this format. I have given it a great deal of thought. My general conclusion is that it stems from the traditional absence in Russia of firm civil rights which has the effect of Russians mistrusting each other and looking to the government to protect them from their fellow-citizens.

FP: Who is your favorite U.S. president of the 20th century? Your least favorite?

Pipes: I don't know that I have a single 20th President whom I would call my "favorite." I would list among them Truman and Reagan. L.B. Johnson was the most disastrous, in my judgment.

FP: Why do you see L.B. Johnson as the most disastrous? For the legacy of his Great Society and all the problems it triggered. His escalation of Vietnam? Both?

Pipes: I consider L.B. Johnson to have been a disastrous president because he was responsible for the so-called "Great Society", including Affirmative Action, which did far more harm than good. And, of course, the Vietnam War which not only claimed thousands of American lives to no purpose, but seriously undermined America's willingness to engage in an active political and military policy overseas.

FP: I am aware that some of these questions cannot be dealt with simply here in this forum. But let me try to at least get a morsel of wisdom from you on anti-Semitism? There is no easy or simple answer of course, but what if you asked to give a sound bite on its causes? I would say envy and jealousy. How about you?

Pipes: Anti-Semitism really cannot be discussed in this format: it is far too complex a phenomenon. Yes, envy plays its part but there is much more to it.

FP: Would Leon Trotsky have been just as big of a henchman and mass murderer as Stalin if he had taken power? After all, for one thing, how do you impose forced collectivization without terror?

Pipes: Trotsky was not the idealist that his admirers make him out to be, but I think he did not suffer from the kind of murderous paranoia that afflicted Stalin. In any event, as he well realized, being a Jew he had no chance of rising to the top of the Soviet political hierarchy.

FP: Fair enough, let's end our discussion by touching on Iraq. Did you support the war? If you were asked to advise Bush on what to do in Iraq now and in the War on Terror in general, what would you say?

Pipes: I support the Iraqi campaign which. I believe, has dramatically changed the balance of power in the Middle East for the better: observe the behavior of Libya and Syria. But I would advise President Bush to forget about installing a western-style democracy in Iraq and concentrate on setting up an effective tribal government.

FP: Fair enough, the argument is clear that perhaps we can't bring Western-style democracy to Iraq for many reasons, etc. But there is a legitimate argument that the effort is worth it. In any case, let's say Bush sets up an "effective tribal government." Could you just expand a bit on a scenario and how this would work?

Pipes: Tribal government: I think I would be willing to let tribal elders run Iraq. Democracy requires that all institutions standing between the individual citizen and the state be eliminated, but this is not possible in countries with strong tribal traditions.

FP: What do you think of how the Democrats are coming off in terms of Iraq and the War on Terror? Would it be a tragedy to our national security if they won the next election? Who are you personally in favor of and why (in terms of leading the U.S.)?

Pipes: I don't think a Democratic administration would be a "tragedy" but a Republican one is preferable, especially because Bush has made the war on terror his personal cause.

FP: Well, our time is up. Thank you for joining us today Dr. Pipes. I would like to take this opportunity to make a brief personal comment. I just want to tell you that, as you might know, my parents, Yuri and Marina Glazov, were Soviet dissidents. I think you met my dad back in the 1970s. He is no longer with us.

My parents admired you greatly and your name was often mentioned in our household. I grew up hearing about you all the time. After our nightmarish experience in the Soviet Union (my parents just barely escaped being imprisoned), we suffered in an environment of Western intellectuals who glorified the Soviet regime and demonized the United States. My parents were university professors in the West and many of their colleagues hated us and what we stood for. These academics were enamored with the Soviet regime and cherished the figures that spawned its bestial terror, especially Lenin and the rest of his crew.

But there was a certain scholar out there, by the name of Richard Pipes, who I heard about as a youngster, who told the truth about Soviet history, and even told the truth about Lenin – the icon of the leftists who berated my family about our anti-communist views. You exposed not only the truth about the pernicious evil of communism, but also about the monstrosity of Lenin and the others who engendered the Gulag Archipelago.

In so doing, you were one of the figures who brought a certain personal affirmation to our family and all of our experiences; you validated our history and reality in a sea where we were told that we didn't live what we lived, didn't suffer what we suffered, and didn't see what we saw.

During all my young years, both my father and mother spoke of you in very respectful and admiring ways.

I would like to take this moment, that I will maybe never have again, to thank you for having the courage to have told the truth about communism, despite the price you had to pay for doing so. Because of people like you, the truth has been engraved in the historical record, which no one can erase. And because of people like you, the human lives that were extinguished by the Soviet killing machine will mean something, will live on in our memory, and will perhaps touch our souls in their own profound and mysterious way – rather than being relegated to the invisibility that the Left has always attempted to impose on the nightmarish outcome of its own ideas.

And I would also like to thank you for your own personal contribution, as a member of the Reagan administration, in helping put Soviet communism on the ash heap of history.

Dr. Pipes, you have always been a hero to me. It was a great honor for me to speak with you. Thank you.

Pipes: I am flattered by your kind remarks Jamie. Thank you.

[Jamie Glazov, "Vixi: Memoirs of a Non-Belonger," Frontpagemag,com, January 19, 2004.]

29. Romancing Opiates – Theodore Dalrymple

Frontpage Interview's guest today is Theodore Dalrymple, a contributing editor to *City Journal* and the author of his collection of essays *Our Culture, What's Left of It: The Mandarins and the Masses.* He is the author of the new book, *Romancing Opiates: Pharmacological Lies and the Addiction Bureaucracy.*

FP: Theodore Dalrymple, welcome back to Frontpage Magazine.

Dalrymple: Thank you. It is an honor to be back.

FP: What attracted you to this particular topic?

Dalrymple: I was attracted to the subject by my contact with hundreds of heroin addicts in my work as a doctor in a prison and also in a general hospital in a British slum. It gradually dawned on me that the official doctrine concerning drug addiction was mistaken and possibly self-serving. Until then, I had more or less believed what I had been taught about it.

FP: Tell us some of the myths in our culture about opiate addiction.

Dalrymple: Perhaps I can best describe what I think most people believe about opiate addiction, particularly heroin addiction. They think that a person, somehow or other, by accident, stumbles across heroin, and is reluctantly persuaded to take some. He likes it, takes another dose, and then, hey presto, he's addicted. If he stops taking it, he has the most terrible withdrawal reaction, so he has no choice but to continue. Unfortunately, heroin is not free and he needs money to pay for it. Incapable because of his addiction of work, he is driven to crime. He cannot stop himself, but fortunately professional help is at hand which, if he accepts it, will stop him from taking more drugs - but otherwise he will continue.

At every point, this narrative is mistaken and obviously so.

FP: But they say that heroine addicts go through hell when taken off the drug, isn't this a fact? Also, can you expand a bit, on each point, how the narrative you illustrate is mistaken?

Dalrymple: With regard to withdrawal, it is grossly exaggerated as a phenomenon. Unlike withdrawal from barbiturates or alcohol, it is not dangerous. There is abundant evidence that a large component of the problem is anxiety, which in turn has been brought about by the uncritical mental absorption of the myth. This myth has been perpetuated in many books and films. In addition, addicts frequently lie about their symptoms in order to obtain drugs from doctors.

At its very worst, withdrawal is like flu, but usually is much less severe than that. We used to withdraw addicts in my hospital, making it clear that we would prescribe for them only when we, the doctors, saw the need, and we would not be influenced at all by anything the addict said concerning his symptoms. After two or three days, the addicts always said, 'Is that all there is to it?' They never suffered severely.

In the prison in which I worked, the addicts did not know that I observed them before they came into my room. Among themselves, they were chatting, laughing and joking. When they came into my room, they claimed to be in the deepest agony. This is an observation that has been made many times, and indeed there is experimental evidence showing that addicts change their behaviour and their story depending upon their interlocutors, and whether their interlocutors are in a position to prescribe or do anything else for them.

The standard view of addiction is wrong because it is not by chance that people become addicted, nor do they get hooked by heroin. It would be truer to say that they hook heroin. Most addicts go through quite a long period of casual use before they 'graduate' to regular use, and so it is a choice. Furthermore, if there is a causative relationship between heroin addiction and crime it is more that a propensity to crime causes addiction than the other way round. The great majority of criminals who take heroin were criminals before they ever took it. A case in point is William Burroughs, a man from a privileged background who was, if I may put it like this, a natural born criminal. He was a criminal before he was an addict, not the other way round.

It is not true that medical attention is necessary to stop taking opiates. Mao Tse Tung managed in his characteristically brutal way to get 20,000,000 people to stop. The fact that threats could achieve this suggest that addiction is not an illness like any other. Furthermore, thousands of American servicemen who addicted themselves to heroin in Vietnam stopped when they came home.

The official orthodoxy is wrong in every particular.

FP: What is wrong with treatments applied by professionals?

Dalrymple: First of all, I don't really like the concept of treatment: it assumes that there is an illness to treat. While addiction has medical consequences, it is not in itself an illness.

But the remedies - usually the prescription of a similar drug, often long term - are of doubtful benefit, and in any transfer the cost of addiction from the individual to society as a whole. The treatments themselves are dangerous, and it is an extremely moot point as to whether they've saved lives or killed people.

FP: So wait a minute, what exactly is addiction then?

Dalrymple: Addiction is a condition in which people grow accustomed to a drug, need to take more of it to achieve the same effect, have withdrawal symptoms on ceasing to take it, and also have a psychological craving for the drug.

FP: So what treatment should there be for addiction?

Dalrymple: I think the very idea of treatment is a mistake, for it suggests a medical condition. Opiate addiction has medical consequences but is not in itself an illness.

Rehabilitation is not treatment and I have no objection to it. By the time they decide to stop taking opiates, if they do, addicts have often sunk further down the social scale, know no one except other addicts and have alienated their family. Because life is a biography, and not just a series of moments, it can take a long time for people to get back on their feet and I see no objection in providing them with sanctuary to do so - provided they realize this is not treatment.

The offer of treatment suggests that there is a 'cure' for the disease, and this I think is nonsense.

FP: You argue that withdrawal from opiates is not actually the crisis our society deems it to be. Can you talk about that?

Dalrymple: The depictions in the newspapers, in novels and in films are gross exaggerations. At worst - and not many addicts suffer the worst - withdrawal from opiates is like the flu. Most addicts do not even suffer to this degree, and it has been comprehensively proven that a large part of the suffering from withdrawal (apart from the lying about it that addicts often resort to in order to fool doctors into prescribing for it) is caused by anticipatory anxiety.

It is curious that withdrawal from alcohol, which - in the form of Delirium Tremens - is really dangerous, does not attract the same degree of literary attention as withdrawal from opiates.

FP: So why do you think that our culture pays so much attention to withdrawal from opiates? And why do you think our culture has engendered these myths?

Dalrymple: Our culture pays a lot of attention to withdrawal from opiates because there is such a long literary tradition, starting with De Quincey (Confessions of an English Opium Eater) and the poet Coleridge, both of whom were first class self-dramatisers. De

Quincey in particular implied that there was a connection between drug-taking and creativity, that drugs opened realms to the mind that others could not perceive, but that the corresponding agonies of withdrawal were of stupendous dimension.

There is a thirst for self-aggrandizement and self-dramatization: it makes small and rather petty lives seem vast and possessed of a tragic grandeur. I believe this to be romantic claptrap. De Quincey was swallowed whole by Dickens, Poe, Baudelaire etc, and his influence (even though he may not be much read any more) stretches down to the present day.

Curiously, in the prison in which I work, a lot of attention was paid to withdrawing drug addicts, but none at all to withdrawing alcoholics, who were genuinely in danger from Delirium Tremens. But then they were just a lot of old drunks, whereas the addicts were the linear descendents of De Quincey.

FP: Theodore Dalrymple, thank you for joining us.

Dalrymple: Thank you Jamie.

[Jamie Glazov, "Romancing Opiates," Frontpagemag.com, July 5, 2006.]

Part VIII: Looking to the Future of Freedom

Introduction:

After digesting the facts, arguments, and analyses from the previous seven parts, it's easy to be overwhelmed by the task facing free societies today. The amount of information out there to understand is complicated and frequently disturbing.

Who is qualified to put the pieces together? Perhaps someone who has spent the last decade doing so five days a week for one of the most important of conservative publications?

For the final discussion of *Showdown with Evil* the tables are turned. I'll be interviewing Dr. Jamie Glazov who will have the last word in explaining the nature of those who fight for tyranny and terror, and, more importantly, what can be done to defeat them. -- David Swindle

30. Showdown with Evil – Jamie Glazov

David Swindle: Dr. Glazov, let's discuss the themes of this collection and what conclusions we can reach from them.

First, in several interviews in this work you discuss your background as the son of two prominent Soviet dissidents. Can you tell us a bit about how you became politically aware over the course of your childhood and adolescence? Most young people are blissfully ignorant of political matters and the often disturbing realities of the world. Given your family's history of fighting tyranny and terror, perhaps you did not have such a luxury?

Glazov: Thanks David. Well I am grateful to God I didn't have this so-called luxury. To say the least, it would be an understatement to say that I never envied a lot of the people I grew up with in the West who walked around without one idea in their head or any yearning for anything. I remember being around certain friends growing up and they would be sitting around aimlessly and complaining that they were "bored." I can understand being happy or sad, or being elated or depressed, but I could never understand being bored. My heart and mind has, from the time I was young, been consumed with worrying for the dissidents back in Russia, and in other totalitarian societies. I am not trying to glorify myself; I'm just being honest in that I was perpetually troubled by the suffering inmates of the communist gulag and I yearned for their release and for the punishment and overthrow of their tormentors.

My soul was intertwined with my dad's and mom's battle and perpetual concern for the martyrs that fell and the heroes that rose fighting against communist despotism. I was forever perplexed not only at the indifference around me about these matters, but, as I grew older and entered high school and the university, at the actual excuse and support for it. Liberal and leftist friends and acquaintances chastised my parents and me constantly about our inappropriate views and concerns, explaining to us that our focus should not be on communism, that really wasn't so bad, but on American imperialism, aggression and oppression -- supposed realities that, no matter how hard I tried, I could not detect my entire life.

These circumstances in which I grew taught me, on many levels, what life was and gave me a priceless gift: the gift of caring for justice, of caring for something greater than just my own immediate material or physical needs. I am forever grateful to my parents for having given me access to the divine gift of having an inner life and world.

My parents took on one of the most evil regimes in human history, a regime that massacred millions of people and brought misery and destitution to millions of others. Because of this background, I think I have a little inkling of what freedom is and what real oppression is. And so I have developed a reflexive nausea when I am confronted with the smug liberal and leftist, of whom I have met a million, who thinks he knows it all, is better than conservatives, and yet, when it comes down to it, has absolutely no concern for the truth or for the millions of human beings who suffer under the tyrannies that he supports and makes excuses for – and under which he himself would perish.

Swindle: Please tell us a bit about your odyssey through academia. What drove you to pursue scholarly work? What were some of the subjects you studied which influenced you the most? How did your studies affect your political philosophy? What was it like being a son of Soviet dissidents in a leftist academic culture which celebrated the monsters who had brought so much pain to your family?

Glazov: Going to university was just a given thing to do. I come from a family of academics and pursuing knowledge is something that you just love and pursue, there's not really a question about it. I did my undergrad in history and then went on to do Ph.D. studies in history as well. I did it because I longed for fighting for the truth about communism and for telling the truth about it. I studied the Cold War because America was a divine entity to me and the Soviet Union was, for anyone with eyes to see, a clear evil empire that represented a toxic threat to every single human being, whether they were under its totalitarian grasp or outside of it.

I detested the leftists in academia who not only apologized for the Soviet Union, but cheered for its victory. I observed the glorification of Mao, Che Guevara, Castro, the North Vietnamese and other mass murderers everywhere I went on campus. No academic professor, with an exception or two, had the courage or integrity to put Solzhenitsyn's *Gulag Archipelago* or Armando Valladares' *Against All Hope* on their syllabuses, even though the Soviet Union and Cuba played prominent roles in their courses. No professor would dare to accompany his reading list full of Noam Chomsky and Howard Zinn with a counter-reading from a David Horowitz or Thomas Sowell. You were only allowed to get one side of the story. And if you thought that capitalism was a good thing or that Ronald Reagan was a great president, you would get a bad mark, because it meant you didn't understand the course and the truth.

It hurt my heart and infuriated my whole being watching these people on campus apologize for evil and heap abuse and slander upon the United States and Israel, the two most beautiful countries in the world that represent and stand up for freedom, justice and equality (well, with the U.S. up until Obama), and are on the frontlines of defending it. In this context, a desire was born in me to expose leftists and their true motives. I wanted to understand and to explain the typical colleague I looked at daily who worshiped societies under which he himself would be exterminated and who heaped criticism at a society that was allowing him every luxury, liberty and material allowance to sit around and think up everything he hated about it.

Swindle: With this background it's quite obvious how you could connect with David Horowitz and the Freedom Center. Could you discuss how you became *FrontPage Magazine*'s managing editor?

Glazov: Back in 1997 I had decided to write a script on how to be a good leftist, a satirical kind of thing. I found leftists so pathetic as I was observing them, that I decided to create a comedic how-to-guide. So I was reading a few books to crystallize my ideas and then, before finishing, I got my hands on *Radical Son*, David Horowitz's memoir. I was totally overwhelmed by it. It had really grabbed me. I remember I had not been that moved by a book for a very long time -- and haven't been since. I was very sad, I remember, when the book ended. I really didn't want to move on to anything else, the narrative had such a hold on me. Picking up another book just wouldn't do, and that really was the situation for awhile. *Radical Son* enters your consciousness in a way that you really can't explain unless you read it. It delivers some of the greatest truths about life, the human condition and the Left in the most powerful of ways.

So I decided to write a letter to David and tell him how much his memoir meant to me and how much I respected him. And when I sent him the letter, I decided to include my script with it, which was called "15 Tips on How to be a Good Leftist." I just included it for something to do, not really expecting to hear anything back. But I did leave my phone number along with my address on the bottom of the letter I wrote.

A few weeks later my phone rang. So I picked it up and said "Hello?" And a voice asked: "Is Jamie Glazov there?" And I said, "Speaking." And the voice said, "Hello Jamie, this is David Horowitz." To say the least, well, it would be an understatement to say that it was quite a surprise. He thanked me for my letter and also expressed an interest in publishing my satire as a little booklet at his Center. So of course I agreed and it became the Center's pamphlet. After that, I started submitting to *FrontPage Magazine* as a regular writer and eventually I became a columnist. One day I got an email from David and it said: "What's your day job?" And well, it all kind of happened from there. I became an assistant editor and then just kind of moved up I guess. And here I am today. David gave me a great opportunity and it has been an honor and privilege to work with him, the Center, and at *FrontPage*. I consider him the most important political thinker and activist of our time. He's a warrior battling on the front-lines. He's a hero. And I am grateful to fight by his side against the totalitarians of our time and their human-hating ideologies.

Swindle: You edited and wrote a very impressive introduction to Horowitz's anthology of his writings, *Left Illusions*. There are few people more familiar with Horowitz's writings and with Horowitz personally than you. What do you think are some of the intellectual lessons that we can learn from Horowitz's work? Are there particular Horowitz books that you especially appreciate?

Glazov: Well, David comes from within the Belly of the Beast. He was in hell and was able to come out of it and to tell us how the devil thinks and what his strategy is. In essence, David demonstrates how the totalitarianism in communist practice is rooted in the socialist idea itself. He has shown, in the most profound way, how the utopianism of the Left leads to the monstrosities of its earthly incarnations. And he experienced all of this personally in terms of what he witnessed as a child of communists and as a leader of the New Left. He has illuminated the belief system of the believer, which envisions replacing this earth and its human beings with a new earth with perfect human beings. This child-like fantasy, as he has termed it, is the "original sin" of the Left. And it is this fantasy that has led to Stalinism, Maoism and all the other communist totalitarian experiments that have killed more than a hundred million human beings and caused mass suffering for millions of others.

My favorite Horowitz books, the ones that had the deepest impact on me, are *Radical Son* and *The Politics of Bad Faith*. *Radical Son*, as I mentioned earlier, was extremely moving. The memoir goes beyond Whittaker Chambers' *Witness* in that it engages in a fearless examination of self, which is almost unprecedented in political memoirs. By going further than any previous narrative in demonstrating how deeply the Marxist fairy tale is entwined with the character and psychology of its believers, David shows how the socialist lie reaches into every corner of its believer's soul. He makes clear why the break from radicalism can be such a personally devastating decision. And that's why, as we know and have seen, a leftist can never look back or say "I'm sorry."

The Politics of Bad Faith builds on this incapacity of the progressive to say "*mea culpa*" and for leftists to say "*nostra culpa*." The book, a collection of essays, is extremely powerful in that it exposes the refusal of radicals to accept the implications of the collapse of Communism for the future of the socialist project. David shows how the Left simply ignored (and ignores) the lessons of communism's collapse, and has just renamed itself and its agendas. And so leftists just continue with their destructive agendas. This is the politics of bad faith. There is really no literature out there that deals with this phenomenon in the way that David's does. This remains really the only book written after the fall of the Berlin Wall that systematically confronts the arguments of the Left with the history that refutes them. Not surprisingly, the Left has ignored it. It deals with David's work the same way that the Soviet regime simply took people out of existence when it rewrote its own history.

Swindle: Let's now discuss the subject of this volume: the ideas you have encountered and promoted at *FrontPage Magazine* over the past decade. What has been your understanding, as the editor of the last nine or so years, of the threat posed by tyranny and terror?

Glazov: Well, radical Islam is now the greatest threat the West faces. We are, as Norman Podhoretz has noted, in World War IV. We face totalitarian and religious zealots who seek to establish an Islamic caliphate worldwide. They hate freedom and liberty, and so they hate and need to destroy the United States and Israel the most, since these two nations are the bulwarks and representatives of freedom in the world.

The threat of radical Islam is rooted in the teachings of Islam, which mandate Islamic supremacism and the subjugation of non-Muslims. Unfortunately, the liberal stronghold on our culture does not allow us to confront this truth, and so it remains a serious challenge how we will be able to defeat an enemy that we cannot name.

We now see this tragedy inherent in the Obama administration, headed by leftists, that somehow cannot see the presence of Islamic jihad in the Fort Hood massacre and in Abdulmutullab's attempt to blow up Northwest Airlines Flight 253. Nidal Hasan and Abdulmutullab themselves insist that they were inspired by Islam and the teachings of the Koran, but the Obama administration treats them as criminals rather than as war combatants. This is simply suicide, it puts American lives and security at risk. And it is, of course, all part of the workings of the unholy alliance that David Horowitz has delineated. It's how the Left makes us vulnerable to our totalitarian enemy. Both seek to destroy our society.

Swindle: Your intellectual background is in a rigorous study of Communism and the foreign policy world of the Cold War. Yet in today's world you, and all of us who are committed to defending freedom, have had to very quickly learn the ins and outs of the ideology of our new opponent: Islamofascism. In this volume you interview several experts on Islam, including Brigitte Gabriel, Robert Spencer, Walid Shoebat and Mohammad Asghar. Could you discuss the evolution of your understanding of Islam and some of the most critical things Americans need to know about this most misunderstood subject? And could you please tell us what are the most important books to read to understand this subject?

Glazov: There are a lot of misunderstanding on the issue of Islam. The problem is not Muslims per se. There are many Muslims who don't know anything about their own religion and also do not practice their religion. There are also many Muslims like Tarek Fatah, Irshad Manji and Thomas Haidon who are trying to bring a reformation to Islam and bring it into the modern and democratic world. Whether that can be achieved or not is another topic of debate.

The key issue is that there is a problem with Islam. It mandates violence against, and the subjugation of, non-Muslims; it teaches Islamic supremacism. And that's why Islamic terrorists quote the Koran when they engage in terrorism. They find inspiration and sanction in their religious texts to engage in their terrorism. This is a problem and until we are honest about it, we will not be able to defend ourselves from the enemy we face in the terror war.

The books by Robert Spencer are the key to understanding the enemy we face. He's a top-notch scholar and he tells it like it is. I have had yet to find any critic of his work that can contest anything he says, since all he does is tell us what Islam itself teaches. His critics call him a lot of names, but they cannot discredit his work, because it is cream-of-the–crop scholarship.

Swindle: One of the most striking interviews in this collection is with the inspirational Dr. Phyllis Chesler. Dr. Chesler has stood up valiantly for women's rights in the Muslim world, showing her true feminist convictions and paying a hefty political cost for it. A *New York Times* article in August of 2009 described this position as being a "Feminist Hawk," though principally focused on David Horowitz and *Frontpage Magazine* with no mention of her unfortunately. (Dr. Chesler authored many articles at *Frontpage* which led to the publication being one of the driving forces on this issue.) I know this has been a very important subject for you that you've written about extensively. Could you discuss her influence on you, your engagement with the issue of Islamic misogyny, and what it means to be a Feminist Hawk?

Glazov: I care about the people who suffer under tyrannical regimes. I care for and worry about dissidents and all freedom fighters who are oppressed and tortured and linger in prisons under totalitarian systems. When it comes to Islam, we know that women suffer tremendously under its ruthless and vicious paradigm of gender apartheid. For many years my heart has been very close to the women who suffer from the crimes of female genital mutilation, honor killings, forced marriage, forced segregation, forced veiling, etc. etc. under Islam's misogynist structures. I want to do something to help them and to prevent future victims.

Within this effort, I have come to see, through my own research and understanding, that it is obvious that woman-hatred is intertwined with Islamic terror. The more fanatical and violent the Islamic terrorist and his milieu, the more misogyny you will find there. So we fight for women under Islam, obviously, for the humane aspect of it in and of itself. We do it because it is the right thing to do to protect a human being. We have to care for women as we care for all human beings. And along with this also comes a common sense ingredient: to fight for women's rights under Islam is also to stick a dagger into the heart of Islamic jihad. Islamo-fascism cannot survive in any environment where women enjoy self-determination and individual liberty.

So when you achieve women's rights in an environment, Islamic fanaticism dies in that environment – it cannot take hold. So it needs to move elsewhere where it can plant itself. Our goal has to be that we create a situation where it has no place to move. Fighting for women's rights is fighting for human rights everywhere. By defeating Islamic fanaticism we free women, and by freeing women we make impossible the growth of Islamic fanaticism, it is a circular paradigm.

The Left has exposed its own agenda as being founded on lies in this context, as it cannot come to the defense of women under Islamic gender apartheid. That's because the Left doesn't care about women or their rights, unless the issue it gets into its hands helps it in its war of destruction against its own society. For the Left, women are pawns to be used in its war against its own society; the Left doesn't care about a woman in and of herself.

Dr. Phyllis Chesler is the leading feminist and scholar on this issue. She has witnessed all of this first hand. She cares for the women who suffer under Islamic gender apartheid and fights on their behalf, and she has exposed the Left's disinterest in those suffering women. She has helped crystallize why and how the Left doesn't care about women under Islamic misogynist tyranny. And I am very moved by her work and have tremendous respect for her courage and honor. She has a true heart. Unlike the leftist feminists I have known all my life, Dr. Chesler cares for the living and breathing real human women who suffer persecution. She's not interested in being popular in trendy lefty communities – which is the priority of the typical leftist feminist in the West.

To be a Feminist Hawk is to fight for women and their rights with no exceptions, something the Left is shamelessly and shamefully unable to do, since anti-Americanism is the altar on which a leftist feminist will sacrifice any persecuted woman who poses a threat to undermining the leftist agenda.

Swindle: One of the sections of *Showdown with Evil* that leaps out the most is Part VI: Leaving the Faith, which includes interviews with those who chose to abandon their leftist or Islamist ideologies. In your years conducting interviews at *FrontPage* you've talked with other ex-believers who have challenged their ideas and emerged on the other side. Do you have any insights into how these shifts take place? In my experience dialoguing with True Believers I've come to the conclusion that it's generally folly to think that it's possible to convert people to the Right through reasoning and debunking ideas. (What was not reasoned in cannot be reasoned out.) There's still value in dialogue; but one should have no illusions that they can effectively change people. The Believer has to learn for themselves through personal experience the fundamentals of capitalism, human nature, the realities of evil, and the beauty of individual freedom. These insights are not gifts that can just be handed to someone who has not grasped them in their own life. Do you agree?

Glazov: Yes of course. But you are implying here that believers are misguided people who are seeking the truth and that something needs to happen in their lives for them to see it. Surely this is true in many cases, but in many other cases this is not true at all. Many believers don't know the truth and do not want to know it. They are not interested in it, and that is clearly discernible upon any conversation with them. They are interested in destruction and in their quest for destruction.

A lot of this goes very deep into the depths of the believer's pathological character. David Horowitz has outlined this well in *Radical Son* and *The Politics of Bad Faith*, where he illuminates how powerfully intertwined the socialist lie is within every corner of a believer's soul. And this explains why a believer is not interested in facts; he is interested in preserving his own identity, which will self-destruct if he accepts certain truths. And there are, for sure, brave and courageous souls who have had the intestinal fortitude to change after a traumatic experience. David Horowitz is one of them. In these cases, it is often a life and death situation. As David wrote about his own decision to leave the faith, he had to move from the space in which he was standing, or he would have died a spiritual death. Pain forced him to move. And I think many of us, in our own lives on different realms, know what this means in terms of the tragedies and difficulties we have had to confront.

Swindle: Part of the mentality of the radical is a need to "solve" a problem or change the world *now*. The radical is unsatisfied with the world as it is now and will not tolerate slow change or the acceptance of an imperfect society. (And you've correctly highlighted how in many radicals this need to change is really a need to destroy.) The understanding of our Islamofascist enemies as articulated in this volume -- they're just doing what the Koran tells them to do and we are not responsible for creating them -- presents a profound problem for the softer radicals who are not outright apologists for totalitarianism in the Ward Churchill mold.

Often in trying to explain these ideas to both so-called "progressives" and Ron Paul-style libertarians (groups with fairly identical foreign policy understandings and temperaments) the answer I've gotten back is the same: "Well you're advocating genocide because the only way to fix this problem is to exterminate every Muslim on the planet." Then the indisputable facts presented are discarded by the radical because the only apparent radical solution is so odious. (There's that disinterest in the truth that you just mentioned.)

No legitimate foreign policy scholar or analyst advocates some kind of obscene Muslim Holocaust to counter the problem of Radical Islam. What is the solution that free societies must pursue in dealing with Islamofacism? What are the policies that should be pursued to defeat this enemy? Further, *can* it be defeated? Or is this a struggle which is likely to continue long after you and I have both been buried in the ground?

Glazov: This is not about demonizing Muslims or attacking Muslims. We are the allies of Muslims. I consider myself pro-Muslim. Muslims are the victims of Islam and its totalitarian structures. I spend a large part of my life fighting for the rights of Muslim women who suffer under Islamic gender apartheid. Does this make me anti-Muslim or pro-Muslim? I fight on behalf of Muslims who want to live in freedom and who don't want to not suffer the harsh punishments of Sharia Law. I fight for a world where young Muslim boys and girls are not brainwashed and forced to blow themselves up. Does this make me anti-Muslim or pro-Muslim?

Pamela Geller is on the frontlines everyday fighting for a young Muslim girl, Rifqa Bary, and it is because of Pamela that this young Muslim girl might not lose her life at the hands of her family. Rifqa's crime was to follow her own human conscience and to believe in a faith that she wanted believe in. For this, she can easily lose her life in an Islamic environment. Does saving her life make Pamela anti-Muslim or pro-Muslim?

If we want to fight for the memory of Aqsa Parvez, a young Muslim girl in Toronto who was murdered by her father and brother because she wanted to live a Canadian life, and if we want to prevent more Aqsa Parvezes, does that make us anti-Muslim or pro-Muslim?

The issue confronting us is Islamic doctrine. Islamic theology has teachings in it that inspire and mandate jihad, misogyny and totalitarianism. We have to be honest about that and we have to be strong in empowering Muslim reformers like Tarek Fatah and Irshad Manji, who are bravely confronting these teachings and trying to have them repudiated and understood in new ways. Can this succeed? I don't know, but it's something we all have to work for. And we have to use military might to confront our enemy, and we have to get ready to fight not for two or five years, but for generations if need be, because our enemy is ready for much more than that.

This conflict will continue long after you and I are buried in the ground. But we can make a difference, in the sense that what we do today can equip our children to defend themselves better against Islamic tyranny and terror.

Swindle: The Left has developed such an effective stranglehold on our culture. Taking a page from Stalinist theorist Antonio Gramsci's playbook, it has embedded itself within journalism, the arts, popular culture, academia, and even many religious institutions. As you've pointed out, this results in an ability to control the flow of ideas.

To make the factual points you've made in this interview is to be branded a racist and for attempts to suppress one's speech to ensue. Can this dominance be overcome so the flow of ideas can begin again? How can the Left be defeated in the world of ideas and relegated to its proper status with comparable crackpot philosophies like alchemy and phrenology?

Glazov: Martin Malia has commented that as long as there will be inequality, there will be the yearning for socialism. Indeed, as long as we are who we are in this human condition, fallen and tainted by original sin, humans will be tempted by that one greatest lie: the lie that a particular entity whispered to someone long ago in a certain garden: you can be God. This is the pretension to equality, and Abel was its first victim, and there would be millions upon millions to come.

I don't really know the answer to any quick fixes or if any of this will come out OK in the end. I just know I will fight till there's no breath left. I know that I am surprised if I ever run into a conservative in my regular walk of life, because you have to be an extraordinary person to have thought through the lies and to have taken the road less traveled. Becoming a leftist is easy and wins you many friends and cultural and material rewards. It can give you great feelings of self-satisfaction. I know that in Toronto, in the "trendy" educated communities, and in all my years in academia, when I just have plainly told a person: "I like George W. Bush," there is a look of horror on their face. They never met anyone like me, and they never read any idea anywhere or spoke to anyone anywhere to have heard why I would have a horrifying disposition like that.

It's also frightening to them because to listen to me will mean that they might be persuaded, and then they will be ridiculed in their communities and lose all their friends -- and a sense of who they are. So they run from me and the facts that I have to impart to them. I have friends who have distanced themselves from me because they are embarrassed to speak with me, because they will lose any argument, and they so desperately need to keep their friends -- friends who will abandon them if they break the Party Line that the liberal world so ruthlessly imposes on its members.

I don't know if we can ever make class hatred synonymous with racial hatred; it's caused far more deaths in the 20th Century. Add up just Mao's, Stalin's and Pol Pot's victims. But the liberal-Left can never accept that, because then its members will lose everything they live for.

What do we do? Well, we stand by David Horowitz's side, right on the frontline of this war, and we do battle for the truth, for justice, and for those who suffer under tyranny and yearn for us to defend and rescue them.

Swindle: The final part of this volume, appropriately titled "The Titans" features interviews with some of the most inspiring minds of our time: Buckley, Hitchens, Coulter, Dalrymple, and Pipes. Each of these figures brings a different approach and identity to the shared pursuit of the defense of freedom.

What lessons can we draw from these figures that we should put into practice in our showdown with tyranny and terror?

Glazov: Well, Buckley was the Godfather of course. An incredibly superior, high intellect that crystallized what made conservatism the right path -- and what made socialism, ultimately, evil.

I find Hitchens top rate. His writing is a pleasure to read and always such a cutting edge to it, something always unexpected. Having turned on the Left in terms of radical Islam, he brings an original and ferocious battle to the arena.

Coulter is extremely sharp and her wit is first-rate. Through her brilliant sense of humor, she effectively cuts to the truth of the conflicts we face. She's also just such a likable person – with a very contagious smile. We have to remember that humor and laughter are the entities that totalitarian structures fear most, so Coulter brings something very sacred and priceless to the arena.

Dalrymple is a first-rate psychoanalyst. He knows humans' psychology and what makes people tick, and especially what makes dysfunctional people and cultures tick. In that way he brings to the forefront the pathologies that confront us -- and the dark places from where they stem.

And Richard Pipes is, of course, the top figure on Soviet history. Courageous and a top notch scholar and intellectual. He deserves the ultimate respect for demonstrating the monster that Lenin was. This is crucial because in academia many Sovietologists, with their leftist illness, are forced to admit who and what Stalin was, but they try to say he was an aberration -- that he didn't discredit communism itself. So they try to avoid criticizing Lenin. But Pipes revealed that Stalinism's roots were in Lenin himself. In this way, and in so many others, Dr. Pipes has made a priceless contribution; he showed the truth about to the idea and system that spawned the *Gulag Archipelago*.

Swindle: Did you have any final words as we wrap up?

Glazov: Well, we've covered a lot of territory. What does one say? What comes to mind, perhaps, as we think about this conflict with evil that we face -- we reflect on what we must do and how we must do it and why. An extraordinary person comes to mind. He was someone who was more than just a person of course; and he visited this earth at one time. And he told us, I think, the most important thing, in the most important way: "You will know the truth, and the truth will set you free."

Swindle: Thank you Dr. Glazov, for taking the time to summarize the themes of this volume.

Glazov: And thank you David for all the help and intellectual nourishment you've brought to this book and discussion.